DISCOVERING RE⌐⌐⌐

Discovering Biblical Texts
Content, Interpretation, Reception

Comprehensive, up-to-date and student-friendly introductions to the books of the Bible: their structure, content, theological concerns, key interpretative debates and historical reception.

PUBLISHED

DISCOVERING REVELATION

Content, Interpretation, Reception

David A. deSilva

WILLIAM B. EERDMANS PUBLISHING COMPANY

GRAND RAPIDS, MICHIGAN

First published 2021 in Great Britain by
Society for Promoting Christian Knowledge
36 Causton Street
London SW1P 4ST

This edition published 2021
in the United States of America by
Wm. B. Eerdmans Publishing Co.
4035 Park East Court SE, Grand Rapids, MI 49546
www.eerdmans.com

27 26 25 24 23 22 21   1 2 3 4 5 6 7

ISBN 978-0-8028-7242-5

Library of Congress Cataloging-in-Publication Data

A catalog record for this book is available from the Library of Congress.

Unless otherwise noted, Scripture quotations are the author's own translation.

Quotations marked NRSV are taken from the New Revised Standard Version of the Bible, Anglicized Edition, © 1989, 1995 by the Division of Christian Education of the National Council of the Churches of Christ in the USA. Used by permission. All rights reserved.

In honour of our three sons:
James Adrian, John Austin and Justin Alexander

Contents

Contents

Contents

Preface

I completed this manuscript just a few days after the global spread of the novel coronavirus responsible for COVID-19 caused the World Health Organization to declare an international health emergency. During the two months or so that have passed between that event and writing this preface, I have had the opportunity to witness once again the fervour and creativity with which some interpreters of Revelation seek to 'discover' new correlations between its contents and events transpiring two millennia later.

When I first read Revelation as a 12-year-old in 1979, self-proclaimed prophecy experts like Herbert W. Armstrong and Hal Lindsey were excitedly looking to the European Economic Community, which at that time was soon to admit its tenth member nation, as the matrix for the formation of the last iteration of the beast's empire, whose ruler would prove to be the antichrist (see Rev. 17.12-13). It has been difficult to explain the swelling of the membership of what is now the European Union to 27 nations, but the new crisis has sparked a new hope for redeeming the older claim. The opening paragraph of an article in the July 2020 issue of *The Philadelphia Trumpet*, a publication of the Philadelphia Church of God, reads: 'Europe's response to the pandemic is accelerating the fulfillment of one of the most crucial end-time prophecies of your Bible! The coronavirus is hastening the arrival of the prophesied Holy Roman Empire.'[1] The author, Gerald Flurry, goes on to predict that, due to the economic crises precipitated by the pandemic and efforts to contain it, 'the EU is about to be pared down to a 10-nation superstate. This prophecy will be fulfilled very soon – I see biblical evidence of probably no more than two to four years, and perhaps even as soon as *this year*.' When the European Union has been thus 'rightsized' back down to its proper biblical number, a 'strongman' – the antichrist – will arise from among its people to give them the leadership they desire for navigating these troubled times.

I have no doubt that, should 2024 arrive without seeing this 'prophecy' fulfilled in this way, some ingenious modifications to the scheme will allow the EU to continue to remain the focus of Revelation's message in those circles.

---

1   Gerald Flurry, 'Europe's response to COVID-19 has set the stage for dictators to rise', *The Philadelphia Trumpet* 31.6 (July 2020): 1–4.

The article claims that 'For over 75 years we' – that is, Herbert W. Armstrong and his successors, like Gerald Flurry – 'have been prophesying the arrival of this empire.' And for 75 years and many more, the devotees of all such interpreters have been distracted from hearing Revelation as something – anything – other than a grid into which events and personalities from their contemporary scene can be made to fit, at least for a time (and times and half a time). Although such readings capture more than their share of attention, appealing as they do to our penchant for the sensational and the eerie, there are other approaches that the faithful in many generations have taken to hearing the book of Revelation and discerning its words of guidance, encouragement and warning to them. I count myself privileged to have been given this opportunity to explore those approaches with the readers of this volume and to suggest ways other than those rooted in prognostication in which we can more fruitfully – and formationally – engage this vitally important text that closes our New Testament canon.

I wish to express my heartfelt thanks to Philip Law, senior editor at SPCK, both for the initial invitation to contribute this volume to his important series and for his extraordinary patience as I took considerably longer to deliver this work than I originally anticipated (#failedprophecies). The same gratitude is owed to James Ernest and Trevor Thompson at Eerdmans, the publisher of this series in the USA, who were also supportive and kindly understanding of my delays. Thanks are due also to Mollie Barker for her diligent work copy-editing this book. I wrote the greater part of the book during a study leave granted to me for the autumn of 2019. I remain grateful to the trustees, administration and faculty of Ashland Theological Seminary for giving such support, costly as it is for an institution, to the production of resources that may serve the goals and interests of theological education more broadly than is possible in any one institution's classrooms. I have now enjoyed such support at Ashland for 25 years and, if I have been productive during that time, it is in large measure because Ashland has respected, and given me space to fulfil, the full scope of my calling.

Finally, it is with great pride and deep love that I dedicate this volume to the three sons I share with Donna Jean deSilva, my wife of 30 years: James Adrian, John Austin and Justin Alexander deSilva, who have all become men since the last time I dedicated a book to them!

David A. deSilva
Ashland, Ohio

Abbreviations

Only abbreviations not currently found in the *SBL Handbook of Style* are included here.

Comm.	Oecumenius, *Commentary on the Apocalypse*
Comm. in Apoc.	Andrew of Caesarea, *Commentary on the Apocalypse*
Exp.	Bede, *Explanatio Apocalypsis*
Hist. Rom.	Dio Cassius, *Roman History*
I. Eph.	*Die Inschriften von Ephesos.* Ed. Hermann Wankel et al. 8 vols in 11. IK 11–17. Bonn: Habelt, 1979–84.
In Apoc.	Victorinus of Pettau, *Commentary on the Apocalypse*
Rhet. Alex.	*Rhetoric to Alexander*
Rhet. Her.	*Rhetoric for Herennius*
Silv.	Statius, *Silvae*
Tract. in Apoc.	Aspringius of Beja, *Tractate on the Apocalypse*

1

Introduction

The Apocalypse of John is . . . the work of a second-rate mind. It appeals intensely to second-rate minds in every country and every century. (D. H. Lawrence)

Between fascination and repugnance

Reactions to the book of Revelation throughout the history of its interpretation seem to vary more widely – and emotively – than reactions to other books of the New Testament. Readers of the Sermon on the Mount in Matthew 5—7, however varied their social locations and interpretative approaches, tend to be agreed at least insofar as they might enquire into what kind of ethic is being promoted in those chapters. Readers of Revelation, on the other hand, are not even agreed that there is anything remotely ethical to be discovered within this book. Friedrich Nietzsche (1956: 185) called the Apocalypse 'the most rabid outburst of vindictiveness in all recorded history'. D. H. Lawrence (1931: 15) considered Revelation to betray the Christian message: 'just as inevitably as Jesus had to have a Judas Iscariot among his disciples, so did there have to be a Revelation in the New Testament.' Literary critic Harold Bloom (1988: 4–5) condemned the work as 'a book without wisdom, goodness, kindness, or affection of any kind' because he found 'resentment and not love' to be its core teaching. Martin Luther, while begrudgingly translating and including it in his 1522 German Bible, held it in little esteem since, in his estimation, 'Christ is not taught or known in it'.

While there is a great deal at stake in the interpretation of any New Testament text, the stakes seem to run higher with Revelation. One approach to the book's interpretation – the approach based upon 'discovering' correlations between the actors and events of Revelation and the contemporary situation and near future of the interpreters – has especially wrought havoc in the lives of thousands over the centuries. Predictions about the imminent end of this world accompanied by the setting of specific dates have prompted the more devoted followers to sell their homes and businesses and give the proceeds away (often to the benefit of the prognosticators and their institutions), leaving them both spiritually crestfallen and financially destitute.[1] The violent fate of more than 80 followers of Vernon Howell, better known as David Koresh, the leader of the apocalyptic Branch Davidian sect outside of Waco, Texas, in April 1993 justifies the claim that 'sober and careful exegesis of the Apocalypse is not just a game; it can be a life-and-death matter' (Paulien 2003: 161). History had already left such warnings to posterity in the fate of the revolutionaries of the Peasants' Revolt of 1524–5 and the Münster rebellion of 1534–5, whose leaders identified themselves with figures in John's prophecy and championed a revolutionary reading of Revelation in ill-conceived calls to arms against the papacy, the state and the authorities of the Reformed churches.

The Revelation of John, however, has elicited deep admiration and enjoyed a long history of positive effects as well. Its call to courageous witness in the face of martyrdom helped sustain Christian identity during the difficult second and third centuries. Its bold declarations concerning God and the Lamb – and their sovereignty over the course of history – contributed substantially to emerging Christian theology. Its striking images and expressions are reflected frequently in the art and liturgy of the Christian churches. Its impact on literary culture, particularly that of Europe and the Americas, has been substantial. For example, John Milton's grand epic on the fall of humankind, *Paradise Lost*, owes as much of its inspiration to the description of the war in heaven related in Revelation 12 as to the Fall narrative of Genesis 3. Its assurance of a future in which God will redress injustice sustained generations of African-Americans enduring slavery, seen particularly in the impact of Revelation's language and images in the tradition of the Negro spiritual. It has inspired cultural critique and non-violent resistance, seen for example in Allan Boesak's *Comfort and Protest* (1987), a disciplined exposition of Revelation brought to bear on the situation under apartheid in pre-1990s South Africa, offering a challenge both to the political structures that sustained these conditions and to the churches complicit in the same. And there is no end to popular fascination with its prophecies as a key to discovering the significance of the present moment and the forthcoming future in the overarching plan of God – though it is especially in this regard that the dangers associated with Revelation emerge once again.

---

1   William Miller, for example, led his followers to expect the second coming of Jesus sometime between 21 March 1843 and 21 March 1844. After a lifelong career as a biblical prophecy expert, Harold Camping definitively set the date for the Rapture (Jesus' secret return to take true believers with him to heaven before the Great Tribulation) for 21 May 2011 (altered to 21 October 2011, shortly after 23 May 2011).

In line with the aims of the series in which the present volume falls, it will be the aim of this book to lay out the various contributions made to the understanding of Revelation through a variety of approaches. Readers may have to work harder to discover Revelation than they would in regard to other books of the New Testament, in part due to pervasive popular presuppositions concerning what this book is 'really' about – presuppositions that will be critically considered in the second chapter. The history of Revelation's effects also suggests that, particularly in regard to *this* book, openness to multiple approaches to interpretation does not conduce to openness to *all* approaches to interpretation. The saying of Jesus in regard to prophets who will claim to speak in his name is especially apt in regard to interpreters and interpretations of Revelation: 'By their fruits you shall know them' (Matt. 7.16).

Reading Revelation

The opening verses of Revelation suggest that the book was written to be read aloud by one disciple to a gathered audience of other disciples: 'Privileged are the one who is reading aloud and those who are listening to the words of the prophetic utterance – and who are keeping the things inscribed therein – for the time is near!' (1.3). As the whole can be read aloud comfortably in an hour and a quarter, it was probably taken in all at once in a single session by its ancient audience, which already suggests that overall impact and impressions may be as important a 'meaning effect' of the book as detailed exposition. What follows is provided as a guide to a first reading (or, at least, a *fresh* reading) of Revelation, and not as a *substitute* for the same. Discovering any text begins with encountering the text itself.

John's commission and Jesus' messages (1.1—3.22)

John introduces his book as a message that originated with God's own self and that is addressed primarily 'to the seven churches in Asia', recalling earlier letters by Paul to specific congregations. John may surprise us by calling our attention from the very outset to the very *end*: 'Look! He's coming with the clouds!' (1.1–8). He introduces himself as a faithful witness whose testimony landed him on the small island of Patmos. While there, the Christ appears to him in overwhelming glory and commissions him to write down what he is about to see and hear, again specifically for Christian congregations in seven cities of the Roman province of Asia (1.9–20).

John then delivers brief prophetic messages from the glorified Christ to each congregation. Each message begins with Christ identifying himself in some way that both recalls elements of John's opening vision of him and suits the challenge that each congregation faces. Christ praises each congregation for its faithful achievements, diagnoses any shortcomings, instructs its members on how to meet the challenges of their situation, and extends promises of rewards for 'conquering' those challenges and warnings of negative consequences for failing to do so (2.1—3.22). The specific elements of these rewards and consequences will return later in the closing visions of judgement and paradise, giving evidence of the whole work's literary unity. These opening chapters establish a strongly situational and pastoral context for the book as a whole: this is a text composed and sent to intervene in the lives of, and provoke particular responses from, Christian disciples living in the shared context of the Roman province of Asia while facing a variety of challenges to persevering in faithfulness.

The three series of God's judgements (4.1—16.21)

A significant shift occurs as John ceases to take dictation for the glorified Lord and is transported 'in spirit' through an open door in the sky to see 'what must come about after these things' (4.1). John views the throne of God surrounded by concentric circles of heavenly beings – 4 living creatures, 24 elders, 7 spirits – who praise God as the Creator of all that is (4.2–11). Then John focuses on a scroll in God's right hand sealed with seven seals and hears an angel invite anyone who is 'worthy' to come forward to take the scroll and open its seals. No one worthy is found until 'the lion from the tribe of Judah' – a slaughtered-but-standing Lamb – appears in the midst of God's throne and entourage. He receives the scroll and the heavenly entourage proclaims the reason: 'You are worthy . . . because you redeemed [people] from every tribe and language and people and nation for God by your blood and made them a kingdom and priests for our God.' The scene closes with every creature in heaven, on earth and under the earth ascribing blessing, honour and power to God and the Lamb (5.1–14).

The Lamb opens the seals one by one, the opening of each seal accompanied by some portent – the four horsemen whose ride heralds conquest, war, famine and pestilence; the revealing of the souls of those slain for their witness to God, crying out for justice from under the altar in God's heaven; the cosmic chaos and universal terror as the 'great day of the wrath' of God and of the Lamb arrives (6.1–17). But the seventh seal is not yet opened. Instead, we see angels with power over the four winds being instructed to hold off on letting their destructive force blow upon the earth while another angel descends with a seal of a different kind – a mark of God's ownership and protection to be placed upon the foreheads of God's slaves. John hears the number of those sealed – 12,000 from each of the 12 tribes of Israel – but then sees an innumerable multitude 'from every nation and tribe and people and language' standing in victory before God and the Lamb, acclaiming them for their deliverance along with the heavenly entourage, and enjoying their protection and care (7.1–17).

The seventh seal is opened, leading to a half hour's silence in heaven. The seven angels that stand in God's immediate presence are given seven trumpets while another angel offers incense at the heavenly altar alongside the ascending prayers of the saints. This angel fills his censer with fiery coals from the altar and casts it down to the earth (8.1–5). The first four angels sound their trumpets in sequence, signalling the scorching of a third part of the earth with fiery hail, the transformation of a third part of earth's seas into blood, the poisoning of a third part of earth's fresh waters, and the darkening of a third part of the sun and moon (8.6–13). The remaining trumpets are introduced as 'woes'. The sounding of the fifth trumpet signals an angel to release a horde of demonic locusts from the underworld abyss, who mercilessly torment all who lack the seal of the living God for a period of five months. The first woe is passed (9.1–12). The sounding of the sixth trumpet signals the angels stationed at the River Euphrates to lead their otherworldly cavalry to destroy a third part of humankind with the fire, smoke and brimstone that proceeds from their horses' mouths. Despite these supernatural visitations, the surviving mass of humanity does not repent of its crimes or its worship of idols (9.13–21).

Once again the seventh event in the series is delayed – ironically by a strong angel who stands upon earth and sea and declares 'there will be no more delay'. The angel holds a scroll that has been opened and invites John to eat it, commissioning him anew to proclaim a prophetic message over 'peoples and nations and languages and many kings' (10.1–11). John receives a measuring rod and is told to measure 'God's temple and the altar and those worshipping there', but not the court, which is given over to the nations to be trampled for 42 months (11.1–2). John is then told of God's 'two witnesses', who will proclaim their message with all the power of Moses and Elijah for 1,260 days, after which they will be killed by 'the monster that rises up from the abyss'. Their corpses will remain unburied 'in the street of the great city' for three and a half days until a breath from God raises them to life. They ascend to heaven in a cloud while an earthquake destroys a tenth part of the city, leaving the survivors fearfully giving glory to the God of heaven. Only now does John tell us that 'the second woe is passed' and that 'the third woe is coming swiftly'

(11.3–14). The seventh trumpet is sounded and a chorus of praise erupts around God's heavenly temple, declaring that 'the kingdom of this world has become the kingdom of our Lord and of his Anointed' and that the time for the meting out of judgements and rewards has arrived at last (11.15–19).

The narrative of John's visions takes a different turn at this point. Rather than encountering still more unfolding series of judgements, we encounter a series of unfolding scenes in a demonic offensive against God and God's holy ones. A woman clothed with the sun, on the verge of giving birth, appears in the sky, followed immediately by the appearance of a great red, seven-headed, ten-horned dragon, waiting to devour her child. He is thwarted, however, as the messianic child is caught up into the heavens and the woman flees into the desert, where she is nourished for 1,260 days (12.1–6). A war breaks out in heaven, resulting in the expulsion of the dragon – now clearly identified as the devil, Satan – and his angels from heaven to earth through a combination of angelic might in heaven and faithful witness unto death on earth (12.7–12). Cast down from heaven, the dragon now rages against the woman, but to no avail, and so he turns to pursue the rest of her children (12.13–18).

He summons, to this end, a seven-headed, ten-horned monster from the sea, who captivates the earth-dwellers, slanders God and God's heavenly hosts, successfully wages war against the holy ones on earth and recovers from some mortal wound to one of its heads. He exercises dominion over 'every tribe and people and language and nation' and receives worship from the earth-dwellers 'whose names are not inscribed in the Lamb's Scroll of Life' (13.1–10). A second monster emerges from the land to promote the worship of the first monster and to guide the earth-dwellers to erect an image of the first monster and worship it as well. Economic embargo and loss of life fall upon all who refuse to worship the image and receive the monster's mark – the brand '666' – on their foreheads or right forearms (13.11–18).

Juxtaposed to this grotesque scene of worship of a beast and image, we see the Lamb standing on Mount Zion with his vanguard of 144,000, 'the first fruits' redeemed from the earth, who bear God's seal upon their foreheads, singing the Lamb's praises (14.1–5). Three angels take flight over the earth-dwellers and over 'every nation and tribe and language and people' to warn them to worship the God who created all things and whose hour of judgement has arrived, to announce the fall of 'Great Babylon', who has corrupted all the nations, and to warn against the worship of the monster and its image, which leads to the experience of God's wrath in all its force and duration. The Spirit pronounces those who die in the Lord, by contrast, 'privileged' (14.6–13). Scenes of ultimate judgement follow: first, the gathering of the 'harvest' of the earth, then the gathering of the produce of the vineyard of the earth and the trampling of the grapes in 'the great wine press of God's wrath', resulting in the release of a sea of blood for hundreds of miles (14.14–20).

John sees a new sign in heaven – seven angels holding the seven last plagues with which 'God's wrath is completed'. A scene of worship follows, in which those who emerged as conquerors from the monster and its image and its number stand before God's throne and acclaim God for his just judgements. The seven angels emerge from the heavenly temple with seven golden libation bowls filled with God's wrath, while the temple is filled with smoke preventing entry until the bowls are poured out (15.1–8). These are poured out in unbroken succession, the first five leading to painful sores breaking out upon those bearing the monster's mark, the turning of the whole sea and all fresh waters to blood, scorching heat from the sun, and complete darkness enveloping the monster's realm. The human response is to continue slandering God (16.1–11). The pouring out of the sixth bowl leads to the dragon, monster and false prophet gathering their armies to 'the place called Armageddon' for 'the war of the great Day of God Almighty' – though a battle is not narrated here. The pouring out of the seventh bowl is met with an ominous word from God's throne in the heavenly temple: 'It has come to pass.' All the cities of the earth, including 'Great Babylon', whose crimes are remembered at last before God, are devastated in an earthquake and hailstorm of unprecedented severity (16.12–21).

The fall of Babylon and descent of New Jerusalem (17.1—22.5)

John draws us in for a close-up look at the overthrow of Babylon, announced earlier at 14.8 and 16.19. An angel takes John 'in spirit' into the desert where he sees (and, thus, we see) a luxuriously adorned prostitute astride a familiar seven-headed, ten-horned monster. He is told that the kings of the earth have committed fornication with this prostitute and that she is herself inebriated not with wine but with 'the blood of the holy ones and the blood of Jesus' witnesses' (17.1–6). The angel then interprets these images. The monster is the one that came up from the abyss, in regard to whom 'those inhabiting the earth, whose names are not written in the Scroll of Life, marvel' (17.8) – and, thus, the monster we met in 11.7 and 13.1–8. Its heads represent 'seven hills' and 'seven kings', of whom 'five have fallen, one is, and the other has not yet come' (17.9–10). The destiny of the whole monster is destruction, but not before it is moved by God's unseen hand to throw off its rider, burning and consuming her flesh.

The prostitute is then identified as 'the great city that has dominion over the kings of the earth' (17.18), which leads to a vision of the city itself now devoid of life and consumed with flames, the target of God's long-awaited judgement, from which God's people are summoned to come out so as not to share in its sins and also, therefore, its punishment (18.1–8). The kings of the earth, its merchants, and its shippers and sailors stand off in the distance lamenting Babylon's sudden and catastrophic overthrow, the collapse of its economy, and the resulting loss of their own pleasures and profits (18.9–20). An angel throws a great millstone into the sea as a parable of the plunge Babylon is soon to take for its violence, economic exploitation and self-glorification (18.21–24), which is met with a liturgy of exuberant praise in heaven, celebrating God's vindication of God's holy ones who have been slain by Babylon's agents (19.1–5).

A transition occurs in the middle of this liturgical moment as John turns our focus away from the judgement and destruction of Babylon to the 'Wedding of the Lamb' with his as-yet unnamed bride, who has attired herself with 'bright, clean linen' (19.5–8). An angel pronounces those people 'privileged' who are 'summoned to the supper of the Lamb's wedding' (19.9), but what follows appears to be a grotesque parody of such a celebratory event. We see a rider, described in ways that link him strongly to the glorified Christ, astride a white horse at the head of the armies of heaven clothed in 'bright, white linen' and then an angel summoning all the carrion birds of the air to 'the great supper of God' – the corpses of the kings, generals, mighty ones, horses and their riders that constituted the fallen armies of the beast and the false prophet, who are themselves plucked up and deposited into the 'fiery lake ablaze with sulphur' (19.11–21).

The Wedding of the Lamb is deferred yet further as an angel descends from heaven to put Satan in chains and imprison him in the abyss for a thousand years, 'so that he might not lead the nations astray until the thousand years are completed' (20.1–3). For the same length of time – indeed, it would appear, during the same time – thrones are set out for judgement, and the souls of those beheaded for their witness to Jesus and obedience to God, and of those who did not worship the monster or its image, come to life to serve as priests and to reign with Christ. John comments that 'this is the first resurrection' and it is a privilege to have a share in it, for it puts one beyond the reach of 'the second death' (20.4–6). At the end of the thousand years, Satan is set free from his prison and leads the remaining nations to besiege 'the camp of the holy ones and the beloved city'. Fire from heaven devours his armies and he himself is thrown into the lake of fire, to join the monster and false prophet (20.7–10). A scene of judgement follows as all the remaining dead are restored to life to face

God upon the throne – from whose face the present earth and sky flee! Scrolls are consulted, both those containing the record of all the deeds of humankind and also the Lamb's 'Scroll of Life'. Those whose names are not found inscribed in the latter are cast into the lake of fire, which we learn is 'the second death', along with Death and Hades themselves (20.11–15).

The theme of celestial marriage returns at last as John sees a new heaven and new earth and 'the holy city, New Jerusalem, descending . . . as a bride adorned for her husband' (21.1–2). The promises of God's dwelling with and sheltering humanity are gathered from across the Jewish Scriptures and presented as fulfilled at last in this vision; all that plagued the present earth is banished: no more sea, night, curse, death, weeping, sorrow or pain (21.3–8; 22.3, 5). An angel invites John to inspect the Lamb's bride, New Jerusalem, more closely, taking him on a tour of its magnificent foundations, walls and gates, through which stream the nations with their glory to walk in its light. God's presence and the Lamb's presence on earth are no longer restricted to a temple but fill the city that itself fills a great deal of earth's real estate. Sun and moon would be superfluous, for the radiance of God and the Lamb illumine the city that has within it the provisions for life and for the healing of the nations (21.9—22.5).

Closing words (22.6–21)

John does not leave us in the utopian destination of the narrative world spun by his recounting of his visions. Rather, he returns us to his lived world as an exile on first-century Patmos as he is addressed again by an angel and, perhaps through the angel, by the glorified Jesus. The angel affirms the reliability of all that John has seen and heard – and thus all that has been communicated to the audience – along with the implicit commission to all who have been privy to this revelation (first and foremost the members of the seven congregations that form his explicitly designated audience) to 'keep the words of the prophetic utterance of this book' (22.6–8). The glorified Christ affirms the imminence of his intervention and, therefore, the privilege that belongs to 'those who wash their robes' as opposed to those who participate in the sorceries, fornication, murder, idolatry and lies that pervade life in and under Babylon (22.13–16). Final warnings are uttered concerning tampering with the text that John has written alongside final prayers that, indeed, Jesus would come quickly to intervene (22.17–21). This literary transition from the visionary world to John's position in this world, with its admonitions and invitations to the hearers (whether direct or implied), reinforces the convictions set forth in the opening chapter and the seven oracular messages that followed: the narrative of what John has seen and heard is to have some effect on the audience's orientation towards their world and their practice in their world.

Structure and interpretation

This reading provides an opportunity to make some preliminary observations about Revelation's structure (or, better, structuring elements) and the implications of structure for interpretation. First, it is immediately apparent that sequences of seven are a major structuring device: seven oracular messages to seven congregations in Roman Asia, the opening of seven seals, the blowing of seven trumpets and the pouring out of seven libation bowls. These groups give order and even a sense of inexorability to the unfolding contents of the book and the forward movement of its plot. The dramatic crescendo of the movement is enhanced by other literary elements, such as the increasing 'symptoms' of theophany, recalling the signs that accompanied God's showing up at Sinai in the biblical tradition. Thus to 'lightning strikes, voices, and thunder' in Revelation 4.5 are added 'an earthquake' in 8.5, 'an earthquake and great hail' in 11.19, and 'a great earthquake . . . and great hail' in 16.18, 21 (Bauckham 1993a: 202) – notably after the seventh event in each series.

At the same time, there are indications that the movement of the plot is not *entirely* linear, but somewhat more complicated. We find ourselves looking at the climactic visitation of God and the Lamb at multiple points within Revelation. We see Christ 'coming with the clouds' in 1.7. We have already arrived at 'the great day of the wrath' of God and the Lamb accompanied by the disappearance of stars, sky and islands with the sixth seal in 6.12–17. 'One like a Son of Man' initiates the harvesting of the earth and the trampling of the wine press of God's wrath in 14.14–20, between the trumpets and the bowls. 'Earth and heaven flee away' (again?) when the enthroned God appears to judge the dead in 20.11–15. With no fewer than four visions of this final judgement, Revelation cannot be reduced simply to a single timeline. As we will consider further in Chapter 8, many interpreters have found some degree of 'recapitulation', of returning to cover the same ground, at work in its plot.

Second, it is equally clear that important scenes interrupt the clean and orderly sequence of sevenfold events. Indeed, it might appear that the orderly sequence exists in order *to be* interrupted: by a scene of sealing and protection and a 'spoiler' vision of the Church Triumphant in Revelation 7 that breaks in between the sixth and seventh seals; by scenes of prophetic commissioning and prophetic witness in Revelation 10—11 that break in between the sixth and seventh trumpets; and by a long narration of a mythic struggle and rebellion against God in Revelation 12—14 that breaks in between the trumpets and bowls. By suspending the sequence and delaying reader expectations, such scenes seem to command greater attention.

Third, parody and contrast appear to be important elements of the unfolding narrative and, thus, significant for guiding the reader's interaction with that narrative and its implications. For example, the scene of the worship surrounding the throne of God and the Lamb contrasts sharply with the scenes of the worship surrounding the dragon and the beast to the extent that the latter might be read as a parody of the former (down to the claims to universal dominion that are made in both). The prominence of the question of whom to worship and the consequences of one's choice in this regard within the narrative world of Revelation highlight this contrast. The visions of Babylon and New Jerusalem as two alternative cities and ways of organizing human society emerge not merely as scenes in a sequence but scenes that sit in meaningful juxtaposition one to the other. The extensive parallelism between 17.1 and 21.9 (the verses in which an angel introduces each vision) sends up a clear verbal signal that these two cities are to be set alongside each other in some way. At a smaller scale, the same can be said for the wedding feast of the Lamb and the great supper of God. The pervasive presence of alternatives – which are presented as mutually exclusive within the narrative world of Revelation – might suggest that the act of interpreting this text should focus not primarily on decoding a linear plot but on responding in one's situation to the alternatives it identifies as these are manifested in that situation.

The following chapter will survey some of the major ways in which Revelation has been interpreted throughout the centuries. A text as rich and multidimensional as Revelation calls for its readers to adopt a rich and multidimensional approach that draws upon a variety of interpretative angles and skills. On the other hand, the history of Revelation's interpretation and effects has uncovered some of the edges of responsible interpretation that readers would do well to consider and, perhaps, commit themselves not to transgress.

2
Interpreting Revelation: strategies for reading

Engaging the 'three worlds' of Revelation

It has become popular to think about approaches to the interpretation of texts in terms of **three worlds** – the world *behind* a text, the world *within* a text and the world *in front of* a text.[1] Examining the world *behind* the text calls for giving attention to the situation within which and the process by which a text was composed, including the broad historical and cultural setting, the more specific occasion or provocation (if available), and antecedent sources. Often, though not always, investigation of the world behind the text focuses the interpreter on the author's method, motives and purposes in composing a particular text, conceiving of 'meaning' as that which the author 'meant' to convey.[2] In an important sense, however, it is impossible to seek after the author's meaning – that is, pursue an **author-centred** reading – apart from the author's text, for in general, and certainly in regard to ancient texts, we have recourse only to the product of the author's attempt to communicate, namely the text, and not to the author's mind.

In regard to Revelation, examining the world behind the text calls for, among other things, (1) the investigation of the historical and social setting of John the prophet and the seven congregations to whom he explicitly addressed his work; (2) the examination of the shared scriptural and other early Christian traditions that John incorporates into his message and how he has deployed these; (3) the exploration of early Jewish and Christian religious practice and its related conventions as a means of illuminating the likely expectations for

---

1   See, for example, the approaches to interpretation outlined in Tate 2008; Carvalho 2009.

2   The classic statement comes from E. D. Hirsch: '*Meaning* is that which is represented by a text; it is what the author meant by his [or her] use of a particular sign sequence; it is what the sign represents.' It is important, however, that Hirsch also gives room for the individual reader's appropriation of meaning, which he calls '*Significance* . . . a relationship between that meaning and a person, or a conception, or a situation, or indeed anything imaginable' (1967: 8).

and functions of the kinds of communication John employs in his text, in particular presenting his own work as a **letter**, a **prophecy** and a **revelation** (see further below); and (4) the analysis of the clues that John's text gives concerning the directions in which he was seeking to guide the emotional, cognitive and behavioural responses of his congregations towards their own lived experience in their local settings.

Examining the world *within* the text calls for a close reading of the composition itself and a thorough and genre-appropriate analysis of its internal dynamics – for example, the use of the tools and lenses of **literary criticism** in the case of narrative texts and the use of **rhetorical analytical approaches** in the case of argumentative or discursive texts. Particularly in regard to narrative texts, exploring the 'world within the text' invites the interpreter mentally to inhabit the spaces, engage the characters, and experience the actions and events that the text creates through its narrative.

Author-centred and **text-centred** approaches to interpretation have frequently been pitted against one another in the recent history of the discipline of literary criticism. Theorists W. K. Wimsatt and M. C. Beardsley coined the term **intentional fallacy** to critique the idea that the meaning of a text is limited by, or accessible by recourse to, the 'design or intention of the author'. The meaning of a text and its success as 'a work of literary art' are to be determined on the basis of what the *text* communicates and the manner in which it does so (Wimsatt and Beardsley 1954: 3). Many biblical scholars, particularly those with an inclination towards reading the Bible 'as literature', have brought this critique and the resulting preference for text-centred *over against* author-centred interpretation wholesale into the study of biblical texts. In so doing, they have often overlooked the very clear limitations that the pioneers of such interpretation placed on their own method, for example their acknowledgement that 'poetry differs from practical messages, which are successful if and only if we correctly infer the intention' (Wimsatt and Beardsley 1954: 5). Genesis, as narrative, might lend itself well to purely 'literary' analysis. But those who first named the 'intentional fallacy' would be among the first to admit that a successful interpretation of Paul's letters, written to provide very practical guidance for his converts facing very specific challenges and circumstances, demands attention to the author's situational purpose (or 'intention').

The question to be addressed in regard to Revelation, then, would concern whether it is a work of literary artistry or a communication of practical guidance. The answer is that it appears to be *both*, and so attention both to the world *behind* and the world *within* the text is warranted. The seven oracles to the seven congregations (2.1—3.22) could not be more practical and situational. The nature of the communication changes with the transition in 4.1 to John's *narrative* recounting of his visionary experiences, which relate a cosmic story with which the members of the congregation are invited to engage, but which affects them and elicits responses to their situations in a very different mode from that of the oracles. Even so, the visions also have a practical claim on John's congregations, for these particular hearers are enjoined at the outset and the close to 'keep what is written therein' (1.3; 22.7) – both the instructions in the seven oracles and the practical implications of the narrative portions.

It is therefore appropriate to give attention to the ways in which Revelation tells 'a story in and through which the people of God discover who they are and what they are to do' as they inhabit that narrative world for the space of the hour or so that it takes to read the text or hear it read (Yarbro Collins 1986: 242).[3] Meaning is communicated and an effect is achieved, in part at least, as the members of an audience allow this particular text to engage their emotions, imaginations, fears and aspirations, reorienting them to the sociospatial world that they actually inhabit.[4] There is a great deal that can deform this engagement, not least of which is coming to the text with inappropriate expectations or not attending adequately to the actual signs (i.e. the *words*) that the text puts forward.[5] It is appropriate and necessary to attend to literary clues that direct our appropriation of the text's meaning – for example, paying attention to John's repetitions of phrases, which often highlight contrasts or make suggestive connections, or to the rigid schema of sequences of seven, which may cumulatively suggest a message ('God is in control'; 'God has a plan') that is more important than the 'meaning' of each discrete event in the sequence (Russell 1994: 111–12).

---

3   The fruits of narrative criticism of Revelation are especially apparent in the commentaries by James Resseguie (1998) and David Barr (2012).

4   David Barr captures this well as he describes the effects on the hearers of simply engaging the narrative world of Revelation: 'The hearers are transformed as they comprehend that it is their suffering witness . . . that brings salvation and judgment to the world, just as the suffering of Jesus was really the overthrow of evil.' The experience of entering into the narrative world 'is a real experience of the community . . . an experience of the "coming" of Jesus' (1984: 48–9).

5   For example, one interpreter asserts that Rev. 17.9–10 'tell us that the seven heads represent *two things*: seven mountains and seven kingdoms (literally)' (Lindsey 1975: 225). This interpreter then identifies those seven kingdoms as the Assyrian, Egyptian, Neo-Babylonian, Medo-Persian, Greek, Roman, and the Revived Roman Empire that the interpreter identifies with the European Economic Community (nearing a total of ten member states at the time of his writing). This interpretation, however, is entirely based on a word that is not *there* in the text – reading 'kingdoms' where every ancient manuscript reads 'kings'. When an interpretation of a text is based on a word that is not in the text, its value as an interpretation is significantly diminished.

Although we might consider John's selection and use of existing sources in connection with the world behind the text, the interpretation and impact of those resources as they are woven into the fabric of the new text – referred to as the study of **intertexture** – is also a key element in exploring the world within the text (here, the internal conversation *between* texts like Daniel 7 and Revelation 13, or Ezekiel 27 and Revelation 18). It is important to attend to macro-level questions concerning a text's **genre** (what *kind* of literature is it) or blend of genres and to think about appropriate reader expectations on that basis, though this, too, overlaps with exploration of the world *behind* the text since genre and generic expectations are based on experiences and material prior to the composition and reading of any given text. Rhetorical analysis – enquiring into how the *text* make claims for its own authority/credibility, potentially arouses emotions (and to what end) or advances argumentative points (and to what end) – also traditionally belongs to literary analysis, although, in the case of a 'practical message' (which *partially* describes Revelation), it too is inseparable from the sociohistorical situation that the text was composed to address.

Examining the world *in front of* the text – the conceptual space between the text and its readers in multiple generations and settings – calls for giving attention to the reception and impact of the text and to the dynamics at work in particular interpretations. Interest in this world does not need to set itself in opposition to either of the other two worlds or their scope of concern. For example, the same investigation of the social and historical situation of the author and audience and of their shared (or non-overlapping!) cultural conventions can help one enquire into how the text was received by its original audience. A thoroughly historical study can thus also be thoroughly reader-oriented.[6] A particular interpreter's reading can be investigated not only as a function of his or her social and theological location, but also as a function of how well or how fully he or she has attended to the particular linguistic and literary cues of the text he or she purports to read and interpret. A reader-oriented interpretation can thus also be thoroughly text-centred.

Broadly speaking, examining the world in front of the text calls for the exploration of what readers bring to the reading of a text and contribute to the interpretation of a text by reason of their own social and cultural location, their personal experience, and their religious beliefs and other values. This might involve appreciating what they are able to see in the text that readers with other backgrounds and commitments might not. It might also involve critiquing

---

6 Pattemore 2004 offers an outstanding example of this kind of study.

how particular readings stand in conflict with elements in the world behind the text, the world within the text, or other readings in front of the text. In regard to Revelation, this facet of interpretation calls for attention to the various interpretations of Revelation that have been offered across the centuries (the **history of interpretation** or **history of reception**), including some account of the decisions and presuppositions that led particular interpreters to their interpretations. It also can call for an analysis of the real-world effects of diverse readings of Revelation on the communities that have embraced (or endured!) those readings, including some evaluation of the **ethics** and the **politics** of these readings.

The evaluation need not be appreciative to be instructive and constructive. For example, postcolonial critics have been interested in exposing the use of Revelation – originally a voice of resistance against the economic, political and ideological colonialism of the Roman Empire – as a resource for colonizing impulses in the history of interpretation. Feminist interpreters have been interested in exposing John's tendency to reinscribe patriarchal images and evaluations of women within his text and the effects of interpretations of Revelation on generations of women readers (or women present, without significant voice or power, in communities of readers), calling both the text and its history of interpretation into question in the light of other values and trajectories.

Because questions concerning the genre of Revelation – decisions concerning what *kind* of literature Revelation is and, therefore, how it is best read and interpreted – have been so important throughout the history of interpretation, the remainder of this chapter will be given to considering the generic cues that Revelation offers its readers and how those cues might orient us towards the history of interpretation and towards discovering Revelation afresh in the contemporary setting.

Reading Revelation through the centuries: a question of genre

Within the first four verses of Revelation, John gives his audience three distinct cues as to what kind of text he has written to them. The very first word in the Greek text is *apokalypsis*, presenting the contents of the book as a 'revelation', the disclosure of material alleged to originate in the divine or spiritual realm (1.1). By the close of the opening paragraph, the content is presented also as 'the words of this prophetic utterance' or 'this prophecy', another label that claims a supernatural origin for the material communicated (1.3). In these opening verses, John refers to himself in the third person ('to his slave, John', 1.2). When John first begins to communicate this 'revelation' or 'this prophecy' in his own voice, that is, in the first person, he does so with a standard form that would immediately be recognized as the opening of a letter: 'John to the seven congregations in Asia: grace to you and peace' (1.4). How did these three signals orient John's audience to his message? How have interpreters throughout history arrived at their different interpretations based on their own negotiation of (one or more of) these indicators of genre?

Revelation as a letter

Letters in the Greek and Roman periods generally began with the formula 'Sender(s) to Recipient(s), greetings'. Numerous examples of this formula can be found opening letters within biblical and para-biblical texts (e.g. 1 Esd. 8.9; 1 Macc. 10.18, 25; 11.30, 32; 12.6, 20; 2 Macc. 11.16, 22, 27, 34; Acts 15.23; 23.26; Jas. 1.1), as well as in actual letters recovered from the ancient world. The 'greetings' might occasionally be expanded to 'greetings and good health' (2 Macc. 1.10; 3 Macc. 3.12; 7.1 NRSV) or some other similar wish. Paul developed a distinctively religious wish, replacing the standard 'greetings' with 'Grace to you and peace from our father God and lord Jesus Christ' in the majority of the letters bearing his name (Rom. 1.7; 1 Cor. 1.3; 2 Cor. 1.2; Gal. 1.3; Eph. 1.2; Phil. 1.2; 2 Thess. 1.2; Philem. 1; compare the shorter forms in Col. 1.2; 1 Thess. 1.1; and the longer forms in 1 Tim. 1.2; 2 Tim. 1.2; Titus 1.4). When John wrote, 'John to the seven congregations in Asia: grace and peace to you from the One who is and the "he was" and the One who is coming', and so on (1.4), he was giving a clear signal that his text was to be read as a letter from an historical author – John – to a particular audience: the seven congregations in the Roman province of Asia that he would go on to specify in Revelation 1.11. The genre of letter suggests that John was most concerned about the audiences he explicitly addressed and that he wrote Revelation with them first in mind, and not later generations of Christians who might eventually read his work, even as Paul was most concerned about influencing the specific choices facing his converts in first-century Galatia or Corinth when he wrote his letters to the Christians in those cities (Mathewson 1992: 211–12).

Particularly since the eighteenth century, many interpreters have taken this as an indication that the message John delivers in Revelation is as time- and situation-specific as any message that Paul or Peter or the Elder or Jude delivered to any of their congregations. Johann Jakob Wettstein articulated this as early as 1752: 'the Apocalypse was written specially for the benefit of certain people who were living at that time, and for the purpose of being understood by them.'[7] With this in mind, two principal goals of the academic study of Revelation have been to 'reconstruct the "question" to which the work itself is an "answer"' (Eagleton 1996: 62) and to discern how Christians in Ephesus or Smyrna or Pergamum would have made sense of John's text, exploring, for example, what referents in their lived worlds *they* would have associated with John's images and how this would have led *them* to respond to various stimuli in the first-century context of the Roman province of Asia in which they lived.

For such interpreters, a great deal of the work involved in reading Revelation is given over to gaining a sufficient familiarity with the social, economic, political, ideological and cultural landscape of Roman Asia Minor – the 'mutual cognitive environment' shared by John and his audiences (Pattemore 2004: 17) – so as to be able to read Revelation 'with' those audiences, discerning both its meaning and its cognitive, affective and behavioural implications for Christians living in that environment. The principal obstacle to understanding John's text is held not to be that John was writing in a mysterious code, but rather the modern reader's distance from the 'mutual cognitive environment' that made John's work intelligible to his immediate audiences.

Such a programmatic commitment undergirds much of the academic study of Revelation. For example, scholars have sought to illumine the local contexts of the seven congregations through the study of the archaeology, inscriptions, regional traditions, geography and local history of the seven cities in which these congregations were located (Ramsey 1904; Hemer 1986; Worth 1999a; 1999b) or of Patmos, where John was located (Saffrey 1975; Rapske 2012; Boxall 2013). They have sought after an ever more precise picture of the kinds of pressures and choices faced by Christians in this environment (Yarbro Collins 1984; Beagley 1987; Thompson 1990; deSilva 1992; Slater 1998; Trebilco 2007). Special attention is often given to the ideology and local representations of the cult of the emperors in Asia Minor (Cuss 1974; Aune 1983a; Scherrer 1984; deSilva 1991; Friesen 1993; 2001; Biguzzi 1998; Frey 2006) and to the economy of the broader Roman Empire (Bauckham 1993a: 338–83; Kraybill 1996) as particularly important facets of this 'mutual cognitive environment'. To this could be added scores of studies of the literary resources used by John that were probably also familiar to his audiences, particularly the prophetic texts of the Jewish Scriptures – in whose tradition John claims his Revelation to stand (see below). A rich history of critical commentaries foreground precisely this kind of contextual reading (see, e.g., Charles 1920; Lohmeyer 1970; Kraft 1974; Roloff 1984; Prigent 1988; Harrington 1993; Aune 1997; 1998a; 1988b;

---

7   Wettstein 1752: 2.893 (tr. from Wainwright 1993: 133).

Beale 1998; Witherington 2003; Smalley 2005; Boxall 2006; Satake 2008; Blount 2009; Koester 2014).

This overall pursuit of reading Revelation as a letter, that is, as a time- and situation-specific communication to its explicitly named audience, is hardly an academic pursuit without significance and relevance. This relevance is not sought, however, by identifying John's images with current events, persons or powers, but rather on the basis of analogy. John's critique of the domination systems of his day and his call to his congregations to respond by witnessing to their underside and to the better alternative of living in line with God's vision for human community becomes the basis for discerning where contemporary domination systems harm human beings and how the scriptural tradition would shape a Christian response (see, e.g., Boesak 1987; Schüssler Fiorenza 1991; Howard-Brook and Gwyther 1999; Maier 2002; Kraybill 2010).

Revelation as a prophetic word

John identifies the contents of his letter at the outset as 'the words of the prophecy' (1.3) and at the close as 'the words of the prophecy of this scroll' (22.7; see also 22.10, 18, 19). In both contexts he pronounces the person who 'keeps' these words 'blessed' or 'privileged', thus promoting the 'keeping' of the prophetic message as a desirable course of action.

John's audience would have been familiar with the genre of prophecy both from the literary heritage of the Jewish community, which continued to be foundational for the early Christian movement, and from the lived experience of that movement. John identifies his message with the former not least in his extensive incorporation of material from the classical prophets of Israel and Judah into his own message and his reapplication of that material to a new situation. This is seen, for example, when he draws upon the four beasts representative of four successive empires in Daniel 7 to depict a new beast representing a further successor in their line of domination (Rev. 13.1–8) or when he recontextualizes material from the classical prophets' denunciation of the violence or economic exploitation of former empires like Tyre and Babylon in his own indictment of the same practices in a new imperial economic and political setting (Rev. 18.1–24).

Prophetic utterances, however, did not only belong to the literary heritage received by the early Church. They appear also to have been a regular part of Christian worship and practice, at least in some early Christian circles. With the conviction that the Holy Spirit was being poured out afresh upon the members of this emerging movement (see, e.g., Acts 2.14–21; Gal. 3.2–5; 4.6–7) came the conviction that God was speaking afresh through that same Spirit, and not merely through the study of God's historic utterances in Scripture. Thus Paul could give extensive instruction concerning the proper exercise of the renewed gift of prophetic utterance alongside other manifest- ations of the Holy Spirit (1 Cor. 12.4–11; 14.1–40) and the author(s) of the *Didache* could give instructions for how to treat the prophets in the com- munity's midst and for discerning the genuine prophet from the freeloading fake (*Did.* 10.7; 11.3—13.7).

Prophetic utterances can have one or both of two elements (Russell 1994: 21–2). The first element, often referred to as **forthtelling**, concerns the com- munication of the divine perspective on the current practices of, or on the challenges facing, the people of God to whom the prophet addresses his or her speech. Thus a great deal of the prophetic corpus of the Jewish Scriptures con- tains indictments of practices that run counter to those prescribed in the his- toric covenant between God and Israel or, more generally, of the practices of foreign nations (often oppressors of Israel) that run counter to God's values and will. To these are often attached promises of restored favour (or, at least, commuted punishment) if the prophetic word meets with a change in heart and practice that brings the people in line with God's covenant and values. One also finds words of assurance to those who are faithful among God's people that they will yet again enjoy the blessings promised under the covenant (for example, deliverance from oppression) if they remain steadfast.

The second element, often referred to as **foretelling**, concerns the commu- nication of future events, usually the immediately forthcoming future. Per- haps because of the emphasis on prophecy and fulfilment in the Gospels and Acts, which foreground Old Testament prophecies as *predictions* of events that would take place in connection with the life and work of Jesus the Messiah and the movement spawned in his name, or perhaps because of the general associ- ation of divine communications ('prophecies') with prognostication through- out the many cultures of the Levant and the Mediterranean, it is *this* element that has tended to prevail when considering Revelation as 'prophecy'. And if identifying Revelation as a letter has served to anchor it in a particular histor- ical context as an interpretative environment for reading the text, identifying Revelation as a 'prophetic word' has served to cut it loose from its moorings and draw it into the eddies of every current in world and church history since.

Three prominent traditions in the history of interpreting Revelation are the **historicist**, **futurist** and **preterist** approaches to the book's contents. All of these traditions of interpretation share a common presupposition, name- ly that calling Revelation a 'prophecy' means that it is filled with *predictions*. Moreover, if Revelation is genuinely a 'prophecy', the figures and events that fill its visions must have a one-to-one correspondence with particular people and events in the unfolding course of the history of the Church and the world. The focus of interpretation is to discover those correspondences either in the history that is past or the history that is *yet* to unfold.

The **historicist** approach treats Revelation's visions as predictions of events spanning the entire time between John's generation – which is addressed by the seven oracles – and the descent of the new Jerusalem.[8] The discrete images and visions provide 'milestones which are able to give the traveler some reasonably clear indication of how far has been traveled and how much further there is yet to go' (Newport 2000: 7). The figure most clearly associated with the emergence of this approach is Joachim of Fiore, a thirteenth-century priest (Wainwright 1993: 49–52). The number 1,260 played into his view that Revelation's visions spanned the time from Christ to the end, marking a period of 42 generations of 30 years each (mirroring the 42 generations from Abraham to Christ in Matthew's genealogy; Koester 2014: 438; Kovacs and Rowland 2004: 124). The seven heads of the dragon represented major opponents of Christ and his people throughout that history, specifically Herod, Nero, Constantius (an Arian emperor), Muhammad, Mesemoth (an otherwise unknown figure possibly associated with the Moors), Saladin (Joachim's contemporary and the victor in the second and third crusades) and the antichrist to come (McGinn 1979: 317 n. 53). Like many historicist interpreters, Joachim located his own generation quite close to the end – during the time of the sixth head.

Once he overcame his initial doubts about Revelation's value, Martin Luther took an essentially historicist approach to the book as well:

> The first and surest step toward finding its interpretation is to take from history the events and disasters that have come upon Christendom till now, and hold them up alongside of these images, and so compare them very carefully. If, then, the two perfectly coincided and squared with one another, we could build on that as a sure, or at least an unobjectionable, interpretation.
> (1546 *Preface to the New Testament*; quoted in Kovacs and Rowland 2004: 44)

Luther's readings often reflect the anti-papal edge that continued to characterize a great deal of Protestant decoding of the book's images (Koester 2001: 11–12). Historicist readings have tended towards Eurocentrism, rarely taking

---

8   See further Wainwright 1993: 49–61.

the historical experiences of the churches in Asia or the southern hemisphere into account (except as the object of European and American missions; Gregg 1997: 37). This stands in some tension with John's own explicitly global view of the Church – a kingdom assembled for God 'from every tribe and language group and people and nation' (5.9; 7.9). The approach remained popular into the nineteenth century.

The **futurist** approach rose to prominence among Catholic interpreters seeking a viable alternative to the Protestants' anti-papal readings of Revelation. It was championed particularly by Francisco Ribera, a sixteenth-century Jesuit priest.[9] He regarded the seven oracles and the first five seals to pertain to the decades immediately following John's writing of the text while the remainder spoke of events yet to come in connection with the final interventions of God and Christ in human history (Wainwright 1993: 61–2; Koester 2014: 56). The seven oracles, in fact, have typically been used ever since by futurist interpreters as a vehicle for bridging John's time with the interpreter's generation by regarding the seven churches as representative of seven successive periods of church history. The futurist approach allows for a largely literalistic interpretation of such hitherto unprecedented scenes as the destruction of a third of earth's trees and grass or the transformation of a third of the seas into blood. It is an essential component of dispensationalism, a theological construct articulated by John N. Darby in the early nineteenth century and widely popularized in the West by means of Cyrus Scofield's *Scofield Reference Bible* (1909), Charles C. Ryrie's *Study Bible* (1978), and such works as Hal Lindsey's *The Late, Great Planet Earth* and the Left Behind series by Tim LaHaye and Jerry Jenkins (starting with LaHaye and Jenkins 1995). This approach to Revelation stands in some tension with John's own conviction that his *whole* message, and not just the opening seven oracles, had immediate relevance for his congregations because 'the time is near' (1.3; 22.10) and that the things revealed would 'come to pass quickly' (1.1; 3.11; 22.7, 12, 20). Hence, unlike the book of Daniel, John's visions were *not* to be sealed up, only to be understood by some distant, future audience (22.10; contrast Dan. 12.9).[10]

---

9 He was not the first, however. See particularly the work of Adso of Montier en-Der (*c*.950), who read Revelation as a prediction of an antichrist who would rebuild the Temple in Jerusalem, demand to be worshipped, and persecute those who would refuse (text in McGinn 1979: 81–7).

10 Hal Lindsey provides an extreme example, suggesting that John himself could not understand many of the things that he was seeing, representing these visions as best he could from his limited frame of reference and first-century vocabulary. In regard to the sixth trumpet, Lindsey (1975: 126) comments: 'The Apostle John describes the army's mounts as horses with heads like lions and with fire, smoke, and brimstone coming out of their mouths. My opinion is that he is describing some kind of mobilized ballistic missile launcher.' When the *interpreter* believes that he or she can reconstruct and

The **preterist** approach, associated particularly with Luis de Alcázar (d. 1613), also became a prominent alternative to Reformation-era anti-papal interpretations of Revelation (Wainwright 1993: 63–6; Koester 2014: 57). According to this approach, Revelation's visions through 19.10 pertain to the distant past, taking the reader up to the 'end' of pagan Rome brought about by the conversion of Constantine. The destruction of Satan, the Last Judgement and the new creation still remain part of the Christian's future hope. Alcázar himself understood the millennium to have begun with Constantine's legalization of Christianity and to mark the whole period of the Church's ascendancy. A more radical preterist approach reads virtually all of Revelation in connection with the events leading up to the destruction of Jerusalem (in the guise of Babylon) – equated with Christ's second coming – at the conclusion of the First Jewish Revolt of 66–70 CE. While this approach is often treated as identical with the more historical-critical approaches, the preterist approach (like the historicist and futurist) is grounded in a very different presupposition, namely, that Revelation's contents were largely *predictions* seeking some *fulfilment* in history.[11]

But what of prophecy as *forth*telling? The words of Jesus to the congregations in Revelation 2—3 are excellent examples of early Christian prophecy, recalling quite directly the oracles of the Hebrew prophets. These are most frequently referred to as the 'seven letters to the churches', but this is a misnomer as far as their genre is concerned. The formula that introduces each message is not the formula that opens a letter but rather a prophetic announcement (Aune 1983b: 275). The formula familiar from the Hebrew prophets – 'Thus says the Lord' – is readily discernible in John's formula, 'The Son of God says these things' (Rev. 2.18), with 'the Lord' now speaking through the Son, who is in turn described with epithets derived (mostly) from the opening vision of the glorified Christ in Revelation 1.12–20 (see also 2.1, 8, 12; 3.1, 7, 14). The contents of these chapters, then, would be far more fittingly referred to as 'seven prophetic messages' or 'seven oracles', and they accomplish precisely what the oracles of the Hebrew prophets set out to do for their audiences: diagnosing

---

articulate John's own visionary experiences better than *John* could, he or she has crossed an interpretative line (not to mention the bounds of hubris).

11 Many historicist and futurist interpreters have pushed beyond interpretation into prognostication, attempting to determine the general or even the precise date of eschatological events such as Christ's return based on their understanding of the correlation between contemporary events and the 'timeline' of Revelation's visions. David Barr says rightly of this line of interpretation that 'every single prediction of the future based on identifying aspects of Revelation with historical events so far has been wrong – and there have been hundreds of them' (Barr 2003a: 97). See the extensive surveys of these attempts in Gumerlock 2000 and Alnor 1989 as well as several examples interspersed in Wainwright 1993: 49–103.

where the hearers are going astray from God's vision for them, affirming those who are remaining loyally obedient, warning of the negative consequences of the former path, assuring those following the latter path of the good that God has in store for them.

Where Revelation's prophecies have the *form* of predictions, must there be a one-to-one correspondence with historical occurrences for the prophecy to be genuine? This is a problem raised in the scriptural tradition, poised particularly acutely in Deuteronomy: 'If a prophet speaks in the name of the LORD but the thing does not take place or prove true, it is a word that the LORD has not spoken. The prophet has spoken it presumptuously; do not be frightened by it' (18.22 NRSV). The prophet Jonah, however, offers an instructive counterpoint. The message that he was given to proclaim was simply a prediction: 'Forty days more, and Nineveh shall be overthrown!' (Jonah 3.4 NRSV). The people of Nineveh responded to the announcement by repenting and changing their practice, with the result that God spared the city and did not bring about its overthrow at the end of the 40 days (Jonah 3.10). The *prediction* failed, but the prophetic word achieved God's goals for it in terms of its impact on, and effects in the lives of, the recipients of that word. Within the narrative world of the book of Jonah, there is no difficulty with this conclusion. Some readers in the Second Temple period, however, still regarded this conclusion to be problematic. Thus when 'the rest' of Jonah's story is told in the *Lives of the Prophets*, he does not return to the land of Israel to reside but instead relocates to Tyre so as to avoid reproach for speaking 'falsely in prophesying against the great city of Nineveh' (*Liv. Pro.* 10.3). One's decision concerning this question will have significant ramifications for one's approach to Revelation – and for what one disposes oneself to discover therein.

Revelation as an apocalypse

A revelation, like a prophetic utterance, was a lived experience in the early Christian communities, especially those associated with the Pauline movement. Paul himself experienced 'a revelation of Jesus Christ' (Gal. 1.12), a visionary encounter with the glorified Jesus (Gal. 1.15–16; 1 Cor. 15.8), the effect of which was to transform the former persecutor of the Christian movement into its fiercest promoter. He speaks elsewhere of other experiences of 'visions and revelations of the Lord', briefly narrating a journey to the third heaven where he was privy to sights and sounds that he does not go on to disclose (2 Cor. 12.1–4 NRSV; cf. also Gal. 2.2; Eph. 3.3). Paul expected that other Christians would narrate, in the context of the worshipping community, 'revelations' that they received for the encouragement and edification of the group alongside other Spirit-inspired utterances (1 Cor. 14.6, 26). When the person who stands to read John's communication out loud to a congregation (Rev. 1.3) announces it as 'a revelation', he or she invites the listeners to attend to it as a narrative relating John's experience of divine mysteries, a phenomenon familiar at least from Pauline Christianity (though likely never of the length and scope of John's book!).

Scholars now use the term 'apocalypse' to refer to the larger body of texts that contain such narratives of divine mysteries disclosed through ecstatic experiences as a literary genre.[12] In one sense, therefore, reading Revelation 1.1 as an announcement of the book's literary genre is anachronistic. In another sense, however, as these texts all represent literary *narrations* of the same kind of (allegedly) lived experience – the revelation of heavenly mysteries through visions, conversations with supernatural beings, and the like – the use of the term to denote a literary genre is quite apt. Other texts that fit this pattern include *1 Enoch, Testament of Levi, 4 Ezra, 2 Baruch* and *Apocalypse of Abraham*, though in one respect these are unlike Revelation in that they are written from the perspective and in the voice of a revered figure of sacred history, whereas John writes from his own perspective and in his own voice. The early Christian conviction that the Holy Spirit was being poured out afresh upon the community gave its members confidence that divine disclosure was a present possibility and not just a characteristic of past generations.[13]

Apocalypses share an interest in what is going on in the unseen realms of God and of the forces of evil and chaos that provide the cosmic backdrop for their authors' and audiences' experiences in the visible world. They also share an interest in the past history and the future events that frame the present moment and interpret its challenges and choices. They place the readers' lived situation within the context of a bigger picture of time and space that provides the interpretative framework for the audience's everyday realities and responses to those realities. The narrative form of apocalypses in general and of Revelation in particular allows hearers and readers to experience vicariously the ecstatic, revelatory experience of the prophet/author, an experience that both legitimates the message as coming 'from beyond' and changes the hearers'

---

12 See Collins 1979; Aune 1986; Bauckham 1993b: 5–12.

13 This is reflected also in the Christian apocalypse *Shepherd of Hermas*, written in the seer's own name rather than the name of some ancient worthy.

and readers' perspectives on and responses to their situation in the light of the same (Aune 1986: 87).

Interpreters of Revelation have often approached the book as if it required a special 'key' to unlock and decode its meaning, as in the title of Joseph Mede's 1627 commentary, *Clavis apocalyptica* ('Key to the Apocalypse'). The very term *apokalypsis* denotes, however, 'the *lifting off* of a veil', not the 'concealment' of meaning. As an unveiling of the larger canvas of divine and demonic activity and agendas, and as an unveiling of what the audience's lived landscape looked like against the backdrop of that canvas, Revelation might be better approached *as* the key that John offered to his congregations to unlock the meaning and significance of their present moment and situation, potentially challenging and changing their own views of and responses to elements of that situation.[14] Thus the visions of Revelation 13.1—14.13 provide an interpretation of the phenomena of Roman imperial rule and emperor cult (and the consequences of participation or non-participation). The visions of Revelation 17.1—18.24 provide an interpretation of Roman economic practices and the policies that preserve the imperial economy.[15] This also may suggest that, as in the case of Jonah's 'prediction', the significance of many of the passages in Revelation laying out visions concerning the future is to be found in the perspective they bring to the present moment and situation of the audience and in the responses they promote, not in their one-to-one alignment with events yet to unfold.[16]

---

14 The fact that the seven congregations see themselves reflected in John's opening vision in the form of the seven lampstands among which the glorified Christ stands (though unseen to them; 1.12–13, 20) might signal to them that they should continue to expect to see themselves and what's going on around them in their setting reflected in John's visions.

15 Nelson Kraybill (2010: 42) helpfully suggests that we think of 'apocalyptic visions [as] political cartoons'.

16 There is another stream of interpretation that, unlike all of those surveyed in this section, is not interested in the connections between Revelation and history – whether the historical situation of its original audience or any subsequent history. This approach is often labelled the 'idealist' reading, though it could also be called a 'spiritual', 'allegorical' or even 'archetypal' reading. It approaches Revelation's images and dramatic actions as symbolic vehicles for transcendent truths valid in every generation, a kind of 'general commentary on the struggle between good and evil' (Newport 2000: 15). This approach has ancient roots in the work of Origen (e.g. *Princ.* 2.11.2–5) and Augustine (e.g. *Civ.*, bk 20). The poet Christina Rossetti (1830–94) exemplifies this approach when she speaks of the struggle against the beast as representing the daily struggle against the 'world, flesh, [and] devil, which are my daily antagonists; of which I must daily, hourly, momentarily beware' (1892: 331). See also, more recently, Delorme and Donegani 2010, who regard attempts to read Revelation in the light of archaeology and late-first-century history to be misguided, since they hold Revelation to be entirely figurative. A purely 'idealist' approach, however, stands in tension with John's own perspective on the imminence and special relevance of the material for his immediate audience – his presentation of his message as particularly 'timely' rather than 'timeless'.

The general approach of this volume

In Chapters 3 and 4 below, significant attention will be given to the world behind the text, first considering some of the basic issues concerning the text's composition (including authorship, date and sources) and transmission (with particular attention to the manuscript tradition and important variants), and then entering into the social and ideological contexts of John and his audience as fully as possible. In the remaining chapters, we will consider how insights from the consideration of each of the 'three worlds' can help illumine the meaning of Revelation, the interpretative decisions made throughout the history of interpretation and the way Revelation's significance might continue to be appropriated. The discussion of Revelation's contents will be guided primarily by the following decisions about the implications of the three kinds of literature it claims to represent. As a letter, Revelation invites interpreters to read it alongside its explicit addressees, seeking to understand how it reshapes their perspective on, and response to, the facets of their situation that John foregrounds. As prophecy, Revelation invites interpreters to read it as a representation of the divine perspective on the addressees' behaviours and on the challenges around them, alerting them to the course they must take to remain in, or return to, favour with God and to avoid judgement. As an apocalypse, Revelation invites interpreters to consider the larger canvas of space and time that John spreads out before the eyes of the Christian congregations in Asia Minor and how that puts their everyday reality, along with its challenges and options, in a different perspective that strategically supports the practical guidance communicated in the text. This journey of discovery will conclude with a discussion of how we might continue to derive contemporary significance on the basis of the reading guided by these principles.

3
The text of Revelation: origins and transmission

Attempting to listen to Revelation in the context of its first performances – to think about its meaning and significance first from the point of view of those congregations whose members were John's foremost concern – involves us in the task of trying to answer a good many questions about the circumstances of those first performances and the parties involved. A number of these questions revolve around the text's origins:

- *Who wrote the text?* Even if a clear identification cannot be made, can we say anything about the authorial persona that the text projects?
- *What went into the production or composition of this text?* In the case of Revelation, addressing this question involves us in reconciling the text's presentation of itself as the transparent transcript of a single, unbroken visionary experience with its intensely literary character as a text seemingly woven together from hundreds of other texts, namely the Jewish Scriptures.
- *When was the text written?* Are there sufficient clues within the text to locate it more precisely in the story of the emerging Christian movement?
- *What does the language of the text tell us?* Beyond the mere fact that John wrote in Greek, what information does the wording give us about its author's social location and his style of communicating?

We also have to reckon with the fact that we have access to the text of Revelation only through the lens of the many manuscripts of the many scribes who copied it – and copied it always with some variations. What happened to the text between John's writing his last sentence on his sheets of papyrus or parchment and the (rather recent) editing of a standard, critical edition of his text? And what might these scribes' and copyists' changes tell us about *their* experience of reading this text?

The writer of the text

The author of Revelation identifies himself simply as 'John' (Rev. 1.4, 9), but John (Greek, *Iōannēs*; Hebrew, *Yohanan*) was a very common name among Jews in the first century CE. Within the pages of the Gospels and Acts we meet a John who immersed people in the River Jordan (Matt. 3.1–14; 11.2–6), a John Mark who accompanied Paul and Barnabas for a brief time (Acts 12.12, 25) and, of course, John the son of Zebedee, one of the 12 apostles of Jesus (Matt. 4.21–22; 10.2). Papias, a Christian leader from the second century, speaks also of a 'John the elder' who was active in Asia Minor in the late first century (in Eusebius, *Hist. eccl.* 3.39.4–6).

From the mid second century on, early Christian leaders connected Revelation with John the son of Zebedee, the apostle of the Lord. This consensus is reflected in the writings of Justin Martyr (*Dialogue with Trypho* 81.4), Irenaeus (*Against Heresies* 3.11.1; 3.16.5, 8; 5.30.3), Clement of Alexandria (*Who Is the Rich Man That Is Saved* 42), Hippolytus (*Antichrist* 35–6, 50), Tertullian (*Prescription against Heretics* 36) and Victorinus of Pettau (*Commentary on the Apocalypse* 11.1; Koester 2014: 66). This might reflect a clear knowledge of local tradition, as in the case of Justin and Irenaeus (who spent time in Ephesus and Smyrna, respectively); it might also reflect a clear desire to regard (or even *promote*) Revelation as authoritative – which meant regarding it as *apostolic*.

Some voices in the early Church dissented from the consensus. The third-century Christian scholar and bishop Dionysius of Alexandria concluded on the basis of significant differences in language and style (and even *competence* in Greek – see below on 'The language of the text') that the same person could not have written the Fourth Gospel and Revelation. Holding that the former was unquestionably written by John the apostle, the latter could *not* have been. Around 200 CE, Gaius of Rome asserted that it was not John but Cerinthus, a gnostic Christian opponent of John, who wrote Revelation in John's name.[1] Both Dionysius and Gaius, however, were also motivated by the debates in which they were engaged to diminish the authority of the book, which was most easily done by disputing its apostolicity.

Almost all modern scholars agree that *someone* named John wrote Revelation – that is, that the book is not pseudonymous, like so many

---

1 His views are recorded in Eusebius, *Hist. eccl.* 3.28.1–5.

apocalyptic writings from the Second Temple period and after.[2] They are divided, however, on the question of *which* John was the author – John the apostle,[3] or an otherwise unknown Christian leader named John. The evidence within the text itself is inconclusive. John speaks of himself, or is spoken about, as a 'slave' of Jesus Christ among a group of such 'slaves' (1.1–2); a 'brother' to and 'partner' with the Christians in the seven congregations that he addresses (1.9); and one prophet among several 'prophets' active among the churches, who are also John's 'brothers' (22.9). While it is in no way demeaning to consider oneself a 'slave' of a divinity (Moses was a 'slave of God', the claim to special subservience to Deity giving him also a claim to authority among human beings), John uses the title democratically by applying it to his fellow believers as well (as in 1.2; 2.20; 7.3; 11.18; 19.2, 5; 22.3). Although some scholars assert that John is the leader of a group of prophets,[4] he himself makes no such claim, presenting himself merely as one of them (22.9). He appears to look upon the circle of the 12 apostles, as also the 12 patriarchs, from the outside (22.12, 14). The reasons that he gives his congregations to listen to him are not rooted in his apostolic status (to which Paul, for example, appeals frequently),[5] but in his status as a prophet, a person specially endowed by the Holy Spirit to receive words and other communications from the Lord (thus words bearing divine authority) for the hearers.

The figure of the Spirit-inspired prophet was familiar to the early Church. Paul expected prophetic utterances supplied by the Spirit to be a regular part of his congregations' gatherings (Rom. 12.4–8; 1 Cor. 12.8–11; 14.1–5, 26–33). Charismatic prophets moved from congregation to congregation already during Paul's time (Paul's troubles reflected in 2 Corinthians 10—13 appear to have been caused by interlopers of this sort) and continued to be a feature of the landscape of the early Church. An early church manual known as the *Didache*, written by the end of the first century, devotes three full sections out of 16 to the phenomenon, laying out guidelines for discerning genuine prophets and for supporting the same as they journeyed from congregation to congregation (chs 11–13). John's presentation of himself *and* his message fits the profile of a prophet far better than the profile of an apostle. The seven congregations that he addresses – while granting that the number seven may also have some figurative significance – were located in seven cities connected

---

2 E.g. *1 Enoch, Apocalypse of Abraham, 4 Ezra* and *2 Baruch*, none of which was written by its purported author.

3 Mounce 1997: 8–15; Osborne 2002: 2–6; Smalley 2005: 3.

4 Schüssler Fiorenza 1985: 146; Aune 1989.

5 Rom. 1.1; 11.13; 1 Cor. 1.1; 9.1–2; 2 Cor. 1.1; Gal 1.1; etc.

by good Roman roads, each about a two-day journey from the next. John may have exercised his ministry primarily in one of these congregations, or he may have travelled regularly between them as an itinerant charismatic prophet.[6]

While apostolic authorship became a cipher for Revelation's authority in the second century and beyond, Revelation's reception among the seven congregations would not have been dependent on such a criterion.[7] Prophets who were deemed to be genuine enjoyed a great deal of authority among the Christian congregations (see, again, *Did.* 11–13) alongside the 'overseers' (*episkopoi*, whence 'bishops'), 'elders' (*presbyteroi*, whence 'presbyters') and 'ministers' (*diakonoi*, whence 'deacons') to whom the day-to-day leadership of the congregations had passed already during the apostles' lifetimes.[8] It was not merely the claim to have seen and heard things that gave a prophet authority, however. These were indeed *claims* to authority on the prophet's part, but authority was granted on other grounds. The early Christian congregations had the tradition and, indeed, the mandate to 'test' prophets, whether resident or itinerant, from their earliest period (see 1 Thess. 5.19–21; 1 Cor. 14.29), to sort out the genuine prophets from the charlatan 'dreamers' (Jude 8). An essential criterion was consonance with the apostolic proclamation and the foundational convictions of the Christian group (Gal. 1.6–9; 1 John 4.1–4). Such 'testing' was a current practice of the congregation in Ephesus, at least, which had recently rejected a group of itinerant teachers (Rev. 2.2) as well as a message that had taken root in neighbouring congregations (Rev. 2.6, 14–15). John abundantly grounds his own prophetic word in the traditions of the Jewish Scriptures (the testimonies and phrases of which he weaves into almost every sentence), their foundational call to the worship of the One God, and the words of and proclamation about Jesus that defined early Christian culture. In the end, it was John's faithfulness to the received tradition as its spokesperson, and not his extravagant claims concerning sights and sounds, that gave his voice authority among Christian churches in ever-widening circles.[9]

John tells his hearers that he 'was on the island called Patmos on account of the word of God and the testimony of Jesus' (1.9) when he received

---

6 See further Aune 1983b: 189–217.

7 Whatever date one assigns to Revelation (see below), the circle of apostles had narrowed considerably – and had perhaps even disappeared entirely – by the time it was written.

8 Or shortly after, if the Pastoral Epistles are understood to have been written by Paul's disciples. See Rom. 16.1; Phil. 1.1; 1 Tim. 3.2, 8; 5.17; Titus 1.7; 3.12.

9 See further deSilva 2009: 142–5, 148–9, 158–74.

his specific commission to write this text to the seven congregations. Early Christian writers including Tertullian, Eusebius and Jerome consistently attribute John's presence on Patmos to a judicial sentence against him.[10] That is to say, John was understood to have been exiled to this particular island because of his subversive preaching.[11] Exile was a common punishment for people convicted of subversive leanings or actions during the Roman imperial period. Philosophers, astrologers, soothsayers, members of suspect religious groups, and unruly gangs might find themselves exiled *from* a city or province or, when a harsher sentence was indicated, exiled *to* a certain location, usually an island. Astrologers and soothsayers could get themselves into trouble by forecasting some unwelcome outcome for the current regime. We can easily understand, then, how *John* found himself in legal trouble given his view of the Roman authorities and his expectation of God's dramatic interventions against them!

Patmos is a smallish and spare island of about 13 square miles (34 sq. km).[12] A hearty person can walk around its irregular shoreline in about 12 hours. It was not, however, a barren, uninhabited rock. Excavations and inscriptions suggest that it was home to a population sufficiently large to support temples to Artemis and (possibly) Apollo, situated upon the two highest points of elevation, and a gymnasium with an array of activities and annual events. It was a frequent port-of-call for merchant vessels travelling between Asia and Greece; it may also have been home to a military garrison during this time, as it certainly was during the late Hellenistic period and Roman Republic.[13] There is no evidence that it was the site of mines or quarries in the Roman period, such that John would have been subjected to forced labour. The proconsul of Roman Asia who exiled John there appears neither to have been overly hostile to John nor to have done him any special favours. It is likely that he selected Patmos as a convenient receptacle wherein to deposit a troublemaker, removing him from his sphere of influence and keeping clear tabs on him, since the island remained within his jurisdiction.

---

10 Tertullian, *Praescr.* 36; Eusebius, *Hist. eccl.* 2.20; Jerome, *Illustrious Men* 9.

11 Leonard Thompson (1990: 173) has argued that the Greek preposition (*dia*) translated 'on account of' could also be rendered 'for the sake of', indicating that John went to Patmos *for the purpose of* preaching the word of God. The Greek *dia*, however, looks backward to a cause: it was John's *prior* activity that landed him, against his will, on Patmos (rightly Yarbro Collins 1984: 55).

12 This compares quite favourably, however, to the diminutive island of Pandateria, whither Augustus exiled his daughter Julia on account of her sexual escapades, affording her less than a square mile (2 sq. km) of earth for the rest of her life.

13 Koester 2014: 239. Helpful studies on Patmos include Boxall 2010 and Rapske 2012.

The composition of the text

How did the book of Revelation come about? What forces were at work in its production as a written text that could be received by the seven congregations in Asia? Some readers might think the answers to these questions to be so obvious as not to require naming: John had visions and conversations with otherworldly beings and Revelation is essentially a transcript of these ecstatic experiences. John tells us as much with every 'then I saw' and 'then I heard' that he writes from start to finish.[14] Early church leaders seem to have adopted this model. Irenaeus speaks of John as he 'who *saw* the apocalyptic vision', which 'was *seen* not so long ago, but almost in our own time' (*Haer.* 5.30.3, my translation). Even Dionysius of Alexandria, who does not grant Revelation apostolic authority, 'will not deny that [John] saw visions and received knowledge and prophetic words' (in Eusebius, *Hist. eccl.* 7.25, my translation). A good number of artistic representations of 'St John on Patmos' across the centuries visually embrace this model, depicting John with eyes aloft focusing on some vision while recording it all on the pages in his lap.[15]

Several scholars, however, have drawn attention to another, equally prominent facet of Revelation that seems to call this traditional model into question. The language of the Jewish Scriptures pervades Revelation. For a work that purports to record an ecstatic experience, it is also a strikingly *literary* work insofar as John has woven together hundreds of identifiable snippets from older texts as he composed his new work. Elisabeth Schüssler Fiorenza draws attention to the ways in which images and phrases from visions recounted in the Jewish Scriptures – for example, the vision of an angel in Daniel 10 – find their way into John's account of his own 'vision' of the glorified Christ on Patmos alongside details traceable to Ezekiel and Exodus (Rev. 1.12–16).[16] She further observes that one can hardly represent in pictorial form the visions John describes, raising doubt in her mind as to whether John himself had ever 'seen' anything. She suggests a different model – that of a scribe with an encyclopaedic knowledge of the Jewish Scriptures and earlier apocalypses like *1 Enoch*, drafting a 'literary vision' as his vehicle of choice for persuading his

---

14 John writes 'I saw' (*eidon*) 45 times and 'I heard' (*ēkousa*) 26 times.

15 See, for example, the representations by Hieronymus Bosch, Hans Burgkmair the Elder, Martin Schongauer, Diego Velázquez and Gustav Doré.

16 Compare the language of Rev. 1.12–17 with Dan. 7.9, 13; 10.5–6, 9–10; also Rev. 10.8–10 with Ezek. 2.8—3.3.

congregations.[17] In a similar vein, Richard Bauckham, with evident admiration for John's literary prowess, suggests that Revelation was 'composed with such meticulous attention to the detail of language and structure that scarcely a word can have been chosen without deliberate reflection on its relationships to the work as an integrated, interconnected whole'.[18]

One might object, however, that such models reflect more the anti-supernatural bias of the Western world (and particularly the academy) and these scholars' own practice of giving 'meticulous attention to the detail of language and structure' than they reflect John's own compositional process.[19] As Leonard Thompson wryly observes, 'among the many explanations for spirit possession, spirits are taboo',[20] at least in some academic disciplines. Anthropologists, however, are not at all reticent to speak of alternative states of consciousness and spirit possession as documentable (and rather *typical*) experiences in many cultures across the globe.[21] An anthropologist might not claim that *God* sent John visions, but she would not dispute that John believed himself, and was probably believed by his audience, to have experienced visions in an alternative state of consciousness (a trance or, in John's language, 'in a spirit', Rev. 1.10; 4.2).[22] And, given the pervasiveness of visionary and other charismatic experiences related across the New Testament and other early Christian literature, 'it would be an excessively suspicious person who would deny that authentic visions lie behind some or all of these literary records'.[23]

This does not invalidate the observations made by Schüssler Fiorenza and others concerning the pervasive influence that the Jewish Scriptures have exercised on the final product, but it does call for a rather more nuanced model than either presented thus far. Just as our dreams draw upon material that

---

17 Schüssler Fiorenza 1991: 29, 51. It is likely that John's only access to Scripture during his time in exile was through memory.

18 Bauckham 1993a: x. Related to this 'literary' model of composition is the intensive investigation of the possibility that the present form of Revelation incorporates earlier source material, whether written by John himself or by another Jewish or Jewish-Christian prophet. For a comprehensive survey of this question, see Aune 1997: cv–cxxxiv.

19 One might also object, with Eugene Peterson (1969: 135), that the model does not account for *both* the similarities *and* the differences between Revelation and the Jewish scriptural texts it incorporates: 'there is not a single exact quotation from any source. It would have been impossible for anyone to copy so many things with such uniform inaccuracy.'

20 Thompson 2003b: 137.

21 See, further, Lewis 1971; Levison 1999.

22 The absence of the definite article ('the') in these verses suggests that we not be too quick to render this 'in the Spirit' (as in KJV, NIV, ESV, NLT). John uses a definite article elsewhere with 'spirit' to indicate a particular Spirit, namely the Holy Spirit (2.7, 11, etc.; 14.13; 22.17).

23 Kovacs and Rowland 2004: 12; see also Wilder 1971: 441; Aune 1986: 91; Hemer 1986: 13–14; Fekkes 1994: 289–90.

we have seen, experienced or imagined in our waking life, so do other alternative states of consciousness. John's lifelong immersion in the Jewish Scriptures and later texts and traditions provided his conscious and subconscious mind with the raw materials for his visionary experiences – the grammar and vocabulary, as it were, with which the Spirit might speak. Such experiences are culture-specific: 'John saw many of the same things in his visions that were described in *1 Enoch*, the *Apocalypse of Abraham*, or the *Ascension of Isaiah*. He did not see what visionaries among the Australian Aranda or the Polynesian Maori saw.'[24] The visionary accounts of the Jewish Scriptures may have exercised so profound an influence on Revelation not because John is cutting and pasting material, but because he himself has used those accounts as the launch pads for his own flights 'in a spirit'. Acknowledging the role of experiences in alternative states of consciousness in John's process of composition helps account for the kaleidoscopic bending and blending of images known from texts across the Jewish Scriptures.[25]

The spaces between visionary experiences (which might well have taken place over some time during his exile) and the writing down of Revelation in its final form also afforded John significant opportunity to ponder further connections between his sacred traditions, his visions and his congregations, joining conscious reflection and ecstatic experience into a persuasive word that would connect those congregations with the larger picture of God's reign that would put their immediate situations into perspective – and clarify for them the paths of faithful response.

The date of the text

Determining *when* a particular text was written can help give interpreters access to the *circumstances* under which a text was written and to which it responds (and calls audiences to respond). Readers of Revelation have been drawn principally to two possibilities: the 'Year of the Four Emperors' (68–9 CE) and the later part of the reign of the emperor Domitian (81–96 CE).

Readers who favour the earlier date base their preference on a number of passages within Revelation. First, they look to Revelation 11.1–2, where John is given a rod and told to measure 'the temple of God, the altar and those worshipping in it', but to exclude the outer court, 'because it was given to the nations, and they will trample the holy city for 42 months'. These readers connect

---

24 Thompson 2003b: 145–6; see also Hemer 1986: 14; Beale 1998: 65–6.
25 See also Fekkes 1994: 289–90; Witherington 2003: 36–8.

this scene with the final stages of the Jewish Revolt of 66–70 CE and, arguing that the Jerusalem Temple is here portrayed as still standing, reason that Revelation must predate its final destruction in 70 CE.[26] One problem here is that every other reference to a temple or its furnishings in Revelation has the heavenly temple of God's realm in mind (6.9–11; 8.1–5; 14.15, 17; 15.5–8; 16.1) and not the physical Temple in Jerusalem – including the reference to a temple that closes this section (11.19).

Second, these readers assert that the beast's seven heads, which John tells us represent seven rulers ('the five have fallen, the one is, and the other did not yet come', 17.9–10), most naturally point to Nero or his immediate successor, Galba, who came to power in 68 CE, as the 'sixth' head – the ruler who 'is' at the implied time of writing.[27] The variation is due to choosing a different starting point for the 'head count', whether Julius as the founder of the dynasty (leading to Nero as the sixth) or Augustus as the first person truly to hold the constellation of titles that would characterize the emperors for centuries to come (leading to Galba). John had observed that 'one of [the beast's] heads' was 'slain unto death' (13.3), which seems also to point to Nero, who had committed suicide in 68 CE, thus placing Revelation decisively in Galba's reign.

Though an attractive hypothesis, this too is not without its problems. Not least of these is the fact that John presents a beast with seven heads not to give us a means of dating his book, but because he regards this particular beast – the regime under which he and his audiences are living – as representing the combined evils of the *four* beasts of Daniel 7.1–7, the regimes whose territories the Roman Empire had encompassed. Where Daniel presented a succession of world empires under the guise of a lion, a bear, a four-headed leopard and a ten-horned monster, John presents the successor of them all as a beast that is part lion, part bear, part leopard, with the seven heads and ten horns of Daniel's four beasts combined (Rev. 13.1–2). It is fortuitous that John can make a connection with the seven hills upon which his 'Babylon' sits; it is probably too much to expect it *also* to correlate with Suetonius's list of Caesars so as to pinpoint Revelation's date. Besides, John's original readers would have simply and instantly connected the ruler who 'is' with whatever emperor was reigning at the time. For them, the point is not where the sequence begins, but their

---

26 Thus Robinson 1976: 238–40; Gentry 1998: 165–92. Whether Rev. 11.3–14 tells a story about Jerusalem or Rome is a matter of dispute hinging on whether one takes the descriptor 'where also our Lord was crucified' as a geographical marker or as another figurative label like the preceding two ('Sodom and Egypt', 11.8).

27 Robinson 1976: 244–8; Gentry 1998: 146–64.

own location near the *end* of the sequence, reinforcing for them what John says elsewhere: 'the time is near' (1.3; 22.10).[28]

It was Irenaeus who first pointed readers towards a later first-century date for Revelation: 'for it [i.e. Revelation] was seen not very long ago, but almost in our own day, towards the end of Domitian's reign' (*Haer.* 5.30.3). Scholars who favour such a date tend not to take Irenaeus at his word, but his suggestion fits well with several further observations about the text. First, the healing of the 'mortal wound' that threatened not only the life of the affected head (13.3) but the beast as a whole (13.12, 14) cannot be said to have occurred prior to the rise of Vespasian and, with him, the founding of the Flavian dynasty that brought stability to the empire again for 27 years. The civil wars following Nero's suicide – during which Galba, Otho and Vitellius all came to violent ends after each reigned for a matter of months[29] – were collectively a gaping wound to the whole imperial enterprise during which some provincials expected the empire itself to collapse.[30]

Second, we may hear in the ride of the third horseman (Rev. 6.5–6) an echo of economic conditions in Asia known from 92 CE. To correct perpetual shortfalls in grain production in Italy and some provinces abroad, Domitian ordered landowners to cut down half of their grape vines to reclaim land for grain production. The elites of Asia Minor lobbied successfully for an exemption, whence perhaps the sarcastic proclamation: 'let the price for a mere quart of wheat or three quarts of barley rise to a day's wage, but don't hurt wine and oil production, whatever you do!'[31]

Third, while the cult of the emperors was a prominent feature of the landscape of Asia since Julius Caesar and Augustus, it experienced something of a revival during the Flavian dynasty, particularly under Domitian. This was not due to Domitian's megalomaniac demands, but to local ambition among the provincial elite and local competition between its cities. John could have lampooned the 'worship of the beast and its image' at any point during the first century, but the phenomenon would have pressed itself upon his mind with

---

28 Bauckham 1993a: 406–7. Not only John's first readers, but readers through the ages have approached this passage from the conviction that they too stood very near the end. Recall Joachim of Fiore's identification of the seven heads as Herod, Nero, Constantius, Muhammad, Mesometh, Saladin and, at last, Antichrist.

29 In the chaos of the year, Vitellius was actually proclaimed emperor by his legions in Germany *before* Otho was recognized as emperor by the Senate in Rome; Vitellius was only recognized by the Senate after Otho's prudent suicide.

30 See, e.g., 2 Esd. 12.17–18; Josephus, *J.W.* 4.657.

31 An admittedly free rendering of Rev. 6.6. On Domitian's edict and its backlash, see Magie 1950: 580–1; Suetonius, *Dom.* 7.2; 14.2.

new urgency – and his words would be heard with a fresh poignancy – in the second half of Domitian's reign.[32]

Finally, there are numerous echoes of the Roman 'urban legend' about Nero returning, whether from the east (at the head of the Parthian armies, to whom he was rumoured to have secretly fled) or from the dead, to reclaim his empire. The shadowy forecast of an 'eighth' ruler that is one of the seven (17.11) and the visions of hordes of hostile forces coming from beyond the River Euphrates (the approximate eastern boundary of the Roman Empire at the time) for a great battle (16.12) are two such echoes. While such a rumour arose fairly early, it gained greater and greater traction as the decades wore on, with pretenders to the imperial throne, claiming to be Nero returning, arising in 69, 80 and 88 CE.[33]

The evidence is susceptible of different weightings. Some have proposed, given the potentially divergent indications within Revelation, that John wrote some of the material (or used previously existing material from) before 70 CE and wove this into the text that he later sent to the seven congregations in Asia nearer the end of the century.[34] The present volume will tend to work from the hypothesis that John's work was entirely composed during Domitian's reign to address the situation of Christians in Roman Asia.

One bugbear that often figures in debates concerning the date of Revelation is the assumption that John wrote *in response* to a significant, recent episode of Roman persecution of Christians – whether Nero's persecution of the Christians in Rome or an alleged persecution of Christians under Domitian (the evidence for which has come under close scrutiny). Only such an experience, some would affirm, could explain the vigour and venom of John's language, 'unless [Revelation is] the product of a perfervid and psychotic imagination'.[35] John certainly knows that significant numbers of Christians have been killed for their faith (Rev. 6.9–11; 17.6) but only speaks of two specific, local acts against Christians: the killing of Antipas (2.13) and his own exile (1.9).

---

32 Two additional, though not major, considerations include the following: (1) it was common to speak of Rome as 'Babylon' after 70 CE, that is, after it had repeated historic Babylon's devastation of Jerusalem and its Temple (compare *4 Ezra* 3.1—5.20; *2 Baruch* 11.1; 67.1); (2) a date later in the century would potentially have been required for Christian congregations to have taken shape in many of the cities John addresses (though this is an argument from the silence of the rest of the New Testament concerning their origins).

33 See, respectively, Tacitus, *Hist.* 2.8–9; Dio Cassius, *Hist. Rom.* 66.19.3; and Suetonius, *Nero* 57.2. Texts speaking of this myth of Nero's return include *Sibylline Oracles* 4.119–27, 133–9; 5.28–9, 33–5, 137–50, 363–9; Dio Chrysostom, *Or.* 21.10.

34 Hugo Grotius (d. 1645) had already proposed that inconsistencies within Revelation reflected John's writing different parts of the book at different times (Kovacs and Rowland 2004: 26). See especially the discussion of the theories of Henri Stierlin and Wilhelm Bousset in Aune 1997: cxii–cxiv, cxvi–cxvii, and Aune's own proposal (1997: cxvii–cxxiv, especially cxxii–cxxiii on the 'earlier' stages).

35 Robinson 1976: 230–1.

The fresh acts of persecution portrayed in the visions themselves are likely not *reflections* of recent events, but *forecasts* of the consequences of heeding John's summons to bolder and less compromising witness in word and practice.

The language of the text

English translations, always smooth and flowing, mask a noteworthy facet of the experience of hearing or reading Revelation in its original language, namely that John 'deploys some of the unruliest Greek grammar in the New Testament'.[36] Dionysius of Alexandria had already pointed this out in the third century, though it was no doubt clear to all its readers and hearers from its very first performances in the churches of Asia: 'his language and style are not really Greek. He uses barbarous expressions and is frequently guilty of grammatical mistakes' (in Eusebius, *Hist. eccl.* 7.25, my translation). Many have tried to account for these 'barbarous expressions' by appealing to John's own Jewish background, suggesting that Greek was his second language and that the structures of his native tongue, likely Aramaic, stand behind his idiosyncratic Greek.[37] Stanley Porter, on the other hand, finds many of John's grammatical 'mistakes' and alleged idiosyncrasies in other Hellenistic writers and suggests 'the conclusion that so many try to avoid: the author of the Apocalypse was not particularly competent in Greek' (1989: 600).

Other scholars, noting the same violations of standard, written Greek and the same (alleged) infelicities of style, have wondered if John might not be intentional in his refusal to make his verbal expression conform to the rules of the dominant culture. Perhaps John knows very well how people who want to be seen to 'behave' and 'fit in' write Greek, and chooses to do otherwise; perhaps John's resistance to the dominant Greek culture within Roman imperialism was so long-standing that he never *bothered* to internalize the 'rules' in the first place. Either way, John's disregard for those rules could replicate on the level of grammar and style what he seeks to achieve also at the level of social, economic and political interaction: distance from and resistance to the way that Roman imperialism has ordered all of life to ungodly ends.[38]

---

36 Maier 2002: 17.

37 See, famously, Charles 1920: cxliii: '*while he writes in Greek, he thinks in Hebrew* and the thought has naturally affected the vehicle of expression' (emphasis original).

38 Thus, for example, Maier, who suggests that John's language 'marks a countercultural Christian identity contesting the ordered syntax of Roman imperial rhetorical culture' (2002: 17), and Callahan, who believes that John 'transgressed grammatic norms as an exercise of his own discursive power' (1995: 464).

Some of John's grammatical irregularities, moreover, may serve yet another end, namely to highlight or draw special attention to some facet of his text – as if a preacher in the ancient cathedral in York were to use the word 'ain't' in a sentence, which would have the effect of underscoring what followed by defying the hearers' expectations for that sentence, jarring them into greater attentiveness. Greg Beale has observed that several of John's grammatical hiccups 'occur in the midst of Old Testament allusions', sometimes because John is preserving 'the exact grammatical form of the Old Testament wording (often from the Greek Old Testament)'. A clear example of this appears very close to the start of Revelation, in 1.4, where John conveys 'grace and peace . . . from "he who is"'. The translation here recreates in English the problem with John's Greek. Just as proper English would have required 'from "*him* who is"', proper Greek would have required John to write the divine name, which John quotes from the Greek version of Exodus 3.14 ('I am "he who is"'), in a different case. John's decision to retain the subjective case from Exodus against those rules, however, makes the connection between Revelation 1.4 and Exodus 3.14 jump off the page.[39]

Handing down the text

Students of the Bible (or any other body of ancient literature) may already be familiar with the discipline known as textual criticism. Particularly in the era prior to the printing press, the dissemination of a text through copying by hand gave rise to variations across a number of manuscripts in spelling, wording, and sometimes even the presence, absence or order of words or whole phrases. The goal of the text critic is to sift through these variations, weighing the probabilities of which variant gave rise to which other variants, with a view to determining which variant most likely represents the author's original wording.

John himself may have been thinking about the vagaries of manual copying of texts when he wrote his stern warning near the close of Revelation:

> I myself attest to everyone listening to the words of the prophecy of this scroll: if anyone adds to them, God will add to that person the plagues written in this scroll, and if anyone takes away from the words of the scroll

---

39 Beale 1998: 320–1, 325. It is clear from what follows that John *knows* the proper case to use, for he goes on to add a pronouncement of grace 'from the seven spirits', putting 'the seven spirits' in the correct (genitive) case.

of this prophecy, God will take away that person's share from the tree of life and out of the holy city among the things written about in this book. (Rev. 22.18–19)

Perhaps these words ought to have been placed nearer the beginning of the book, for by the time the scribes got to the end, almost every one of them had introduced additions, omissions and changes to 'the words of the prophecy of this scroll'.

Many variants between the ancient manuscripts of Revelation simply reflect scribes' mistakes – skipping over a few words as their eyes moved back and forth from the manuscript before them to the copy they were making, subconsciously harmonizing a phrase later in Revelation to an earlier one, or simply mistaking one word for another. A good number of variants in the manuscript tradition of Revelation reflect the efforts of scribes to smooth out the rough spots in John's Greek, bringing his text into closer conformity with the normal rules of Greek grammar or inserting a word or two to supply elements of the sentence the scribes thought to be missing.[40] Andrew of Caesarea, who has left us a complete commentary on Revelation from the seventh century, seems to have been aware of this trend and speaks out against it – notably in his remarks on Revelation 22.18–19. When scribes copying the works of the revered pagan authors encounter grammatical irregularities, they respect the integrity of the author's work; how much more, Andrew suggests, ought scribes to respect the integrity of the work of the authors of the scriptural texts when they are 'contrary to the rules', for the Scriptures are 'more trustworthy and venerable than Attic compositions'.[41]

Stylistic improvements rarely change the meaning of John's original text; this does not hold true for a good number of other scribal changes (whether accidental or intentional), which do materially change the meaning. Only a few examples can be given here.

1 A number of scribes were dissatisfied with the glorified Christ's threat to the unrepentant prophet in Thyatira, labelled 'Jezebel', that he

---

40 For example, the song in Rev. 5.9–10 celebrates the fact that the Lamb 'was slain and redeemed for God from every tribe and language and people and nation'. Some scribes were troubled by the absence of a clear direct object in this clause and added the word 'us' after 'redeemed', even though the song is not sung by the redeemed themselves (who are spoken of in the third person as 'them' in 5.10) but by God's heavenly entourage. The final chorus in Handel's *Messiah* ('Worthy is the Lamb') incidentally includes the added word 'us', following the tradition of the KJV. Or, in Rev. 11.1, John wrote that 'a rod was given to me, saying . . .' The lack of a clear antecedent motivated some scribes to supply one: 'a rod was given to me, *and the angel stood*, saying . . .'

41 Andrew of Caesarea, *Comm. in Apoc.* 24.69 (Weinrich 2011a: 206).

was about to throw her 'into a bed' (Rev. 2.22). Perhaps some felt the significance of this to be ambiguous (perhaps even suggestive); perhaps, understanding this (rightly) to mean a 'sickbed', some felt it wasn't nearly severe enough. So we find the threat heightened to 'a prison' and even 'a furnace' in some manuscripts!

2 In the passage that describes the ride of the four horsemen (Rev. 6.1–8), some scribes read the summons pronounced by each of the four living creatures in turn – 'Come!' – as addressed not to each horseman, ordering him to begin his ghastly ride, but to John the visionary, expanding the command to make this clearer for other readers: 'Come and see!'

3 Though the flight of eagles or vultures is appropriately ominous, some scribes appear to have thought it inappropriate to attribute speech to them, even in a vision. Thus the declaration of woe pronounced by an eagle in most manuscripts (Rev. 8.13) is pronounced by an angel instead in many later manuscripts.

4 John himself appears to have intended the terse sentences that close the introduction of the first beast (Rev. 13.9–10) to reinforce the inevitability of persecution: 'If anyone [is] for captivity, to captivity that one goes; if anyone [is] to be killed with a sword, with a sword that one [is] to be killed.' Perhaps influenced by Jesus' warning to his disciples in Matthew 26.52, quite a few scribes wrote instead: 'If anyone *kills* with a sword, with a sword that one [is] to be killed.'[42]

5 The closing wish for grace in Revelation 22.21 reveals how scribes could switch over to autopilot. Familiar with a number of ways of ending the sentence 'the grace of our Lord Jesus [be] with' from the other epistles in the New Testament, different scribes ended the wish with 'all', 'you all', 'us all', 'the saints', 'your saints', 'all the saints' and 'all his saints'!

Quite a few of the differences that set the King James Version (KJV) apart from more modern translations can be attributed to decisions about which variant represented John's original wording. In this regard, modern translations have the benefit of a great deal more – and much older – manuscript evidence than was available to the editors of the Greek text on which the KJV was based in the early seventeenth century.[43]

---

42 The Geneva Bible (1560) goes even further, adjusting the first maxim as well to read: 'If anie lead into captivitie, he shal go into captivitie.'

43 A thorough, but still quite accessible, resource in this regard is Comfort 2008: 809–72.

The attitudes of Christian scholars of earlier periods varied in regard to alternative readings within the manuscript tradition. As early as the second century, Irenaeus of Lyons draws attention to a rather significant variant of the number of the beast, with some manuscripts reading 616 rather than 666. Irenaeus is himself convinced that 666 is the correct reading and warns those who follow the variant to desist 'so that they may not be counted among the false prophets' (*Haer.* 5.30.1–2)! His attitude is very similar to, if somewhat more spirited than, that of many text critics of the nineteenth and twentieth centuries: find and stick to the author's original wording.

Andrew of Caesarea, on the other hand, mentions a number of variant readings in the course of his commentary and seeks to draw meaning from *each* variant, if he finds therein something that might edify his readers.[44] He mentions two variants explicitly. In some manuscripts of Revelation 3.7, Jesus identifies himself to the Christians in Philadelphia as the one who holds, not 'the key of David', but 'the key of Hades' (probably recalling Rev. 1.18). Drawing attention to the fact that the latter appears 'in some copies', Andrew simply proceeds to remark that 'through the image of the "key of Hades" the authority of life and death is ascribed to Christ', untroubled by any concern that only one of the two readings could be original.[45] Similarly, the seven angels of the seven last plagues emerge from the heavenly temple 'in pure linen' (Rev. 15.6 in most manuscripts), 'or, as some copies have it, in a "pure stone"'. Andrew weaves the two images together in a single interpretation: 'Their dress indicates the purity of their natures and the proximity they have to Christ, their cornerstone.'[46] While impatient with stylistic improvements of John's language – the kind of scribal editing he considered 'arrogance' – Andrew is patient with variations among texts where each promotes orthodox theological thought.

Both author-centred and text-centred interpretation – as well as reader-centred interpretation where we are interested in the experience of the *first* readers – require knowing as fully as possible what *John* himself wrote. Traditional text criticism, which requires making the kinds of decisions Irenaeus made, will therefore always be foundational for exegesis. But the textual variants themselves provide material for another kind of reader-centred interpretation, namely the investigation of how Christian scribes were reading Revelation across the centuries – and perhaps even, with Andrew, finding some value in what these variants might tell us.

---

44 These have been identified and discussed in Hernandez 2011.

45 Andrew of Caesarea, *Comm. in Apoc.* 3.8 (Weinrich 2011a: 125).

46 Andrew of Caesarea, *Comm. in Apoc.* 15.45 (Weinrich 2011a: 169).

4

The world of John the Seer: locating the text historically and socially

John refers to figures, activities, institutions and systems throughout his work in ways that suggest that these were objective facets of his landscape and the landscape of the congregations he addresses. The *manner* in which he makes these references is highly interpretative and ideological – that is, it is clear that he wants his hearers to see these realities in a particular way that is strategic to John's goals for his hearers' orientation to them. But it seems equally clear that he is interpreting *realities* in the lived landscape he shares with his audiences. This is especially evident in the seven oracles to the churches (Rev. 2—3), which have long been regarded as the most transparent windows into the historical settings of and challenges facing John's audiences (see Ramsey 1904; Hemer 1986; Worth 1999a; 1999b). But it is also clear in regard to certain features of the visionary chapters of Revelation, which highlight conditions that all seven of John's congregations face in common – such as the ubiquitous phenomena of idolatrous religion (9.20–21) and emperor worship (13:4, 11–18) and the economic practices that have formed around the needs of the imperial centre – 'the great city' set 'upon seven hills' that 'has authority over the kings of the earth' (17.9, 18).

Many readers throughout the centuries have intuited some correlation between the images in the text and realities in the lived world, though the history of interpretation shows a propensity to look for these correlations in the lived world of the *interpreters* and not of the Christians in the seven congregations addressed by John. While this no doubt reflects a conviction on the part of readers in every generation that Revelation, as part of Scripture, has a word for them in their setting, it potentially suffers from not at least pausing to consider what word Revelation had for the Christians to whom it was originally addressed and whose concerns and challenges were of vital importance to John as he prayed, meditated, was caught up in the Spirit and set down in writing the word he believed he had received *for them*. Taking the time to hear Revelation's *historic* word to the churches, moreover, may be a particularly helpful step on the path to hearing Revelation's word in a new setting both on analogy with well-established practices in the interpretation of the prophetic and epistolary texts in the scriptural canon and as a methodological restraint upon the book's peculiar penchant for being pressed into the service of the interpreter's situational agenda over and above any consideration of John's historic agenda.

In this chapter we will look at the principal realities to which John draws attention, but from perspectives other than his own or those of his book. Then, in the chapters that follow, we will give close attention to how John's text potentially shapes his audiences' perceptions of and responses to those elements of their shared, lived context.

The religious and ideological context

After the opening of the seals and the sounding of six of the seven trumpets, John reports that, contrary to all expectation, the survivors 'did not repent from their handiwork, so as to cease to worship the demons and the idols of gold and silver and bronze and stone and wood' (Rev. 9.20). In the oracles to the congregations in Pergamum and Thyatira, the glorified Christ makes mention of teachers within the congregations seeking to make room for 'eating what had been offered to idols' (2.14, 20). The inhabitants of the earth are said to have 'worshipped the dragon, because he gave authority to the beast' (13.4), and they go on to worship the beast and eventually an image of the beast (13.4, 8, 12–15). Whether or not a person engages in such worship becomes a determining factor in his or her temporal fate and eternal destiny (13.15; 14.9–11; 15.2–4; 20.4).

Religious activity – whom and in what contexts one worships – is clearly a matter of principal concern to John, as it was indeed in the environment of his congregations. Public spaces in each of the seven cities addressed by Revelation were dominated by buildings and activities that were particularly religious in nature, but always directed towards a deity other than the God of Israel and of Jesus Christ. The world of the early Christians, moreover, knew no separation of religious activity from every other sphere of social activity. There were public, civic officials dedicated to the regulation and promotion of traditional religious cults. City councils often deliberated on matters that modern people would call religious, such as the establishment, funding and staffing of local temples to one or more of the gods (including the emperors). Regional councils were similarly tasked with promoting and regulating the worship of the Roman emperors at the provincial level. Social and political advancement within the elite often necessitated holding official priesthoods and subsidizing cultic activity. Important religious festivals brought a city's entire population together to honour the gods with processions and sacrifices and to enjoy a state-sponsored meal, the main courses of which were provided from the sacrificed animals. Private dinner parties included the offering of incense and wine to the gods who were also 'present'. Traditional piety also embraced the commercial life of the city. In port cities, the shipping season was opened with religious rites invoking the favour of the gods (Kraybill 1996: 123–7). Associations of artisans of particular crafts or merchants dealing in particular goods included religious rites in their meetings and meals.

Artemis (or Diana, as she was called in the Roman pantheon) was particularly revered in Ephesus, where a massive temple had been erected to her. With a footprint four times the size of Athens's Parthenon, the Artemision was regularly listed as one of the top seven tourist destinations by ancient travellers.[1] There was also a smaller shrine to the goddess, eventually to be shared with Julius Caesar, in the civic forum, the administrative centre of town. Archaeological work on Pergamum's acropolis has identified a monumental altar to Zeus and temples to Athena, Demeter, Dionysus and Hera, as well as a shrine to Hermes and Heracles in the gymnasium complex. An Asclepion (an ancient health spa) about half a mile (1 km) distant from the acropolis included a temple to Asclepius, the god of healing. Excavation in Smyrna is extremely limited due to the presence of the major, modern city of Izmir, but literary and inscriptional references name temples to Zeus, Cybele (the mother goddess) and Dionysus. The discovery of scores of small bronze statuettes of various deities along with small stone altars for offering incense bear witness to pious devotion in domestic settings as well.

The gods' favour was held to be the bedrock for human flourishing. Showing them the proper gratitude was the responsibility of every citizen, for the good not only of each individual but also of the city – even the empire – as a whole. Piety towards the gods and solidarity with one's fellow citizens went hand in hand. Thus, when certain Jewish communities pressed to be given the rights of citizenship in their host cities, the Gentile citizens objected that their lack of piety towards the gods revered by the city undermined any such claim (see the reports in Josephus, *Ant.* 12.121–6; *Ag. Ap.* 2.65). Political ethicists like Cicero warned that 'the disappearance of piety towards the gods will entail the disappearance of loyalty and social union among people as well, and of justice

---

1   See the remark by Antipater of Sidon in *Greek Anthology* 9.58. A description of the temple appears in Pliny the Elder, *Nat.* 36.21.95–7.

itself' (Cicero, *De natura deorum* 1.2.4, LCL; see also Dio Cassius, *Hist. Rom.* 52.36.2). Significant social pressure upheld traditional piety.

One particularly prominent cult in Asia Minor (and, arguably, in the book of Revelation) is the cult of the Roman emperors and the goddess Roma. This cult is both a result of and a promotional tool for a larger empire-wide ideology concerning Roman domination of the greater part of the known civilized world. It would not be too much to call this ideology a 'gospel', not least because an inscription found in Priene and several other cities of Roman Asia spoke of the birth of Augustus (emperor from 31 BCE to 14 CE) as 'the beginning of the gospel ['the good news'] for the world'. According to Virgil, one of the great evangelists of this gospel, Zeus (or Jupiter), the supreme god, raised up the Roman people to 'rule the sea and all the lands about it' (Virgil, *Aen.* 1.236–7), referring to the *orbis terrarum*, the 'circle of the lands' about the Mediterranean. These 'lords of the world' (*Aen.* 1.282) would enjoy 'rule without end' (*Aen.* 1.279), bringing 'the whole world under the rule of law' through its military power (*Aen.* 4.232).[2] This notion that Rome ruled 'the whole world' is pervasive in literature from the period (see even Luke 2.1), though the empire's residents remained aware of nations independent from and hostile to Rome.

Augustus himself would usher in a new 'golden age' (*Aen.* 6.792–3) and was destined to 'extend his rule to regions beyond the stars', beyond the horizon 'where Atlas shoulders the sky' (*Aen.* 6.794–6). In keeping with this conviction, a new calendar began to be used in Roman Asia in 9 BCE. New Year's Day would henceforth be observed on 23 September – Augustus's birthday. Since Augustus's reign marked the beginning of a new era, his birthday would mark the start of each new year.[3] Virgil, like many in his world, embraced a view of history according to which civilization passes through periods of increasing decline and corruption – first a golden, then a silver, then a bronze, then an iron age – before a renewal of the golden age. The gospel of Rome thus included a view of time in which the best of all possible worlds had already been restored and would last for ever (Friesen 2001: 122–31). It proclaimed a world with Rome at the centre of the conceptual map and Roman rule as the instrument by which the gods showered unprecedented favours upon humanity. Awareness of the dominant view of time and history helps us to hear the

---

2   I focus here on literary witnesses, but see Smith 1987 for an excellent study of the visual representations of this ideology at the Temple of Augustus (the 'Sebasteion') at Aphrodisias, a city some 37 miles (60 km) distant from Laodicea, and Zanker 1990 for a more general study of the visual representations of imperial ideology.

3   The text of the relevant decree can be found in Danker 1982: 215–22 and Friesen 2001: 34–5.

polemical edge to John's reconfiguration of time. The present age (the eternal 'golden age' of Rome) is temporary and fleeting, soon to be brought to a cataclysmic close by the God whom Rome ignores. By contrast, the time of God's future vindication of God's faithful ones is vast – a whole millennium – and the true golden age of eternity will occur in a renewed creation far removed in time from Rome's brief span to strut and fret its hour upon the stage of history (see also Friesen 2001: 159–61).

Alongside this ideology emerged the cult of the emperors, beginning with Julius, but gaining in momentum with Augustus. Nicolaus of Damascus, a contemporary and friend of Herod the Great, explained the phenomenon as a proportional response of gratitude to the immense scale of the benefits Augustus had brought to the whole world (see his *Life of Augustus* 1). Augustus would be hailed as 'saviour of the world' after his victory in the civil wars against Marc Antony and Cleopatra VII of Egypt (Propertius, *Elegies* 4.6.37–40). The rhetoric of 'peace' was particularly important in connection with Augustus's rule, in regard not only to ending a string of civil wars that stretched across two decades but also to restoring peace to unruly provinces in the west, and, with peace, the return of prosperity. One illustrative anecdote can be found in Suetonius's *Life of Augustus*. While an Alexandrian grain ship was moored in the port of Puteoli, the sailors and merchants, putting on white garments and placing wreaths upon their heads, offered incense and praise to Augustus as his ship was passing by, exclaiming: 'It is through you that we live, through you we sail the seas, through you we enjoy our freedom and our fortunes' (*Augustus* 98). Successive emperors would continue to benefit the province of Asia in impressive ways. Tiberius gave substantial financial assistance to restore several cities after an earthquake. Nero undertook the dredging of Ephesus's harbour, ever in danger of silting up. Vespasian constructed a highway from Pergamum to Smyrna to Ephesus and to Thyatira and Sardis beginning in 75 CE, greatly facilitating trade and earning him accolades as 'Benefactor of the World and Saviour and Benefactor of all Mankind' in multiple inscriptions around the province (Magie 1950: 570, 572). Since the emperors brought gifts that were usually the subject of prayers offered to the gods, it seemed appropriate to render to the emperors the honours and thanks given to the gods.

The worship of the emperors and, alongside them, the deified personification of Rome itself was a prominent feature of the urban landscape of the seven cities named by Revelation.[4] Cults were organized, and temples com-

---

4   See the detailed catalogue in Price 1984: 254–60, 264–5. The studies of Price (1984) and Friesen (1993; 2001) are the most important for both the significance and the incidence of the imperial cult in the province.

missioned, at both the local and provincial levels. Sponsoring a provincial temple brought significant recognition to the city, as the emperor himself would select which city making application would be awarded the honour of becoming the 'temple keeper' (in Greek, *neōkoros*) of his provincial cult site. Pergamum was the first city in Asia to win this honour in connection with its bid to erect a temple to Augustus and Roma in 29 BCE. In 26 CE, Smyrna would beat out ten sister cities for the privilege of erecting a temple to Tiberius, along with Livia and the personified senate (Friesen 2001: 36–8). Ephesus would finally win its first *neokorate* in 89 CE in connection with its temple to the Flavian emperors – probably originally dedicated to Domitian but rededicated to Vespasian after the former's fall from grace with the senate after his death (Friesen 2001: 43–52).[5] A 7.5-metre-high (24 ft) cult image of Domitian once stood therein, presenting the emperor as the larger-than-life figure he was widely believed to be.[6] Imperial cult rites would be brought to life by professional choirs singing hymns to the emperors as to gods, by processions within the city precincts, by athletic and other competitions held in connection with imperial festivals, by the drama of sacrifice and, of course, by the fellowship meal enjoyed by participants (often involving the entire civic body; Thompson 1990: 162; Friesen 2001: 104–13).

The connection between civic pride, civic competition and imperial cult is evident from a number of inscriptions involving the coveted title *neōkoros*. Following the inauguration of its temple to Domitian, official Ephesian decrees were issued in the name of 'the council and citizenry of the temple-warden city of the Ephesians'. The Pergamenes, who had not before incorporated the title into their civic inscriptions, immediately reacted to the upstart city by naming themselves 'the council and citizenry of the *first*-to-be-named "temple warden" Pergamenes'. The rivalry heated up in the early second century when Pergamum was awarded the right to build a second provincial temple, this time dedicated to Trajan, after which it referred to itself in inscriptions as 'the council and citizenry of the *twice*-named "temple warden" city

---

5   Beyond these structures, a local temple to Augustus and Roma with a footprint of 15 by 22 metres (50 x 72 ft) (Wilson 2010: 209) sat in the centre of Ephesus's administrative forum, turning the whole forum into a kind of sacred precinct for the temple. Statues of Augustus, Livia and Tiberius also dominated one end of an enormous portico in the forum, with a dedicatory inscription to them and to Artemis conspicuous on the side facing the open courtyard. Sardis had a temple to Augustus as well and Laodicea built a local temple to Domitian and Domitia towards the end of the first century.

6   There is some dispute as to whether the head and forearm of this statue found in the remains of the temple depicted Titus (Friesen 2001: 46, 50) or either Vespasian or Domitian (so Price 1984: 187, 197, 255).

of the Pergamenes'. Ephesus was prepared to counter and, having won the bid to erect a monumental temple to Trajan's successor Hadrian, flaunted its new status as 'the council and citizenry of the first and great mother city (*mētropolis*) and *twice*-named "temple-warden-of-the-emperors" city of the Ephesians'. Pergamum predictably countered: 'the council and citizenry of the mother city of Asia and *first*-to-be-*twice*-named "temple warden" city of the Pergamenes'. This rivalry recorded in stone may strike us as amusing, but it also reveals some important facts about the imperial cult. For one thing, there is nothing to suggest that it was imposed upon the province 'from above'. Rather, it was enthusiastically promoted at the level of the local elites and may well have garnered a great deal of popular support as a cipher for civic pride.

The ubiquity of expressions of piety towards the traditional and imperial deities, together with the civic virtues that participation in such worship was understood to signal (and the corresponding vices that non-participation signalled), presented Gentile converts to the Christian movement with significant challenges. Diaspora Jews, whether Christian or not, had always been met by a good portion of their Gentile neighbours with suspicion, derision and occasional backstreet hostility for their views towards the city's gods and their neighbours' piety. Gentiles who made the conscious decision to withdraw from their previously typical engagement with the gods – and their neighbours in connection with the gods – engendered even greater reproach and animus. There were significant additional problems associated with the Christian 'gospel' (versus the Augustan gospel!) beyond those associated with monolatry, for example the fervent hope that the present world order welcomed by so many would be abruptly shaken in favour of some new 'kingdom of God' with a revivified crucified rebel at the helm. It is not surprising that several early Christian communities wrestled with how low these particular boundaries could be set so as to maximize the benefits of showing solidarity with their neighbours in religious contexts while not violating their more exclusive faith.[7]

The economic and military contexts

John is not only concerned about the religious activity surrounding his congregations and some converts' desire to discover a modus vivendi with their religious environment. Other facets of the social and economic contexts of empire also concern him, particularly the ills that an economy shaped by the

---

7   See deSilva 2020b for an imaginative attempt to recreate how these tensions manifested themselves in a variety of social contexts in Ephesus on the eve of the inauguration of the Temple of Domitian.

interests of the people at the heart of the empire inflicts upon the people at the margins of the empire (thinking of 'margins' not just geographically, but socially). This is prominent in his portrayal of 'Babylon' as a prostitute and in his prophetic denunciation of the 'city that rules over the kings of the earth' in Revelation 17.1—18.24.

The appetite of the city at the centre of empire was truly staggering, first and foremost in a quite literal sense. Rome's population during the first century is estimated at about 200,000 family units, perhaps yielding an overall figure of one million inhabitants. The heads of these families enjoyed regular access to a free, fixed amount of grain – probably only enough to sustain one person in the family, with the remainder of the unit's needs being purchased on the open market (Kraybill 1996: 107). The provinces (particularly Egypt, North Africa, Syria and the Black Sea region) had to ensure a steady supply of grain to meet these needs, whether supplied as part of the province's tribute or sold at fixed prices. In times of shortage, it was the province and not the city of Rome that had to cope with the shortfall. Monte Testaccio, a 35-metre-high (115 ft) mound on the south side of the city by the River Tiber, stands as a monument to the capital's consumption of olive oil. This artificial mountain consists of an estimated 50 million broken amphorae once used to import olive oil into the city.

Rome was omnivorous in its appetites, however, craving not only the necessities of life but, among its upper echelons, whatever luxuries every corner of its empire could supply. Aelius Aristides, a celebrated Greek orator of the second century CE, paints this picture of the movement of goods in the imperial economy:

> Around lie the continents far and wide, pouring an endless flow of goods to Rome. There is brought from every land and sea whatever is brought forth by the seasons and is produced by all countries, rivers, lakes, and the skills of Greeks and foreigners . . . Anyone who wants to behold all these products must either journey through the whole world to see them or else come to this city . . . One can see so many cargoes from India or if you wish from Arabia . . . that one may surmise that the trees there have been left permanently bare, and that those people must come here to beg for their own goods whenever they need anything!
> (*To Rome* 11–13, LCL)

As this paragraph appears in a speech *praising* Rome's stature and achievements, Aristides may himself have been oblivious to the problems of an economy that left the provinces at the periphery bare and their inhabitants having to come to Rome to recover some portion of their produce. From the viewpoint of the imperial markets and the houses of the elite families in the capital, however, the availability of (literally) a world of goods was seen as a sign of Rome's unparalleled achievements. The penchant for luxury, overconsumption and self-indulgence did not go unchallenged within Rome itself. Seneca, for example, reproached Rome's 'insatiable present hungers for every luxury and excess of food, clothing, and shelter, which stand against the simplicity of earlier times and the little that is required for Nature's need (*Helv.* 10.3–11.4)' (Rapske 2012: 336), as did Lucian in his *Nigrinus* (Royalty 1998: 123).

Thyatira, Sardis and Laodicea occupied places in the land trade and production of wares. Ephesus and Smyrna were major port cities sending goods westward and receiving some Western luxuries for the province's elite. It is not unreasonable to think of John himself standing on the upper tiers of the great theatre in Ephesus overlooking the wide street that led to its harbour and watching cargoes making their way from the various commercial forums down to the ships waiting in the harbour:

> cargoes of gold and silver and precious stone and pearls and fine linen and purple goods and silk and scarlet goods and goods of every kind of citrus wood, and ivory vessels and vessels made from most precious wood and bronze and iron and marble, and cinnamon and amomon and incense and myrrh and frankincense and wine and olive oil and fine wheat flour and wheat and cattle and sheep, and horses and chariots, and bodies (that is, human lives).
> (Rev. 18.12–13)

An inscription on the mausoleum of one Titus Flavius Zeuxis just outside the city gate of Hierapolis, a close neighbour of Laodicea and Colossae (see Col. 4.13), speaks of its occupant's successful shipping business. Zeuxis had made 72 trips around the coast of Cape Malea in the south of Greece to Italy, presumably starting from the port of Ephesus (the most convenient for a resident of Hierapolis), transporting his cargoes. In John's vision, Zeuxis would have been among those standing at a safe distance from the smouldering ruins of Babylon, lamenting the loss of its business (Rev. 18.15–19).

The Roman provinces were divided into two classes: imperial and senatorial. The provinces that posed potential problems were administered directly by the emperor through his own agents, and the legions were stationed in these provinces. Secure provinces were entrusted to senators to govern. Asia was a senatorial province, whose population had long since made peace with Roman rule and, at some echelons, was profoundly supportive of Roman rule. It is unlikely that anyone in John's congregations would have had even great-great-grandparents who had been alive to see the last violent clash between Roman armies and the local population, which would have occurred in 88 BCE with the suppression of anti-Roman factions (who had even murdered Roman citizens seeking sanctuary in the Temple of Artemis). Asia appears to have been particularly content with the rule of the Flavian emperors. Statues, altars, buildings dedicated to Domitian – above all the temple in Ephesus – bear witness to the province's general satisfaction with him, and he is reputed to have kept a close watch on the senatorial governors to ensure their honesty and fairness (Magie 1950: 577).

Nevertheless, the final argument in the discourse of empire was violent force. While some kingdoms came voluntarily under the aegis of Rome, the empire grew significantly through the conquest of territories and kingdoms (including Gaul, Germania, Britannia, Egypt and Judea), subjugating them to the empire and its interests as 'provinces'. Rome also acted decisively to suppress provinces whose residents sought to 'opt out' of empire, most famously, for students of the New Testament, in Judea – a province in open rebellion from 66 to 70 CE. The celebrated Roman peace was established, extended and maintained with a heavy price tag in human life, exacerbated by the inhumane treatment of thousands upon thousands of those who resisted and survived (whether their destiny was the slave market, the arena or the cross). Hordes of carrion birds circling in to feast upon the bodies of the slain were not only to be seen in John's apocalyptic imagination (Rev. 19.17–18); they could have been seen over many a battlefield throughout the empire in the first century, and not least over Jerusalem in 70 CE. Not all Romans were oblivious to the underside of their accomplishments. Imagining how a chieftain in Britannia would comment on the Roman 'achievement' in his native land, the Roman historian Tacitus wrote: 'to violence, rapine, and plunder they give the name "government"; they make a wasteland and call it "peace"' (*Agricola* 30).

The conquest and retention of these territories was a prerequisite to the centre of empire (and the provincial elites partnering with the empire) enjoying the lifestyle that the tribute, produce and products of the widely diverse provinces made possible. Rome brought benefits to its subjugated territories, to be certain. But if it could be called a 'symbiotic' relationship rather than an outright parasitic one, Rome derived the greater share of the benefit in the relationship by far. And the economy of the entire Roman world was unquestionably parasitic in one important respect, namely the reduction of a full one fifth of the population to the status of 'living tools' (to quote Aristotle's infamous definition from *Politics* 1.4 [1253b27–33]) to be used as slave labour.

The gross inequities in access to goods and distribution of resources created by the imperial economy, the violence that kept a sufficient number of territories tethered to the capital to create the requisite conditions for the economy, and the human cost (both in terms of lives exterminated and persons enslaved) of maintaining the economy all led John to believe that one could not participate in and profit from this economy without becoming liable also for its crimes (Rev. 18.4). As Harry Maier (2002: 61) observes so well:

> For audiences convinced of the reasonableness of a Roman military order whose economic prosperity was bought at the price of incalculable human suffering, John the troublemaker from Patmos unsettles reason and asks his audience to reconsider what counts for sanity.

We will have occasion to explore further some facets of the environment specific to just one or two out of the seven congregations below in Chapter 6. If John's first audiences were given to the same impulses as so many audiences of Revelation since – namely, to seek out what correlations might exist between these images in his vision and features of the landscape of their lived reality – we will need to keep the realities of Roman imperialism as experienced in all seven of these cities in mind in order to discern how Revelation interpreted the world for those first hearers.

5

A revelation of Jesus Christ (Revelation 1)

The opening words declare the book to be 'a revelation of Jesus Christ' (1.1). The sense of this phrase is ambiguous. On the one hand, it may be heard to indicate that this is 'a revelation that came from Jesus Christ', that is, 'something that Jesus Christ revealed'. This well suits the immediate context, in which we are told that God gave this content to Jesus 'to show his slaves what must quickly come about' (1.1). As such, it raises interesting questions about the authorship and authority of the book for, though every word was written down by John, John practically denies with every word that his was the creative mind behind any word! This is true both in regard to his claim that the text's origins lay in experiences in which John himself was but a passive observer and listener (perhaps occasionally an *interactive* observer and listener at most) and to the manner in which John incorporates extensive material from older texts and revelations into his new text. Craig Koester (2014: 847) observed that 'the principal function' of Revelation's opening and closing sections (1.1–20; 22.6–21) 'is to shape the way readers receive the text' and, in regard to establishing the nature and sources of the authority that John claims for his text – and that he hopes his hearers will ascribe to the same – he is certainly correct.[1]

On the other hand, it could indicate that this is 'a text that reveals Jesus Christ' in the same way that Paul experienced 'a revelation of Jesus Christ' (Gal. 1.12), that is, was shown something important about Jesus Christ (indeed, according to Acts, shown Jesus Christ himself!) that deeply influenced his own life choices. This option, too, has strong contextual support, for the hearers will be shown Jesus 'coming on the clouds' less than a full minute into the public reading of this text (1.7). John will also reveal Jesus to them as Jesus revealed himself to John, standing before John on the island of Patmos (1.12–20).

---

1 See the discussion in Chapter 2 above of the indications of genre in Revelation 1.1–4 (as letter, 1.4; as 'prophecy', 1.3; and as 'revelation/apocalypse', 1.1) for another facet of the way Revelation's opening shapes 'the way readers receive the text'.

This suggests that we might read Revelation specifically for its theological – and, above all, its *christ*ological – contributions. While some weighty voices have contested Revelation's value in this regard, even questioning to what degree John's Revelation is a 'Christian' text, others have valued it specifically for its christological affirmations. It is certainly a text that foregrounds encounter with the glorified Christ, not least in presenting the encounter with Christ on the eschatological horizon as the principal crisis facing humankind in general and John's hearers in particular.

Authorship and authority in Revelation

Who is the author of Revelation? From one perspective, of course, it is John the visionary prophet who puts ink on parchment, even as he is twice commanded to do by the glorified Jesus (1.11, 19). The authority of a prophet, however, comes not from his or her speaking in his or her own voice, but being heard to speak the words of another, supernatural figure. As Revelation opens, it is indeed not John's voice at all that one hears, but an impersonal, anonymous voice presenting the text as a message that originated with God and that was communicated by Jesus through an angel to John for the benefit of God's many servants (1.1; see also 22.6). This voice also commends John as one who 'bore witness to the word of God and the testimony of Jesus in regard to whatever he saw' (1.2), drawing attention both to John's fidelity (for such witness will be lifted up as a primary virtue throughout Revelation)[2] and once more to the origin of the message *outside* of John's creative mind in the visionary experiences he was given. He does not claim to invent the content, but rather claims that the content came to him 'in a spirit', that is, in a visionary trance (1.10). Indeed, the opening is similar to – and may purposefully recall – the openings of several of the prophetic books of the Jewish Scriptures (see Isa. 1.1; Mal 1.1), presenting John's work as one more text in that authoritative line. In a situation of competing prophets, John's message receives supernatural endorsements. Angelic voices – and God's own voice, it appears, at one point – authenticate particular utterances or larger blocks of material as 'genuine words of God' (19.9), 'reliable and genuine' (21.5; 22.6), sent from God for God's servants (22.6).[3]

The focus throughout Revelation remains on John's 'seeing' and 'hearing', not 'creating'. John's voice recedes beneath the voices of otherworldly beings.

---

2 See 1.5, 9; 2.13; 6.9; 12.17; 19.10, 13.

3 Indeed, the pronouncement in 22.6 may be heard to authenticate the entire text of Revelation, since it explicitly and extensively recalls the language of 1.1, 3.

The glorified Christ speaks to commission John (1.17–20)[4] and to rebuke certain practices and persons in the seven congregations (2.1—3.22). The souls of murdered Christians cry out for vindication (6.9–11) and praise God when God enacts judgement against their persecutors (16.5–7). Angels and other heavenly voices challenge allegiances and behaviours (14.6–13) and denounce 'Babylon' for its crimes against humanity and God (18.1–24). God himself speaks to declare his identity (1.8), announce the fulfilment of his ancient promises (21.5–7) and pronounce warnings against the unfaithful (21.8). When John does speak in his own voice, it is to report his own experience of 'seeing' or 'hearing' or perhaps communicating with an angelic figure and thus, ironically, to continue to remind the hearers of the otherworldly sources of the content he discloses.[5] John's description of his own visceral and very physical reactions to these visionary encounters – falling down in awe, overcome by the experiences (1.17; 19.10; 22.8) – strengthens the impression of their 'reality'. A clear rhetorical gain of this tactic is that it is now the voices of the glorified Christ, angels, the Spirit and other supernatural beings who both confront and assure John's congregations.[6] To the extent that his audiences accept John's text authentically to represent the utterances of such figures, they are more likely to accept the content and its implications for their own practice.

The topic of urgency seems to support the authority – the weight – that John's Revelation will carry. Whereas Daniel's visions and interpretations of visions concerned 'what things must necessarily happen in the last days' (Dan. 2.28), John claims his revelation to concern 'what things must happen quickly' (Rev. 1.1; 22.6; Beale 1998: 166–7). Where Daniel was told to 'seal up' the contents of his book for a much later time (Dan. 8.26; 12.4, 9), John was told *not* to seal up his book, 'for the time is near' (Rev. 22.10). In Daniel, as in other pseudonymous books, this was a device used to account for the book's not having come to light until long after the death of the alleged author, the exilic-period prophet Daniel. John's departure from this device has been taken to suggest that, 'from its inception, Revelation was designed to be an open book that addressed issues facing its earliest readers, and modern historical interpretation takes that setting into account when exploring the significance of the text' (Koester 2014: 852). John's own perspective is contradicted by readings

---

4 This is not a prophetic 'call' narrative so much as an authorization of this particular message. John had been 'called' long before (rightly Karrer 1986: 139–41; Koester 2014: 249).

5 John refers to his 'seeing' no fewer than 45 times (1.12, 17; 4.1; 5.1, 2, 6, 11; 6.1, 2, 5, 8, 9, 12; 7.1, 2, 9; 8.2, 13; 9.1, 17; 10.1, 5; 13.1, 2, 11; 14.1, 6, 14; 15.1, 2, 5; 16.13; 17.3, 6; 18.1; 19.11, 17, 19; 20.1, 4, 11, 12; 21.1, 2, 22).

6 So, among others, Yarbro Collins 1984: 145; Kirby 1988: 199; Schüssler Fiorenza 1991: 115, 137–8.

that presume that the twenty-first-century interpreter knows far better what John's images signify based on his or her experience, even though the book was not sealed for a later time but left open for the first-century congregations to understand.[7]

This impression of imminence or urgency is reinforced throughout Revelation: 'the time is near' (1.3); Jesus is 'coming quickly' (2.16; 3.11; 22.7, 12, 20) or suddenly 'as a thief' (16.15). Urgency potentially heightens the hearers' attentiveness and amplifies their emotional responses (deSilva 2009: 180–1). As Dale Allison observed in regard to the historical Jesus' declaration that God's kingdom was close at hand, 'Proclaiming a near end confronts people with a decision that cannot wait' (2009: 98). It facilitates a more radical willingness to alter the shape of one's life in the present by communicating the ultimate stakes of doing so (or failing to do so) in a manner that can be readily apprehended 'like advertising with its urgent appeal to buy "while quantities last"' (Maier 2002: 130–1).

This technique, however, creates the problem of the 'soon' or the 'quickly' of Jesus' promised intervention. This would not have been a problem for John's original audience, of course, but it becomes an increasingly pressing problem after one century, then another, then *another* passes. Interpreters have dealt with this problem in a number of ways over those centuries. The sixth-century Greek commentator Oecumenius, for example, attributes this to God's perspective on time, according to which 'a thousand years in your sight, O Lord, are as yesterday when it is past, or as a watch in the night' (*Comm.* 1.1–2 , quoting Ps. 90.4; Weinrich 2005: 2), a solution promoted also in the annotations in the Geneva Bible (p. 1195 on 22.20). Andrew of Caesarea ventures that the impression of the imminence of the end indicates 'either the shortness of the present time in comparison with the future age or the sudden swiftness of the death of each person. For the departure from here is the end of every person' and standing before God and the Lamb at the last day is never further away than one's own death (*Comm. in Apoc.* 22.7; Weinrich 2005: 395). John's text, however, also prepares for this tension of a 'soon' that takes for ever to arrive by juxtaposing statements concerning the imminence of the 'end' and spinning a narrative that frequently delays progress towards that end, as seen in our survey in Chapter 1. Even the announcement that 'there will be no more delay' – made when the larger half of the book lies still in front of this announcement rather than behind it! – renders questions of time more complex

---

7 Hal Lindsey (1975: 295) applies the language of Daniel concerning that book's relevance for a later time (that is, its being 'sealed up' for a later generation) to Revelation, overriding Revelation's own claim to the contrary.

than they might seem. Christ also promises to come to intervene in the history of the congregations he addresses 'soon' (2.5, 16), but this seems to indicate a 'soon' that is not a final intervention in history (Koester 2014: 222).

The authority of John's text is also heightened by the fact that blessings are pronounced upon those who attend to its message, to 'keep' it (1.3; 22.7), while curses are pronounced upon those who presume to alter it or, perhaps, apply it selectively (22.18–19). Even before the opening 'title' of 1.1–3 is over, the anonymous voice pronounces 'privileged' or 'favoured' the person reading the text out loud to the congregation and those who are hearing *and* heeding the message and its implications for their allegiances and practices (1.3). Essentially the same pronouncement is repeated in 22.7, appropriately omitting the blessing of the one reading aloud and those hearing, for they all have arrived at the conclusion and all that remains is the 'keeping', the obedient heeding, of the message.[8] Such people are 'privileged' because they stand in a better position to overcome the challenges of the forthcoming future successfully and encounter Jesus favourably when he returns to reign and to judge. There are seven such 'blessings' or 'macarisms' in Revelation (1.3; 14.13; 16.15; 19.9; 20.6; 22.7, 14). Each proposes conditions that lead to a highly desirable state (being 'privileged', 'favoured', 'blessed'), and thus motivates the hearers to align themselves with those conditions.[9] Cumulatively they provide a summary of the postures John wishes for all his congregations to adopt and ambitions he wishes for them to prioritize (Bauckham 1993a: 30).

At the same time, Revelation concludes with the pronouncement of curses – quite probably to be heard as uttered by Jesus (compare 22.18 and 22.20) – upon those who fail to respect the inviolability of this prophetic utterance by adding to or taking away from its contents (22.18–19). This recalls similar curses warning against tampering with the text of the Mosaic law (Deut. 4.2; 12.32), including its Greek translations (*Let. Aris.* 311; Koester 2014: 845). Given John's own expectation of Christ's imminent intervention, he was himself probably not concerned for the integrity of the precise wording of his text over the course of a long history of transmission. Perhaps he sought to prevent local readers or others in the congregations from adding qualifying glosses or omitting details to lessen any discomfort when reading the indictments of

---

8 'Keeping' consistently has behavioural implications. See the use of the term in 2.26; 3.3, 8, 10; 12.17 ('those keeping the commandments of God'); 14.13 (the same, conjoined with keeping 'faith with Jesus').

9 Dissatisfaction with the adequacy of 'blessed' as a translation has led to several alternative suggestions that better capture the force of a macarism, for example 'How honoured!' 'How privileged!' 'How favoured!' (Hanson 1996: 90; deSilva 1998: 104).

the churches and local figures within them (one thinks of the awkwardness of reading Revelation 2.18–29 with the Christian prophet whom John labels 'Jezebel' sitting in the room!), or of the Roman domination system as a whole. Perhaps he sought to guard against selective application of the message while still maintaining some accommodating practices. Either way, setting readers between blessing and curse depending on how they treat a message is a bold claim for the text's authority and power.

Another pervasive source of authority for John's message is the scriptural tradition shared by church and synagogue, together with the tradition of Jesus' sayings. The voices of the prophets, psalmists and other scriptural authors speak throughout Revelation by virtue of John's incorporation of phrases, clauses and sometimes whole sentences from the older, authoritative texts. On the one hand, Revelation gives new voice to the familiar voices of the Jewish Scriptures; on the other, it invites the older texts to lend the authority of their voices to John's new utterance. A clear example confronts the audience as early as 1.7:

> Look! He is coming with the clouds,
> and every eye will see him,
> and whoever pierced him,
> and all the tribes of the land will wail on his account.

The italicized text shows the verbiage taken over by John from Daniel 7.13, used to speak of the coming of the Son of Man to receive authority over the kingdoms of the earth, and Zechariah 12.10–14, used to articulate the significance of the event for the majority of humankind. The combination already appears in traditions ascribed to Jesus (Matt. 24.30 and par.), suggesting that not only the texts but also their combination and interpretation would be received as 'traditional' and, therefore, authoritative here.

While not every hearer would recognize every possible allusion to an older text – indeed, even John, who made the diction of the Scriptures so fully his own, might not have been aware of many of them – they would hear sufficient resonances in sufficient bulk to recognize that they were hearing a message that claimed to stand in faithful continuity with the messages of Scripture. The pervasive incorporation of texts already accepted as divine revelation helps John's vision come across as an authentic revelation. John gives the texts new shape, referents and direction, but the older texts lend their authority and power to that new shape. The Venerable Bede had noticed the 'considerable harmony between this book and the prophets, not only in their meanings but also in their vocabulary. For what verse can you find that is not from Isaiah or

Zechariah or another of the prophets?' (*Exp.* 22.9; Weinrich 2011b: 193).[10] This has become an area of intensive investigation for scholars of the book, and thus a topic to which we will frequently return.

Since John speaks his prophetic word in an early Christian culture well accustomed to testing prophetic utterances to determine their genuineness and, thus, the authority to be accorded them, it is not the implicit and explicit claims to authority – to mediate the speech of God, the glorified Christ, the angels – that will persuade the congregations to 'keep the words written therein' (1.3; cf. 22.7). Rather, it is the consonance of John's message with the scriptural tradition and the apostolic preaching, combined with John's record for reliably representing the same, that will win an obedient hearing. And in regard to such consonance, John offers a great deal of evidence (deSilva 2009: 147–74).

Encountering Jesus in Revelation

Some readers have not found John's revelation to be, in fact, 'a revelation of Jesus Christ' in the sense of imparting any valuable information about or experience of the Church's Lord. In his 1522 *Preface to the New Testament*, Martin Luther expresses a low estimation of the book because, in his opinion, 'Christ is not taught or known in it; but to teach Christ is the thing which an apostle above all else is to do'.[11] D. H. Lawrence found Christ in the Apocalypse, but did not at all approve of the Christ he found therein:

> Always the titles of power, and never the titles of love. Always Christ the omnipotent conqueror flashing his great sword and destroying, destroying vast masses of men, till blood mounts up to the horses' bridles. Never Christ the Saviour: never.
> (Lawrence 1931: 34)

Rudolf Bultmann, a celebrated German biblical scholar and theologian of the post-Second World War era, suggested that Revelation was barely even Christian.[12]

---

10 John does not explicitly *cite* his sources as, for example, do Matthew and Paul. For John to say 'as it is written in the prophet Isaiah' would distract his hearers from the immediacy of experiencing John's vision (just as footnotes in a novel would disturb the readers' immersion in the narrative world) and suggest that John's own experience was derivative rather than an original, ecstatic encounter.

11 1522 *Preface to the New Testament* 12, quoted in Kovacs and Rowland 2004: 44.

12 Bultmann (1984: 525) found the book to represent 'a weakly Christianized Judaism'. In an important article, Eduard Lohse (1988b) took up the question prompted, in part, by Luther's and Bultmann's verdicts: 'How Christian is the Revelation of John?' His own findings were significantly positive.

There is ample reason in the text and in the history of its interpretation, however, to reject these positions as inadequate assessments of Revelation's witness to Jesus. Jean-Pierre Prévost speaks for this more appreciative tradition when he writes:

> If we read [Revelation] to discover something about Jesus Christ, we shall be served royally! Do it for that reason alone, to reveal the riches of the person of Christ and the significance of the events of his death and resurrection for the future of the world.
> (Prévost 1993: 1, 3)

Against Luther's initial assessment of the book, Jesus emerges in fact as the focal figure of several visions. John describes his own visionary encounter with the glorified Jesus as he exists on this side of his resurrection (1.12–20). He presents Christ as the Lamb whose singular achievement (at a singular cost) won for him the unique authority to take the scroll in God's right hand and, with it, authority over the end of this world's history and the transition to God's everlasting kingdom (5.1–14). Finally, John shows the returning Christ coming at the head of the hosts of heaven to destroy the destroyers of the earth and prepare the way for the new ordering of human community (19.11–16).

While Lawrence claimed that we find in Revelation 'never Christ the Saviour: never' but always the destroyer (1931: 34), a more sympathetic reader of John's text might find significant attention given to the redemptive and constructive side of Christ's work. This emerges as a major theme in the book's opening – the place authors typically announce the major themes that will occupy their work as a whole. Jesus first emerges in Revelation as 'the one who loves us and released us from our sins by his blood' (1.5), a reference to Jesus' death as an act of redemption and supreme love that will emerge again in 5.6–14 as the distinguishing feature of the Lamb's work and achievement. In both passages, this redemption 'from' is also a redemption 'for': 'and made us a kingdom – priests to his God and Father' (1.6). Nelson Kraybill (2010: 21) observes that this 'is political language, calling followers of Jesus Christ to alternative allegiance and alternative identity'.

One theme that runs throughout Revelation is the history of this 'alternative sovereignty' (Friesen 2001: 181), consisting of those who persevere in living faithfully under the rule of the One God and the Lamb in the midst of Satan's attempts to expand his own empire, as John sees it, through the activity of Rome, its rulers and its legitimation mechanisms like the imperial cult.[13] The capacity of Revelation's language concerning Jesus' achievement to bestow dignity on the oppressed is sensitively captured by Allan Boesak, writing about Revelation from a prison in apartheid South Africa:

> It does not matter what the powers of this world have made of us, what labels they have put on us – 'kaffirs,' 'niggers,' 'coloureds' – to force us to accept subhuman status and to hide their own desperate, fearful uncertainty. The Lord of lords, the King of kings, has made us kings and priests for his God and Father.
> (Boesak 1987: 49)

To be a 'kingdom' for God in the present age, however, also requires 'endurance' because of the 'tribulation' brought about by those vying with God for dominance (1.9).[14] Boesak is also helpful in revealing the pastoral relevance of those qualities of Revelation's Jesus that Lawrence found unwelcome, namely the future activity of the Lord who vindicates his faithful ones, oppressed and slaughtered by the powers of this age:

> Those who do not know this suffering through oppression, who do not struggle together with God's people for the sake of the gospel, and who do not feel in their own bodies the meaning of oppression and the freedom and joy of fighting against it shall have grave difficulty understanding this letter from Patmos.
> (Boesak 1987: 38)

Lawrence also failed to give weight to the images of the Lamb's continuing care for the redeemed on the far side of death. The passages that speak of the Lamb shepherding these souls and leading them beside streams of living water (7.13–17), keeping them by his light and presence from the reach of darkness, sorrow, pain, death and curse (21.4, 22–23), have consoled Christians facing their own deaths – whether natural or as the result of the hostility of those around them – or the deaths of their loved ones throughout the centuries.

---

13 One way in which the reader can trace out this contest in Revelation is by paying close attention to the references to 'nations, peoples, languages and tribes' (with slight variation) throughout the book. See 5.9; 7.9; 10.11; 11.9; 13.7; 14.6; 17.15.

14 By presenting himself as one who is willing to share the present cost of faithful witness to the kingdom and faithful obedience to God's rule, in contrast to others who seek avenues of accommodation with the rival sovereignty, John incidentally also advances his own credibility.

Commentators, particularly during the patristic period, have looked to the specific titles and descriptions of Jesus in Revelation as bearers of significant christological weight. Andrew of Caesarea entertained the possibility that 'the One who is and the "he was" and the One who is coming' (1.4) masked a Trinitarian self-identification, with the Father as 'the One who is' (as God identified himself in Exodus 3.14), the Son as 'the "he was"' (as the Word which *was* God and *was* in the beginning with God; John 1.1–2), and the Spirit as 'the One who is coming', who would be poured out on God's children at their baptisms.[15] This statement is more typically read as a statement about the nature of God as a unity rather than parsed out in Trinitarian terms. It is particularly interesting to hold it up against a near-contemporary acclamation of the chief god of the Greco-Roman pantheon: 'Zeus was, Zeus is, Zeus shall be: O great Zeus!' (Pausanias, *Descr.* 10.12.10; see the additional texts collected in Aune 1997: 31–2). The God of Revelation, however, is not merely the one who 'shall always be', who exists in a static eternity, but 'the one who is coming', who is even now on the way to intervene in human affairs. John's title for God thus also contributes to the sense of imminent confrontation with the one who will determine the eternal destiny of John's hearers and their neighbours.[16]

Other titles have been found to hold more promise for Christology specifically. God identifies himself as 'the Alpha and the Omega' in 1.8 and 'the beginning and the ending' in 21.6, but Jesus takes these titles for himself in 22.13. Jesus identifies himself also as 'the first and the last' both in 1.17 and 22.13, using an expression that God applied to God's own self in Isaiah 44.6: 'I am the first and I am the last; apart from me there is no god.' John reveals thereby a 'mystery, which becomes explicit as we travel through the Apocalypse – that the standing one and the sitting one share a Name', that is, the name of Deity (Humphrey 2007: 191; see also Fekkes 1994: 71–4). Such observations became important in the christological controversies of the fourth century, providing additional ammunition against Arius's claim that the Son was subordinate to

---

15 *Comm. in Apoc.* 1.4 (Weinrich 2005: 3). The context of a Trinitarian faith has often led interpreters to regard the 'seven spirits of God' as the one Holy Spirit, with the result that Revelation is heard to open with 'trinitarian blessing' (Bauckham 1993b: 164). One is left to wonder, however, why John would refer to the Holy Spirit here as a plurality of seven spirits but elsewhere in the same book straightforwardly in the singular (see 2.7, 11, 17, 29; 3.6, 13, 22; 14.13; 22.17). A Trinitarian interpretation may obscure a background closer to home for John the Jewish seer, namely the seven chief angels of God's presence (see further below on Rev. 4—5), a possibility noted as early as Oecumenius in the sixth century (*Comm.* 1.4b; Weinrich 2005: 4).

16 The familiar hymn 'Holy, Holy, Holy' by Reginald Heber (1861) misses an essential element of John's portrayal of God when Heber speaks of the one 'which wert, and art, and evermore shalt be'.

the Father.[17] They also came to expression in hymnody, as in a fourth-century hymn of Prudentius that continues to be sung in many churches today:

> Of the Father's love begotten
>   ere the worlds began to be,
> He is Alpha and Omega,
>   he the source, the ending he.

The Greek letters A and Ω become increasingly common in Christian iconography from the fourth century on as a visual reminder of Christ's co-eternity with the Father. The fact that Christ comes in Revelation 'to repay each according to his or her works' (22.12), an activity expected of God throughout the Old Testament (see, e.g., Ps. 61.16; Prov. 24.12; Jer. 17.10; Lam. 3.64; Sir. 16.14; 35.22–24), reinforces the embeddedness of the Son in, and equality of the Son with, the Father. Jesus' appropriation to himself of the titles 'Root and Offspring of David' (22.16) was read as a scriptural affirmation of the two natures of the Christ. Claiming to be David's *root* refers to the Son's pre-existent divinity as Creator or source of David, while the expression 'offspring of David' refers to the Son in his Incarnation and, thus, his human nature.[18]

The first 'revelation' or 'vision' in the book is specifically a vision of the glorified Christ. The language that John uses to describe the resurrected and glorified Lord is largely drawn from the visionary encounters that Old Testament prophets like Isaiah and Ezekiel had with the One God (Fekkes 1994: 53–7). By presenting his own vision of Jesus in line with his audiences' scripturally informed expectations for such encounters, John gives his experience greater credibility (Whitaker 2015: 62–3). John's reported reaction to the vision also confirms its authenticity, since Daniel and Ezekiel reacted similarly to their ecstatic encounters with the divine (see Ezek. 1.28; Dan. 8.17; 10.9–10; Koester 2014: 247).

Patristic interpreters were keen to find meaning atomistically in each of the details of John's description. Thus the priestly garment represented the flesh in which the Son was robed and which he offered as a sacrifice (Bede, *Exp.* 1.13; Weinrich 2011b: 116). He was girded about the breasts rather than the loins, because the gospel restrains passions from the very heart and not

---

17 See Ambrose, *Fid.* 2.4.34–5; 4.9.108; *Ep.* 63.49 (Koester 2014: 36, 220); Gregory of Nazianzus, *Or. Bas.* 29.17; Athanasius, *Discourses against the Arians* 3.4; Primasius, *Commentary on the Apocalypse* 22.13 (collected in Weinrich 2005: 7, 401–2).

18 Oecumenius, *Comm.* 22.15–19 (in Weinrich 2005: 405). So also Bede, *Exp.* 22.16 (in Weinrich 2005: 405–6; 2011a: 194).

merely in the fleshly act (Jerome, *Homilies on Mark* 75.1 and Andrew of Caesarea, *Comm. in Apoc.* 1.12–13; Weinrich 2005: 12–13). The breasts are the two
testaments by which believers are nourished 'as by holy paps' (Caesarius of
Arles, *Exposition* 1.13; Weinrich 2005: 13; also Bede, *Exp.* 1.13; Weinrich 2011b:
116). The whiteness of Christ's head betokened the antiquity of divinity (Victorinus, *In Apoc.* 1.2; Weinrich 2005: 13) – an observation that has merit insofar as John has combined the description of the 'Ancient of Days' in Daniel
7.9 with that of 'one like a son of man' in the same chapter. The hair white 'as
wool' signifies the sheep of Christ's flock (Caesarius of Arles, *Exposition* 1.14;
Weinrich 2005: 14). The feet resembling bronze that has passed through the
fire represent either the apostles, who preached the word while being refined
through suffering as if in a furnace (Victorinus, *In Apoc.* 1.5; Weinrich 2005:
14) or the Church in the end time yet to come, when it will face severe afflic-
tions (Bede, *Exp.* 1.15; Weinrich 2011b: 117). The sharp sword emerging from
Christ's mouth might indicate the word of judgement (Victorinus, *In Apoc.* 1.4;
Weinrich 2005: 15); the word of Christ's teaching, double-edged because both
the literal and allegorical sense bear meaning (Jerome, *Homilies on the Psalms*
59; Weinrich 2005: 16); or the Holy Spirit, which emerges with the resurrected
Christ's breath in John 20.22 (Fulgentius of Ruspe, *Letter to Peter on the Faith*
11.54; Weinrich 2005: 16).

The impetus to decode Revelation's images admittedly arises within Revelation itself, for Christ is seen to interpret the lampstands among which he
stands in this vision as the seven congregations to which John is to write and
the stars that he holds in his right hand as the angels of the congregations
(1.20). The question is: how far should one go with this approach? One is left
to wonder once more whether Revelation is best *decoded* or *experienced*. Does
the vision yield its meaning when its details are interpreted severally or when
they exercise a cumulative impact upon the audience, mediating an encounter between the members of John's congregations and the glorified, awesome
Lord whom they serve, under whose protection they stand but also to whom
they will give account? The latter would be the consensus position of a number of scholars who regard John's vivid description of the figure of the glorified
Christ and other visions to be an instance of the rhetorical technique of *ekphrasis* – 'descriptive language', the goal of which is to bring 'what is portrayed
clearly before the sight' (Aelius Theon, *Progymnasmata* 118.7–8; tr. from Kennedy 2003: 45).[19] The result is a more immediate encounter with the thing de-

---

19 See especially Whitaker 2015; Barnhill 2017; Stewart 2017. Peterson 1969 also stresses the importance
    of the imaginative and emotional impact of the visions on the hearer or reader over the reduction of

scribed, which also has the capacity to produce 'emotions ... just as if we were present' (Quintilian, *Inst.* 6.2.32, LCL).

John's own narrated response to the vision provides his audiences with guidance for their own emotional reaction. His falling down before this Jesus 'like a corpse' (1.17) mirrors the fear and awe that the audience is to feel as well at this encounter (deSilva 2009: 182; Barnhill 2017: 249). Awareness of the importance of the Roman imperial cult and representations of the emperor in the seven cities addressed by John suggests that he sought to arouse such a response, at least in part, to remind his congregations that their Lord was a far more impressive and powerful figure than the temporal lords in Rome. A genuinely divine figure, Jesus trumps the pretensions of human rulers and their manufactured glory. But fear is a stage in a process, not an end. Christ himself places a hand on John and seeks to change his emotional state: 'Don't be afraid.' Christ's assurances that follow are meant to inspire confidence as one considers this awe-inspiring figure to be on one's side and *at* one's side (Barnhill 2017: 250). The Roman magistrate might be able to kill the faithful witnesses of the One God and his Anointed, but those witnesses have a far greater ally who holds the keys to death and the grave (Blount 2009: 46).

If the encounter with the glorified Jesus mediated by John's description of his visionary experience in 1.12–18 pushes his congregations in the direction of alignment with what this Jesus values and divestment from what this Jesus finds objectionable, the universal encounter with the returning Jesus does so more and more. It is indeed revelatory for John to lift the gaze of the members of his congregations – a gaze often fixed upon their neighbours' disapproval and growing hostility, the growing tensions with the local Jewish community, and the challenges of maintaining a somewhat stable situation for one's family in the midst of such social pressures – to an event as yet unseen, namely the coming of Christ 'with the clouds', potentially to universal regret (1.7).

John here at the outset of, and elsewhere throughout, Revelation vividly presents the primary 'crisis' to which his hearers must attend (e.g. 6.12–17; 14.14–20; 19.11–21). The stakes of this critical encounter are amplified by the forecast that it will have a sorrowful outcome for many (even 'all'). The recapitulations serve to underscore the paramount importance of this encounter and of being prepared for this encounter. By this means, John guides his hearers to choose the response to the more immediate challenges before them that will most closely align with 'the commandments of God and faithfulness towards Jesus' (14.12) so as to position them to successfully meet that greater challenge – to

---

the details of the text to theological propositions or an end-time playbook.

encounter the Christ who returns to judge the living and the dead. At the same time, John's portrayal of Jesus not as distant, but as standing even now among his congregations (1.12–13, 20), 'adds urgency to his message' (Whitaker 2015: 103): the crisis of that encounter is here and now, not entirely deferred to a future (even if imminent) coming. This provides the framework, then, for the further messages about to be revealed in the voice of the glorified Christ himself (mediated through John's transcript).

6

Oracles from the glorified Christ (Revelation 2—3)

If the opening sentences of Revelation pronounced privileged 'those listening to the words of this prophecy and keeping the things written therein' (1.3), chapters 2 and 3 present the first and clearest instances of such prophecy. Here John presents his transcripts of the messages that the glorified Lord has for these particular seven congregations designated as the recipients of Revelation as a whole (1.11) and of each oracle individually (2.1, 8, 12, 18; 3.1, 7, 14). These chapters contribute a great deal to our understanding of Revelation and the situations that called it forth. First, they are primary sources for refining our picture of the kinds of challenges and tensions that John's congregations are having to navigate beyond the more general and widely shared challenges of living in the midst of Roman imperialism and the pressures to participate in the religious cults that legitimize Rome's hegemony. Second, they spell out fairly clearly the directions in which John would steer these congregations to respond, giving us a fuller inventory of the rhetorical goals potentially supported by the whole work. Third, they provide rich examples of early Christian prophecy – an important and pervasive phenomenon that lies beyond our reach save for the scattered examples in the New Testament itself.

One question that has perennially occupied interpreters is: why *these* seven congregations? Congregations had been planted in Colossae and Hierapolis, both within 10 miles (15 km) of Laodicea, already during Paul's lifetime (Col. 1.2; 4.13). Congregations probably already existed in Magnesia and Tralles, close by Ephesus, for Ignatius of Antioch would write letters to both on his way to martyrdom in Rome early in the second century. In keeping with the symbolic nature of the number seven throughout Revelation (and throughout Scripture), the third-century commentator Victorinus regarded these seven churches as representative of the Church universal, even as the Church universal is also the ultimate audience of the letters Paul addressed to seven specific churches (Rome, Corinth, Galatia, Ephesus, Philippi, Colossae, Thessalonica). The Venerable Bede, a scholar and monk active at the turn of the eighth century, also held to this opinion, though he affirmed that, at the same time, the oracles also accurately reflected the conditions in seven real congregations.[1]

Another explanation popular in the history of interpretation is that these seven congregations were selected because they were representative of successive periods in the Church's history spanning from the time of John's writing to the end time. Such a reading particularly allows futurist interpreters to account for the distance between the first-century churches that John addressed and the events they allege to lie in their own (immediate) future beginning in chapter 4. While hints of this were present in earlier interpretation,[2] it blossomed in the Reformation period and came to dominate popular interpretation through the *Scofield Reference Bible* (Scofield 1917: 1331–2) and the work of Hal Lindsey (e.g. 1975: 26–54) and others. Ephesus is consistently taken to represent the apostolic period; Smyrna, the period of Roman persecution (Augustine was already aware, though critical, of interpretations of the 'ten days' as the ten major persecutions of Christians from Nero to Maximin; *Civ.* 18.52); Pergamum, the compromised Church of Constantine and his successors; and Thyatira, the Catholic Church of the medieval period. During the Reformation period, Thomas Brightman (d. 1607) could view the congregations of Sardis, Philadelphia and Laodicea as different branches of the Church of his own time – connecting Sardis with the Lutheran Church, Philadelphia with the Calvinist Christians (his own leaning) and Laodicea with the Anglican Church (Wainwright 1993: 72; Kovacs and Rowland 2004: 54–5). With the passage of more time, Sardis alone came to represent the period of the Reformation and Enlightenment, Philadelphia the time of the Great Awakening and the missionary endeavours it spawned, and Laodicea the Church of the present age.

It is highly questionable, however, whether such hindsight truly grants a clearer understanding of the text (as Lindsey 1975: 23 affirms) or, rather, obscures the complexities of the history of the Church and its present condition. Aside from presenting a gross caricature even of the Western Church, this popular scheme is starkly Eurocentric and, more particularly, Protestant-centred. It turns a blind eye to the state of the Church in the southern hemisphere and the Middle and Far East throughout this history. And if the oracle to Laodicea is meant to characterize the Church of the present age, the glorified

---

1 See Victorinus, *In Apoc.* 1.7 (Weinrich 2005: 10; 2011a: 3) and Bede, *Exp.* 1.11 (Weinrich 2011b: 116).

2 See Tyconius, *Exposition of the Apocalypse* 3.9–10 (Weinrich 2005: 45–6); also the work of Peter of Tarentaise (d. 1174) and Joachim of Fiore (d. 1202), discussed in Koester 2014: 232.

Christ would himself be turning a blind eye to the millions of faithful Christians in the developing world whose fidelity to God under great pressure and whose enthusiasm for evangelism far more closely resemble the conditions in Smyrna and Philadelphia than Laodicea. There has hardly been an era in which the diversity of the congregations addressed by Revelation failed to be represented, nor is it 'viable to reduce entire periods of history to single categories, as if the early church were known only for persecution or the modern church for complacency' (Koester 2014: 233).

A third explanation appeals to John's personal acquaintance with *these* seven churches, perhaps as a result of exercising an itinerant ministry around this circuit. Good roads connected these seven cities, most of which fell within a two-day journey from the next. Some scholars working from this hypothesis have sought connections between the messages to the churches and the history and geography of the city in which each congregation was located, suggesting many particular, local references in each message (see, especially, Ramsey 1904; Hemer 1986; Worth 1999a; 1999b).[3] These studies take seriously the local context of each congregation and the oracle addressed to it, though they occasionally err on the side of stretching the connections between the message to the church and either the *distant* history of the city or some aspect of the city that was not truly peculiar to *that* city. For example, Smyrna is not the only city that would resonate with 'being dead and living again' (cf. Rev. 2.8), for Sardis, Philadelphia and Laodicea also had to come back to life after devastating earthquakes; Ephesus is not the only city whose residents would resonate with being removed from their place due to earlier relocations (2.5), for Smyrna had similarly been moved in the Hellenistic period (Koester 2014: 233; against Ramsey 1904: 269–70; Hemer 1986: 52–4).

The form and message of the oracles

Many excellent commentaries treat the oracles in depth one by one. Space constrains us to think of them collectively – an approach facilitated by the fact that these oracles all follow a consistent pattern with most of the formal elements achieving similar ends across the group of seven. Indeed, most of the elements of these oracles reflect the style and content of the oracles of God recorded in the Hebrew prophets – the opening 'Thus says [the Lord]', the divine speaker's use

---

3   A great deal of scholarly material exists to help interpreters enter more fully into the local contexts of these congregations. See the essays on the individual cities in Beitzel 2019: 537–53, 629–96 and the bibliographies ending each entry.

of titles and descriptors to identify salient features of his character or power, commendation for faithful responses, confrontation of practices that show disloyalty or disobedience, and announcements of positive or punitive consequences. Both at the level of form and of content, the oracles presented by John align with the sacred tradition – and its values – that he shares with his congregations.

1 Command to John to write

Each oracle is introduced by the same formula, in which the glorified Christ commands John to write (thus reminding the members of each congregation that what they hear comes by way of divine dictation) specifically 'to the angel of the congregation in' each city in succession. Interpreters have come to different understandings of these angels. Some have regarded them as human figures, whether the bishops or priests of the churches or just human messengers.[4] Given the use of 'angels' to denote supernatural beings everywhere else in Revelation, others regard them essentially as the guardian angels of each assembly, an extension of the belief in guardian angels for individuals (Tob. 2.14–16; *Jub.* 35.17; Matt. 18.20; Acts 12.15) and for nations (Dan. 12.1).[5] Still others have regarded them simply as figures standing for the congregations themselves, even as what is written 'to the angel' becomes, at the conclusion of each oracle, 'what the Spirit says to the churches'.[6] Rhetorically, addressing the 'angels' of the congregations allows the hearers not to experience Jesus' words as *direct* confrontation, though even here the speaker frequently slips from the singular 'you' (*su*) addressing the (fictive?) angel to the plural 'you' (*hymeis*) addressing the members of each congregation directly.[7] The speaker, moreover, does not threaten the angels with punishment, but only the guilty among the listeners.

2 Identification of the speaker

The oracle proper begins with a variation on the prophetic formula, 'Thus says the Lord', with 'the Lord' being identified now by one or more of the traits seen in the vision of the glorified Christ that preceded the seven oracles

---

4   Bede, *Exp.* 1.20; 3.1 (Weinrich 2011b: 118, 121); Alexander the Minorite, *Expositio* 22–49 (Wainwright 1993: 54); Hemer 1986: 32. See discussion in Aune 1997: 108–12.

5   Koester 2014: 248–9.

6   Oecumenius, *Comm.* 2.1–7 (Weinrich 2005: 19–20).

7   For but one example, see Rev. 2.10: 'Fear nothing (singular command) that you (singular) are about to suffer. The devil is about to throw some of you (plural) into prison in order that you (plural) might be tested, and you (plural) will have tribulation during ten days. Be faithful (singular command) unto death, and I will give to you (singular) the crown of life.'

(1.12–20).[8] These traits remind the hearers of the awesomeness of the figure – before whom John could only fall down as a corpse – who is addressing them, commending them, confronting them, calling for specific responses, promising consequences. The oracles' persuasive power depends to a great extent not merely on *what* is said but on *who* is saying it – one who has the power to enforce it.

The way in which Christ identifies himself often has some bearing on the particular congregation's situation. For example, the glorified Jesus introduces himself to the congregation in Smyrna as the one 'who was dead and came alive' (2.8). While this is, of course, a central feature of Jesus' story in Christian faith generally, it is particularly relevant to the members of the congregation in Smyrna as they are summoned to find the courage to remain loyal to Jesus unto death (2.10). Similarly, he introduces himself to the congregation in Pergamum as 'the one holding the sharp, two-edged sword' (2.12), a sword he threatens to use against those who hold the teaching of the Nicolaitans (2.15–16).

3 Commendation and instructions

Jesus affirms that he knows the challenges each congregation faces and what each congregation has been doing in the face of those challenges ('I know your works', 2.2, 9, 13, 19; 3.1, 8, 15), though in the case of two of these statements Jesus surprises the congregations by rebuking them from the outset on the basis of what he knows (3.1, 15). A great deal of what is commended has to do either with continued investment in the life of the Christian community and its members ('your labour', 'your love', and the like; 2.2, 19) or with continued perseverance in the face of pressures from outside the community ('your endurance', 'not denying my name', 'not breaking faith', and the like; 2.2, 3, 13, 19; 3.8; cf. also 2.9; 3.4). As a corollary of the second, discernment and rejection of preachers whose message changes the contours of the faith and faithful response is also commended (2.2, 6).

We will explore the sources of these pressures and the alternative response to the same being urged by some Christian teachers among the seven congregations in the second half of this chapter. For the present, we may observe how John positions his congregations to think about the source of these tensions. In several cases, the glorified Christ identifies Satan, the arch-rebel against

---

8 Some of these descriptors make connections beyond 1.12–20 as well. For example, 'the one holding the seven spirits of God' in addition to 'the seven stars' (3.1) looks forward to 5.6 as well as back to 1.19–20. 'The one holding the key of David' (3.7) recalls Jesus' claim to hold 'the keys of death and Hades' (1.18), but also transforms the claim in the light of Isa. 22.22 (see Fekkes 1994: 130–3).

God's order and source of the misdirection that has led the nations astray, as the ultimate force behind the challenges, whether posed by the actions of a local Jewish community (the 'synagogues of Satan' in Smyrna and Philadelphia; 2.9; 3.9), the actions of Gentile neighbours, generally on the basis of their own commitment to their gods and piety (the 'test' of imprisonment leading to death, instigated by Satan; 2.10; the hostility of the city 'where Satan has his throne', 2.13),[9] or the deviant Christian teachers (who initiate their disciples into 'the deep things of Satan', 2.24). Yielding in the face of any of these challenges thus means accepting defeat at the hands of God's principal enemy and rival.[10]

Within the commendatory remarks and the instructions given on the basis of the same, the glorified Christ offers several kinds of incentive to faithfulness. To those in Smyrna who persevere in faithfulness even if this were to require submitting to execution, Christ promises 'the wreath of life' (2.10), a familiar image in Smyrna and throughout the Greco-Roman world whether given to the winning athlete or adorning the military conqueror. Wreaths also showed up in funerary settings, both around the heads of the deceased and engraved on their grave steles. Such wreaths were testimonies to a life well lived, the value and virtue of which were sealed by death, not ended by it. The image assures the Christians that dying for loyalty to Jesus did not mark one as a deviant or as a loser, but rather as a winner, a conqueror, a person who lived and died virtuously, and who would continue to live and enjoy honour in the greater empire of God.[11] Christ claims to have set 'an open door' before the Christians in Philadelphia, probably signifying his assurance of their

---

9 Does John's characterization of Pergamum as the city 'where Satan's throne is' and 'where Satan lives' (2.13) refer to some local landmark? Some have suggested that John is referring specifically to the Temple of Roma and Augustus, the seat of the provincial cult of Augustus (Hemer 1986: 87; Witherington 2003: 103; Wilson 2010: 285). Others think it more likely that John refers here to the altar of Zeus, a distinctive landmark on the Pergamene skyline. This was a massive throne-like altar complex resembling an open-air temple, complete with columned porticoes surrounding its staircase and inner courtyards. The whole had a footprint of about 36 by 35 metres (120 x 110 ft), rising to a height of 12 metres (40 ft) (Wilson 2010: 285). The correlation of Zeus, the king of the gods, with Satan, the chief of the demons, better suits the general Jewish tendency to identify the pagan gods with demons (Bar. 4.6–7; 1 Cor. 10.19–21; Rev. 9.20–21; Kästner 1998: 143; deSilva 2009: 43). The Temple of Roma and Augustus in Pergamum is a manifestation of the cult of the beast and its image, not of the dragon that gives the beast its power (Rev. 13.1–4, 7–8). Craig Koester (2014: 286–7), however, rejects all such references to local landmarks in favour of a reference to a local event: 'What distinguishes Pergamum from other cities is that Antipas was put to death there, which is understood to be evidence of Satan's presence.'

10 John will also bring this strategic perspective to bear on pressures to participate in the imperial cult and its legitimation of Roman rule in 12.1—13.18 – strategic, because it fosters perseverance in resisting.

11 See also the use of the image in 4 Macc. 17.15; 1 Cor. 9.25; 2 Tim. 4.8; Jas. 1.12; 1 Pet. 5.4.

entrance into the new Jerusalem (rather than some missionary opportuni-ty).[12] Such assurance of the end facilitates perseverance in the 'in between'. On the basis of the shared value of reciprocity, Christ assures the members of this church, who have 'kept' Jesus' instructions to persevere, that he will 'keep' them through the period of testing about to come upon earth's inhab-itants (3.10). Through such promises, the glorified Christ helps the congre-gations persevere in the commitments that, in themselves, yield no hope of visible rewards in the here and now.

4 Rebuke and call for change

The glorified Christ also offers his diagnosis of what is amiss in each congrega-tion, where relevant (there are no words of rebuke for the Christians in Smyrna or Philadelphia). Three times this is introduced with the words 'I have against you that . . .' (2.4, 14, 20); twice it is introduced, somewhat ironically, with the words 'I know your works', which more generally introduce commendation (3.1, 15). Hearing the glorified Lord, about whose awesomeness (1.12–16) and imminent intervention (1.7) the congregations have just been reminded, say 'I have this against you' will certainly elicit the hearers' attention and, in all likelihood, a disposition to distance themselves speedily from whatever pro-vokes Christ's displeasure. The portrayals of judgement at Christ's coming (14.14–20; 19.11—20.15) and the pervasive connection between one's eternal fate and Christ's pleasure or displeasure in one's deeds (e.g. Rev. 14.9–11) will reinforce this effect.

We will consider the challenges facing the congregations in Pergamum and Thyatira more fully in the second half of this chapter. Here we will consider the rebukes particular to the congregations in Ephesus and Laodicea. The glorified Christ warns the Ephesian Christians, 'You have forsaken your first/former love' (2.4), admonishing them to correct this deficit. No further explanation is given, leaving interpreters with little guidance when it comes to determining what specifically might have been lacking. Some believe that a cooling of a for-mer fervent love for God or for Christ was the problem (Prigent 1988: 42; Beale 1999: 230); others suggest that love for others is more in view (Loisy 1923: 89; Lohse 1988a: 25), perhaps a casualty of their zeal to detect and guard against heresy (Murphy 1998: 115–16; Koester 2014: 269) – if, indeed, a choice ought to be made (Hemer 1986: 41). The Ephesian Christians would no doubt have

---

12 On the open door as 'opportunity for witness', see the use of this imagery in Acts 14.27; 1 Cor. 16.9; 2 Cor. 2.12; Col. 4.3; Lohse 1988a: 33; Aune 1997: 236; Murphy 1998: 152; as the congregation's assur-ance of entry into God's kingdom, see Rev. 3.12; Beale 1999: 287; Friesen 2006: 140; simply as 'access to God', see Koester 2014: 324.

had to examine their hearts and practice to discover in what regard this charge was true. Love is commended as the *sine qua non* of discipleship within *many* streams of Christian culture, so there would be no disagreement that a failure of love would be a serious matter.[13]

The sharpest rebuke seems to have been reserved for the Christians in Laodicea, whose tepidity elicited nausea from the glorified Lord. The images of 'hot', 'cold' and 'lukewarm' have invited a great deal of speculation concerning the more precise nature of the Laodiceans' problematic performance and attitude. Early interpreters suggested that the essential issue was a lack of fervour for Christ and his mission. It would have been preferable had they remained zealous (i.e. hot) or had they never been converted in the first place (i.e. stayed cold), since then a true conversion would still have been possible (Oecumenius, *Comm.* 3.14–22; Weinrich 2005: 51; Bede, *Exp.* 3.15; Weinrich 2011b: 123; see also Loisy 1923: 117; Murphy 1998: 161). Other interpreters find it difficult to think that Christ would actually prefer drifting Christians never to have become disciples in the first place. They note that both hot water and cold water served healthful and welcome purposes – indeed, both might be served at banquets (to warm or chill wine, for example), whereas tepid water might be served as an emetic (Keener 2000: 159; Koester 2014: 343–4).

The more specific critique of Laodicea in 3.16–18 might provide clearer guidance concerning the meaning of these images. What is lukewarm 'is like . . . its surroundings; it does not distinguish itself . . . By analogy, nothing distinguishes the works of the Laodicean Christians from the common practices of their society' (Koester 2014: 344). It is no accident that their boast will be heard as an echo of the boast of Great Babylon itself (18.7) and both boasts will prove to be deceptive. These disciples have prospered in their corner of the Roman imperial economy, and the resulting complacency has left them unaware of their spiritual poverty. The danger facing 'those who dwell in Babylon', who have come to blend in so well with its practices and spirit, is that they 'do not know they are there' (Berrigan 1983: 107). The glorified Christ enhances the hearers' attentiveness to the need to address the matters he has identified as deficiencies with warnings (or, perhaps truer to the reality, *threats*). At the same time, he shows himself easily reconciled with those willing to heed his admonitions, offering the congregation in Laodicea, for example, both the harshest rebuke and the most tender promises of restored fellowship.

---

13 See, e.g., Mark 12.28–34; John 13.31–35; 15.12–14; Rom. 13.8–10; 1 Cor. 13; Gal. 5.13–14; Eph. 5.1–2; Heb. 13.1; Jas. 2.8; 1 Pet. 1.22; 2.17; 3.8; 1 John 3.11–18.

5 Promises to 'the one who conquers'

In order to motivate the perseverance or the course changes promoted in each oracle, the glorified Christ closes the oracles with promises to 'the one who conquers' the challenges in each situation (both peculiar to each locality and common to the province), announced as prizes to be awarded to the victors. The call to 'conquer' or 'overcome' strategically frames the hearers' current situation as one of contest or even war (so Bauckham 1993a: 213), with goals to be won and antagonists or enemies to be identified and resisted. It also reinforces the oracle's commendations and rebukes by retrospectively defining them as pictures of what 'winning' and 'losing' look like in each congregation's situation, orienting the hearers strategically towards that situation. The exhortations to 'conquer' in each of the seven oracles connect also with images of conquering throughout the visions, particular the manner of the Lamb's 'conquering' in 5.5–6 and the manner in which the faithful conquer both the dragon (12.11) and the beast and its image (15.2). It is significant that the path to victory is defined as one that involves temporal loss, hardship and even death. The image transforms these experiences, the consequences of faithful witness and withdrawal, from degrading defeat into a noble victory before God's eternal court (deSilva 2000: 68–70).

Many of these promises (and the warnings as well) look ahead to the unfolding narrative of the future that God has prepared for his faithful and for the world, particularly in 7.9–17 and 20.11—22.5 (Wilson 2007b: 173–230). The visions to come will confirm the reliability of the promises made and warnings posed by the glorified Christ in chapters 2—3 as the audience hears of all these ends, wonderful or tragic, coming to pass (Maier 2002: 80). Such recurring images include the tree of life (2.7; 22.2, 14); preservation from 'the second death' (2.11; 20.6, 14–15; 21.8); the morning star (2.28; 22.16); receiving white robes (3.5; 7.9–14); having one's name retained in the scroll of life (3.5; 20.11–15; 21.8); 'installation' in some sense in the new Jerusalem (3.12; 21.2). A number of these promises are admittedly never mentioned again, for example the 'white stone' and the 'hidden manna', leading to the need to look elsewhere for clues to how John's hearers would have processed these images. Thus 'hidden manna' might be heard to resonate with end-time expectations for God's provision (see 2 Baruch 29.8; Koester 2014: 290), while a 'white stone', perhaps better translated as a 'white ballot' in keeping with a common civic use of the noun psēphos (often inscribed with the name of the voting body), might be heard to signal Christ's casting of a vote for acquittal for the 'winners' when he comes to judge the world.

6 Admonition to all the assemblies to 'listen'

At or near the conclusion of each oracle falls the verbatim admonition, 'Let the one who has an ear hear what the Spirit is saying to the assemblies' (2.7, 11, 17, 29; 3.6, 13, 22).[14] The saying recalls a phrase associated with the historical Jesus, particularly in connection with his teaching in parables: 'let the one with ears listen!' (Matt. 11.15; 13.9, 43; Aune 1997: 150). The oracles reverberate elsewhere with the idiom of Jesus as he was known to have spoken in the flesh: 'unless you/they repent' (Rev. 2.5, 22; Luke 13.3, 5); 'I will confess his name before my father and before his angels' (Rev. 3.5; Matt. 10.32); 'be watchful' (Rev. 3.2; Matt. 24.42; 25.13; Mark 13.35, 37); 'you do not know in what day/hour' in connection with the image of the thief breaking in upon the householder (Rev. 3.3; Matt. 24.42–43). These connections support the authenticity of the oracles both in terms of their content, which is heard to align with the historical Jesus' teachings, and in terms of the claim that they represent the speech of the Lord who continues to live and to guide his assemblies on this side of his resurrection and Ascension (Aune 1997: 264–5; Vos 1965: 224).

This particular admonition also highlights (seven times over!) the public nature of all seven oracular pronouncements (Aune 1990: 184; Witherington 2003: 109). The circle of churches bears witness to their Lord's commendation of each congregation's achievement (where such is noted) and his rebuke of each congregation's failure to live up to the mark (again, where such is noted). This dynamic emerges also in 2.23, where the fate of the prophet whom John labels 'Jezebel' and those who follow her teaching will become a public occasion by which 'all the assemblies will know that I am the one who searches minds and hearts'. Each congregation is reminded that its sister congregations are looking on to witness their responses to the challenges before them – whether they will repair their reputation in Christ's and one another's eyes or prove shameless in the light of Christ's correction.

Local challenges facing one or more congregations

Some of the challenges named in the seven oracles – whether in the context of commendation or censure – merit closer attention as significant features of the lived situation of multiple congregations. These include tensions between

---

14 In the first three oracles, the admonition precedes the word of promise; in the last four, it follows the word of promise.

the Christian and Jewish communities (the reconstruction of which is problematized particularly by the history of anti-Judaism in the Christian Church), tensions between the Christians and their host cities (a subject on which we touched in Chapter 4 but can further nuance here), and alternative strategies for navigating these tensions being promoted by other teachers among the seven congregations.

1 Tensions with the synagogue

The oracles to the Christian assemblies in Smyrna and Philadelphia identify one source of tension to be a group of people 'claiming themselves to be Jews and they aren't, but [are] a synagogue of Satan' (2.9; see also 3.9). This group is said to be the source of 'slander' in Smyrna, at least. Some translations, such as the KJV, New American Standard Version (NASV) and New Living Translation (NLT), read 'blasphemy' here, but the Greek word *blasphēmia* covers a wider range of abusive speech and denunciation than the English 'blasphemy'. It is less likely that the speech of this group is directed against God and far more likely that it pertains to the Christian congregation. Koester (2014: 274) suggests that 'denunciation' is a particularly apt equivalent in English, as the speech of the 'synagogue of Satan' is connected at least implicitly with the hardships endured or about to be endured by the Christians in Smyrna and Philadelphia.

New Testament scholars and Christian theologians have become very sensitive to the problematic ways in which New Testament texts and our interpretation of them have contributed to the anti-Judaism (or anti-Semitism, though that is a broader term) that climaxed in the Holocaust in Hitler's Germany. Passages like the oracles to Smyrna and Philadelphia and the mutual antagonism between Christian assembly and Jewish community they reflect need to be understood and interpreted thoughtfully and carefully.

For John to call the rival community a 'synagogue of Satan', though the language is certainly strong, is not unprecedented in inner-Jewish conflict. The authors of the Dead Sea Scrolls call fellow Jews outside the Qumran covenant community the 'congregation of Beliar' (1QH 2.22; 1QM 4.9), using another of the names of God's arch-enemy. In the Fourth Gospel, Jesus denounces opposing Jewish leaders as belonging to their father, the devil (John 8.44), while his own detractors call him demon-possessed (Matt. 9.34; Luke 11.15; John 7.20; 8.48). The author of the Johannine letters divides humanity into children of God and children of the devil (1 John 3.8–10), placing those who seceded from his own congregations in the latter category, calling them 'antichrists' as well (1 John 2.18). It is also important to note that, while there were certainly

Jewish communities in Ephesus and Sardis, and probably the other cities as well, John does not say anything disparaging about those synagogues – only the Jewish communities whose activity is putting Christians in some jeopardy (Friesen 2006: 141).

John's use of the label 'synagogue of Satan' probably does not reflect a debate over which community could rightly claim the label 'Jew' or 'Israel' (Friesen 2006: 138) as in Paul's letters, wherein Paul claims the Christian community to be 'the [true] circumcision' (Phil. 3.3) or the genuine sons and daughters of Abraham (Gal. 3.6–9; 4.21–31) or the 'Israel of God' (Gal. 6.16; as opposed to 'Israel according to the flesh', 1 Cor. 10.18). It may rather reflect John's opinion of his co-religionists' acceptance of the penalty imposed upon them by the emperor Vespasian in the wake of the failed Jewish Revolt of 66–70 CE. Prior to 70 CE, Jewish males throughout Israel and the Diaspora paid an annual tax of a silver half shekel for the support of the Jerusalem Temple. With the destruction of the Temple, Vespasian ordered the tax (reckoned at two denarii or drachmae) to continue to be collected from a larger pool of Jews of both genders and designated for the renovation and support of the Temple of Jupiter on the Capitoline Hill in Rome.[15] Vespasian may have believed himself to be showing considerable leniency to require so little of the members of a rebellious *ethnos* by way of war reparations. However, he put the Jewish people in the difficult position of having to purchase continuing toleration at the cost of supporting a pagan cult, quite literally taking what had belonged to God and giving it to Caesar (or, at least, Caesar's gods). Given John's uncompromising attitude towards pagan religion, he might well have regarded his fellow Jews as having betrayed their witness and exclusive loyalty to the One God for the sake of peace with the beast (Kraybill 1996: 184). Following in the long-standing Jewish tradition of associating the gods of the Gentile nations with demons,[16] John connects idolatry with the worship of demons (Rev. 9.20–21). Connecting Satan, the chief of demons, with Zeus/Jupiter, the chief of the Greco-Roman gods (to whom the funds once meant to support the worship of the One God were now being diverted), would be a natural inference.

John does not flesh out what kinds of speech or action constituted the 'slanderous speech' of the Jewish community where the Christian assembly in Smyrna was concerned. Relationships between the non-Christian Jewish and Christian communities showed marked tension wherever the New Testament

---

15 Josephus, *J.W.* 7.6.6, §218; Dio Cassius, *Hist. Rom.* 46.7.2; see discussion in Smallwood 1976: 371–6,

16 See, for example, LXX Ps. 95.5, which claims the gods of the nations to be 'demons' (where the Hebrew Ps. 96.5 reads 'idols'); similarly LXX Isa. 65.3, which specifies 'demons' as the objects of worship wherever worship is directed away from the One God. See also Ps. 106.37; Bar. 4.7; 1 Cor. 10.20–21.

authors remark on the same. The Jewish community would have ample cause to respond negatively to Christian claims concerning the 'true' identity of God's people and the heirs of God's promises, the identification of Jesus as the Messiah, and the significance of the coming of Jesus and the Spirit for the binding authority of the law of Moses. Jewish communities would have even greater impetus to dissociate themselves from a break-away, revolutionary Jewish group that expected a duly executed Jew to return to establish a new world order where Rome currently held sway. Christian success in turning Gentiles 'to God from idols, to serve a living and genuine God' (1 Thess. 1.9), could further motivate such dissociation, since Roman authorities historically reacted negatively when they believed Jews to be making 'atheists' out of good gods-fearing Gentiles (Leon 1995: 17–20). The speech that John has in mind might refer to open denunciation (such as we see in Acts 18.12–17; *Martyrdom of Polycarp* 12.2; 13.1).[17] It might refer just as plausibly to the local Jewish community simply making it known which individuals out of the local residents belong to their number and which residents might behave like Jews in some regards (like abstaining from all worship of other gods) but are not truly 'of them'. The latter possibility would nevertheless still expose the local Christians to danger if it were to lead to closer investigation on the part of the authorities concerning this anomalous group. This provides a plausible scenario in which 'slander' or 'denunciation' concerning the Christian group's *not* being a part of the Jewish community (and therefore not enjoying legal toleration) might eventuate in imprisonment leading to death. We have the later testimony in the *Martyrdom of Polycarp* (19.1) that 12 Christians in Smyrna would meet with execution on account of their faith by the year 154.

The precise nature of the hostility between the Jewish community and Christian congregation in Philadelphia is even murkier. If the reversal of the problem involves the members of the synagogue discovering that God's Anointed One 'loved' the Christian disciples, it seems plausible that the problem itself had to do with the synagogue's disavowal of Christians (perhaps particularly *Jewish* Christians, whom they would be expelling from their own community) as people whose new commitments and practices have removed them from the faithful people of God. The promise that the Jews would one day 'bow to the ground at the feet' of the Christians represents a reconfiguration of the promises spoken through Isaiah that Gentile rulers would do the same before Israel after bringing those Israelites who had been deported and scattered throughout the Gentiles' lands back to their inheritance (Isa. 45.15–23).

---

17   Witherington 2003: 100–1; see also Beale 1999: 240; Keener 2000: 115.

This, too, speaks of Christ's vindication of the Christian community's value in God's sight, which is currently disputed (so also Koester 2014: 331).

2 Pressures and hostility from Greco-Roman neighbours

Several of the oracles suggest that some of these congregations were enduring pressure from their Gentile neighbours as well. The Christians in Ephesus and Thyatira are commended for 'bearing up' on account of Christ's name (Rev. 2.3, 19) and, in Pergamum and Philadelphia, for 'not denying [Christ's] name' when circumstances might have made it advantageous to do so (2.13; 3.8). The oracle to Smyrna announces the presumably credible prospect of imprisonment leading to execution (2.10), an effect connected with the actions of the local Jewish community in Smyrna in some way, but beyond the purview of a Diaspora Jewish community even over its own members and thus suggesting readiness on the part of Gentile authorities to act against the group.[18] Pergamum has already provided the venue for a martyrdom in John's recent memory – one Antipas (2.13), though it is far from clear whether this was the result of official, legal proceedings or of a back-alley murder.

At and prior to the time of writing, John's congregations were most likely being subjected to the insults, physical abuse and disenfranchisement that were the common lot of Christians throughout the eastern Mediterranean (see Heb. 10.32–34; 13.3; 1 Pet. 2.11–12, 18–25; 3.13–17; 4.1–4, 12–19; 1 Thess. 3.1–6; 2 Thess. 1.3–9) – imposed as much to reclaim the deviant as to dissuade others from joining the disfavoured group – rather than any kind of systematic elimination as would become official policy during the third century.[19] In Chapter 4, we considered at some length the causes behind and motivations for this animosity. Throughout Revelation, John connects the hostility and violence directed against followers of the One God and his Christ with their refusal to worship the gods of their neighbours and, particularly, to participate in the worship of the emperors – thus also ceasing to show solidarity with their neighbours both in symbolically important, public contexts and in many private contexts as well.

The common assumption that Revelation is written to Christians suffering harsh and bloody persecution at the hands of the empire, however, overstates

---

18 Imprisonment was not a judicial punishment, but was used to detain someone before a trial, 'as a means of coercion to compel obedience to an order issued by a magistrate', or a place of detention until execution could be carried out (Aune 1997: 166).

19 See deSilva 1991: 197–201; 1992: 286–91; 2009: 50–5; Slater 1998: 241; Worth 1999a: 124–5; 1999b: 112–30. On the social goals of such harassment, see deSilva 1995: 146–64; 2000: 44–50.

the evidence (e.g. Boesak 1987: 15; see the helpful re-evaluations of the ancient evidence in Yarbro Collins 1984: 69–73; Thompson 1990: 95–132). John certainly remembers the violent persecution that has taken place since the crucifixion of Jesus and the victims whose blood cries for justice (6.9–11; 16.5–7; 17.6; 18.20, 24; 19.2; 20.4–6), no doubt including many of the original apostles and the bloodbath of Christians in Nero's Rome, exacerbated by his cruel inventiveness in ways to torment and degrade the victims. This would still be remembered by the Roman historians Tacitus (*Ann.* 15.44) and Suetonius (*Nero* 16) writing in the early second century. How much more would it weigh upon the mind of John, who sees the imperial power so fully through the lens of Nero's cruelty and career, as if the beast showed its colours most fully and truly in *this* head?

John, however, points to only one violent fatality among the Christian communities of Asia in recent memory (2.13), though he sees in both Nero's Rome and this more recent event the shape of things to come if the Christians persevere in 'keeping the commandments of God and the testimony of Jesus' (12.17; cf. 14.12) – as they *must*. The number of martyrs remains ominously incomplete (6.11); the career of the archetypal witnesses ends in execution (11.7–10), though that is not *God's* final word on their story. Fervour for the worship of the beast would reach such a pitch that those who refused to honour their ruler thus would meet with economic embargo and, eventually, death (13.15–17; 20.4–6). From start to finish, John will encourage Christians to 'love not their lives unto death' in the face of such pressure and, thus, to participate in the defeat of the dragon alongside Michael and his angels (12.10–11), standing up for and, thus, standing *beside* the Lamb whose testimony they bear and in whose steps they follow – wherever it might lead. To a very real extent, he accurately foresaw the course of the two centuries that followed his visionary experiences.

3 A gospel of accommodation

John's response to the hostility of those with power to withhold the means of thriving and inflict suffering in its place, however, was by no means the only one being proclaimed and embraced among the seven congregations. The fate of Antipas revealed something of how precarious the Christians' position had become – and why finding a means of peaceful coexistence, even if it meant significantly muting one's Christian witness and exclusive devotion to the God of Jesus Christ, might be highly desirable. Indeed, discovering a long-term modus vivendi might have been regarded by some as an urgent matter for the survival of the Christian movement in *some* form.

This appears to have been the goal of the teachers whom John labels 'Nicolaitans' and 'Jezebel', whose agenda he (or, rather and strategically, the glorified

Christ) summarizes as 'teaching my slaves and leading them astray to commit fornication and eat food that had been sacrificed to idols' (2.20; cf. 2.14–15).[20] We have seen in Chapter 4 how it would have been advantageous for Christians to make room for participating in the social occasions where meat once sacrificed to an idol might be served. It is unlikely that John also accuses these teachers of promoting fornication in any literal sense. Idolatry and sexual immorality were admittedly linked in Jewish anti-Gentile polemics (see Wisd. 14.12; Rom. 1.18–32; *Let. Aris.* 152; Duff 2001: 56) and perhaps also in actual practice (possibly reflected in 1 Pet. 4.3–4). However, John uses the imagery of sexual relations and partners (e.g. a great prostitute who seduces the kings of the earth!) extensively throughout Revelation in ways that suggest a metaphorical significance. 'Fornication' is probably a figure for all improper intercourse with Roman society and its gods, while sexual purity represents loyalty to the One God and his Christ (suggested as early as Tyconius, *Exposition of the Apocalypse* 2.14; Weinrich 2005: 31; see also deSilva 1992: 294; Duff 2001: 56).

John connects the Nicolaitan movement that has gained a foothold (not surprisingly) in Pergamum with the historic figure of Balaam, known from Numbers. Having failed to curse the Hebrews as Balak, king of the Moabites, had hired him to do, Balaam masterminded another plan for defusing their threat: the Moabite women were to seduce the Hebrew men, lead them into worshipping the Moabite deities alongside their own, and thus become one people together rather than encounter one another as invader and invaded, conqueror and conquered (Num. 25.1–2; 31.16; Josephus, *Ant.* 4.129–30; Philo, *Mos.* 1.294–9). By associating the Nicolaitans with Balaam, John leads the Christians in Pergamum to regard their boundary-relaxing position as a grave threat to the integrity and safety of God's new congregation.

John goes further when he refers to a woman prophet and teacher in the congregation at Thyatira as 'Jezebel', fusing the horizons between John's rival and the Old Testament figure he wishes his audience to regard as her prototype.[21] Jezebel was historically a patroness and protector of the prophets of Baal, whose worship she promoted in Israel. Just as the author of 2 Kings summed up her activity as 'fornication' (2 Kings 9.22), so John uses sexual

---

20 John also mentions 'those who call themselves apostles' but who, John avers (and the Ephesian Christians have agreed), are not (2.2). If these represent a different group, John gives no indications of their message and agenda.

21 John's issue with Jezebel is not her gender, as if women ought not to be prophets or engaged in teaching, but her message and its implications for the boundaries of the group (Schüssler Fiorenza 1991: 133; Koester 2014: 299). This is demonstrated from the fact that John believes the glorified Christ to have given her an opportunity to repent and, thus, preserve her ministry in that congregation (2.21; deSilva 2009: 69).

imagery for her teaching and influence (Rev. 2.20–22). Indeed, John will use this same language to characterize 'Babylon', the economic, political, military and ideological domination system with which Jezebel would allow some measure of partnership for the sake of short-term security (compare 'her fornication' in 2.21; 14.8; the activity of 'leading astray' in 2.20; 18.23). John underscores that the ministry of the Thyatiran prophet leads believers into the webs of 'fornication' (that is, entangling alliances with an idolatrous and victimizing system) spun by Babylon.

The oracles do not give clues as to the arguments that Jezebel or the Nicolaitans might have advanced in support of their position, but one encounters similar social dynamics – and a similar solution being proposed – in Corinth, where those urging greater accommodation to their neighbours' sensitivities suggested that, since 'an idol is nothing' and 'there is no God but the One' (1 Cor. 8.4), no real spiritual harm would follow ingesting meat that had been offered to an idol. They might have remembered Jesus' teaching that 'there is nothing outside a person that, by going in, is able to defile him or her' (Mark 7.15). Why, then, should Christians unnecessarily provoke their neighbours to their own hurt?

Such reasoning may have undergirded the Nicolaitans' and Jezebel's arguments – arguments that were proving persuasive among Pergamene and Thyatiran Christians to a fair extent – advocating such practices as would alleviate the tension and perhaps even restore good will and reciprocity between the members of the congregations and the host society.[22] The summons of the glorified Christ in regard to these teachers and their agenda is to repent of *tolerating* their presence and activity (2.14–16, 20), to dissociate themselves from their teaching and to shut down their influence in the congregations. Indeed, the whole of Revelation advocates the sharpening of difference and distance in religious practice and, therefore, heightening the tension.[23] As Yarbro Collins (1984: 88) rightly observes: 'At stake here was the question of assimilation: what pagan customs could Christians adopt for the sake of economic survival, commercial gain, or simple sociability.' But also at stake was *witness* (a key word in Revelation), the testimony to the world that 'The LORD is God, and God alone!' (cf. Deut. 6.4). Participating alongside their neighbours in the religious rites that legitimate Roman rule and practice, the Christians would cease to raise the problematic issues regarding Roman imperialism in their

---

22 So also Caird 1966: 39; Schüssler Fiorenza 1985: 195; Hemer 1986: 128; Talbert 1994: 19; Mounce 1997: 81.

23 deSilva 1991: 207–8; 1992: 292–6; 1993: 55–7.

neighbours' consciousness that had precipitated their own withdrawal. Moving away from their prophetic practice, they would relinquish the space that non-participation creates for critical distance and the discovery of alternative ways of being human together.

A number of modern critics have sharply criticized John for his intolerance towards Jezebel and her position. Some have regarded Revelation as essentially an attempt on John's part to assert his own power and influence over the churches over against the growing influence of rival teachers (Duff 2001: 49; Royalty 2004: 285–6). They take issue with John's failure to show 'tolerance for dissent and alternative points of view' and to provide 'the means of expression for all voices', such as one would expect in a 'just society' (Royalty 2004: 286), suggesting that John's practice imitates instead that of the empire, for 'neither allows dissent' (Carey 1999: 117). Toleration of alternative viewpoints and the provision of 'the means of expression for all voices' are important indeed in a modern, pluralistic society – and values particularly important for the empowered to embrace. One wonders, however, if it is appropriate to level such criticisms against John's rhetoric and place such expectations upon his own practice in his very different and distant situation.

First, both John and Jezebel stand on a level and equal playing field (indeed if anyone is disadvantaged it is *John*, who speaks from exile). John does not have the power to exclude or silence Jezebel. He has only the power to persuade people in the congregations that Jezebel's accommodationist teachings, if heeded, will lead them to betray the witness and obedience to which Christ has called them. Jezebel has freely enjoyed 'the means of expression' prior to John's writing Revelation and would have been on hand to present a rebuttal if she desired after Revelation was read in her congregation. The community would decide which prophet spoke with the more genuine authorization – that is, it would 'test' the prophets in what was, to all appearances, a setting that was fair to both. If the community members decided that Jezebel was indeed leading them down a path that would compromise their identity and witness, they were within their rights not to give her teachings a further hearing.

Second, both John and Jezebel speak within a situation in which a dominating power has been at work silencing or subduing the voices of a number of minority cultures, in this case the Christian minority culture. The dominant culture had terminally silenced many Christian witnesses over the decades from notable early leaders of the movement to members en masse in Rome. Its local representatives pressure Christians to mute their own witness and return to practices that show affirmation of (or at least acquiescence to) the dominant culture's legitimacy to rule (e.g. by participating in the imperial cult). Jezebel speaks essentially on behalf of the dominating power, seeking to make room within the minority group for those very behaviours that would satisfy the dominant culture and its representatives. John speaks on behalf of the subaltern culture, its tradition *and* its silenced voices (see, e.g., 6.9–11; 16.5–7!). He encourages his Christian hearers to find and sustain their voice in a situation of protest against oppression and injustice. The ascendancy of Jezebel's voice would mean the silencing of the voice of Christian witness. In short, there is far more at stake in this situation than preserving *Jezebel's* right to speak.

Finally, to demand of John that he be tolerant of all voices and viewpoints is to demand that he betray his own tradition for the sake of accommodating himself to values foreign to that tradition. The Jewish Scriptures proclaim a God whose first commandment was 'You will have no other gods before me' (Exod. 20.2–3; Deut. 5.6–7) and whose second commandment prohibited any form of idolatrous worship (Exod. 20.4–5; Deut. 5.8–10). The tradition made no room for the prophet who might wish to lead God's people to worship other gods in violation of the covenant (Deut. 13.1–5), and John speaks in line with his received tradition rather than in judgement upon it. Modern readers need to take care not to replicate in their own responses to John the dominant Roman culture's distaste for the exclusive claims made by a particular subaltern people (the Jews and their spiritual offspring, the Christian Church).

John's concerns about the Roman imperial economy, the ills that both maintained and devolved from it, and the significance of Christian participation in it emerge also in the seven oracles as the likely background for what makes wealth 'poverty' (3.17–18) and the impoverished 'rich' (2.9). Where idolatry and commerce are closely intertwined, 'poverty' (Smyrna; 2.9) and lack of worldly clout (Philadelphia; 3.8b) are appropriate for those whose loyalty to the One God makes them unwilling to compromise (Kraybill 1996: 171; Duff 2001: 30). John does not oppose wealth in and of itself, for he will depict New Jerusalem in the most opulent terms (Duff 2001: 63). He is, however, deeply concerned about the compromises necessary to obtain wealth within the Roman imperial economy. Among the seven oracles, the message to the Christians in Laodicea (whose experience seems to demonstrate that the promise of prosperity under Rome is no mere myth) expresses this concern in the starkest terms.

Conclusion

Former generations of scholarship tended to focus too exclusively on the external pressures – even persecution – faced by (some of) the Christians addressed to the exclusion of other concerns, like the *flourishing* of some Christians in their idol- and exploitation-infused environment. Scholars of a more recent generation tend to focus too exclusively on what they consider to be 'power plays' between John, the prophet whom he labels 'Jezebel', and other such figures vying for influence in and control over (some of) these congregations (e.g. Duff 2001; Royalty 2004).[24] A careful reading of the seven oracles and, indeed, the whole of Revelation shows John to be concerned with multiple issues, some overlapping and some not, facing his seven congregations (Yarbro Collins 1984: 4–7; deSilva 1992: 286–96).

The oracles to the seven assemblies are favourite texts for preaching because church leaders rightly intuit that reflection on what the glorified Lord commended and rebuked in those ancient congregations can assist congregations in other times and places discern what pleases and what provokes the still-living Lord in their practice. In this regard, the *Scofield Reference Bible* (Scofield 1917: 1331–2) helpfully suggests that all seven oracles speak to the Church in every age as tools of ongoing discernment of their state in God's sight. Or as Craig Keener suggests, the essential principle in applying these oracles to new congregations is: 'If the shoe fits, wear it. To whatever degree our lives or churches reflect symptoms analogous to any of the churches the risen Lord addresses . . . we must take heed to "what the Spirit says to the churches"' (2000: 109). This signals the interpretative approach that has probably generated the most healthful insights and least empty speculation for Christian churches.

---

24 For a review of, and answer to, criticisms of John's authoritarianism and intolerance of dissenting views, see deSilva 2009: 66–9, 142–5, 315–24.

7
Visions of the cosmic centre (Revelation 4—5)

The chapters that begin the visionary portion of Revelation in earnest establish a centre for the cosmic map that John draws, and thus a reference point for the evaluation of other features of that landscape. At the centre of this map is not Rome or even Jerusalem, but the throne of God in the realm beyond the visible earth and heavens. It is from this centre that John himself takes his bearings and invites his audiences to do the same in regard to the choices, challenges and enticements that confront them in their immediate locales. Reference will be made back to this centre throughout Revelation as its agents break forth upon the earth and its inhabitants who have been swept up in the cosmic rebellion of Satan, 'the old dragon'.

Getting 'there'

We encounter here a major and sudden shift of scene. In the first three chapters, John related a vision on earth in which the glorified Christ appeared to him and gave him messages for each of the seven congregations to which he is writing. Now, without transition, that same voice that accosted him from behind on Patmos addresses him from the heavenly realm and summons him to 'come up' and enter the same. In John's view of the cosmos, God's realm exists in a place beyond the visible, material earth and heavens, and thus a 'door' must open in the sky to allow him access to this realm beyond. God is not merely 'up there', as moderns tend to caricature early Christian cosmology, but 'beyond *this*', where *this* is all that can be seen with the eyes of sense, all that is ultimately secondary and temporary vis-à-vis God's eternal realm. John's view is not unlike that of the author of the letter to the Hebrews, for whom the physical earth and heavens must be shaken and removed in order for the way into the divine realm to become accessible (Heb. 12.25–28).

John draws attention again to the non-rational state in which he finds himself. He was 'in a spirit' on Patmos when the glorified Christ appeared to him from behind (Rev. 1.10); he is 'in a spirit' again as he views the spaces inaccessible to the minds and bodies of human beings.[1] English translations commonly render the phrase as 'in the Spirit', as if John is indicating the Holy Spirit as the medium of communication (as in the NASV, NIV and NLT), though the absence of a definite article might suggest otherwise. John seems to call attention to the same distinction Paul makes in 1 Corinthians 14 when he contrasts praying 'with my mind' and 'with my spirit', the latter referring to praying with ecstatic speech (1 Cor. 14.14), and determines that he will pray and sing both 'with mind' and 'with spirit', both with rationally directed utterances and ecstasy-inspired utterances. Both Paul and John would attribute the latter to the inspiration of the Holy Spirit, but the phrase itself seems to denote merely an alternative state of consciousness.[2]

Dispensationalist interpreters find here, in this shift in location from Patmos to the divine realm, an anchoring point for their belief in a 'rapture' – the instant and sudden transfer of faithful Christians from the earthly realm to the heavenly realm immediately prior to the beginning of the 'seven last years' of tribulation and upheaval narrated in the remainder of Revelation, which they thereby escape. One major problem with such an inference is that John does not *remain* in heaven but will find himself in all manner of places – for example, back down on earth to meet the angel who hands him the scroll to eat (10.2–3, 8–10) or out in a desert in which the prostitute Babylon is revealed to him (17.3) – where dispensationalists would not wish for the raptured Church to follow! It also runs counter to John's own clear pastoral goal for Revelation, which is precisely to prepare Christians to remain faithful in the face of increasing hostility and even to invite increasing hostility through their uncompromising obedience to the One God and their uncowed testimony to God's Anointed One.

The heavenly court

John sees – and his highly detailed descriptions invite the hearers also to 'see' in their own imaginations[3] – the very throne of God and the celestial attendants that constitute the divine court. Such visions have been communicated before in the sacred tradition John shares with his audiences. Isaiah 'saw the Lord

---

1 John will make this declaration twice more in Revelation – at 17.3, when he views 'Babylon the Great' in the desert, and at 21.10, when he sees and tours the new Jerusalem. The expression seems to underscore the importance of the sights described.

2 Thus the CEB, 'a Spirit-inspired trance'.

3 Whitaker 2015: 34–5, 58.

sitting upon a throne, exalted and lifted high', surrounded by six-winged seraphim exclaiming 'Holy, holy, holy is the LORD of armies' (Isa. 6.1, 3). Ezekiel
saw God enthroned and moving by means of God's otherworldly chariot, at
once constituted and driven by bizarre otherworldly creatures (Ezek. 1.4–28).

Several writers from the Hellenistic and Roman periods also described visions of God's throne and ever-increasing entourage. The *Testament of Levi*,
part of the collection known as the *Testaments of the Twelve Patriarchs*,[4] presents a picture of God enthroned in the highest of seven heavens – essentially
in the holy place of the heavenly temple – attended by the seraphim of Isaiah
6.2–3, still shouting their song of 'Holy, holy, holy' (*T. Levi* 3.5; 5.1). The 'angels
of the Presence' occupy the next tier of heaven. This elite order of angels per-
forms a priestly function, offering bloodless sacrifices for the sins that the
righteous commit in ignorance (*T. Levi* 3.5–6).[5] A third tier is home to a lower
order of angels who serve as mediators and messengers (*T. Levi* 3.7), while a
fourth features another celestial order, the 'thrones and powers', who offer
ceaseless praise to God (*T. Levi* 3.8). The section of *1 Enoch* known as the Parables of Enoch – dating perhaps from the early or mid first century – portrays
God enthroned as Daniel's 'ancient of days', surrounded by different orders
of angels, including the Seraphim, Cherubim and Ophanim (those 'who do
not sleep, but keep watch over the throne of his glory', *1 Enoch* 71.7); by chief
angels including Michael, Raphael, Gabriel and Phanuel (71.9); and finally by
'a thousand thousands and ten thousand times ten thousand' (71.8).

These precursors inspire and inform John's own visionary experience (and
his reflection on and written description of the same), but his is not constrained
by nor merely derivative of them. Nevertheless, the fact that John's description
of God and God's entourage has marked similarities particularly with those of
the scriptural tradition (Isaiah, Ezekiel) potentially facilitates his audiences'
acceptance of his visions as 'accurate', since they align with their scripturally
informed expectations for such an experience of seeing the divine.[6]

John directs his audience's mental gaze first to the throne on which God
sits. Focusing on the throne makes a strong statement concerning who rules,
who exercises ultimate authority in the cosmos John and his audiences inhabit.
For John, the answer is clear: 'The Lord, *our* God – the Almighty – reigns'

---

4 The best available translation is Marinus de Jonge, 'Testaments of the Twelve Patriarchs', in Sparks
   1984: 505–600. The collection has been preserved in Christian circles and gives blatant evidence
   of Christian editing but is likely to have been Jewish in origin. On this question, see deSilva 2012:
   194–222.

5 See Lev. 5.18 on sins committed in ignorance.

6 Thus also Whitaker 2015: 62–3.

(Rev. 19.6), and alignment with the One who occupies *this* level of cosmic governance will always prove advantageous in the end. The absolute rule of God is a conviction nurtured in the worship life of both synagogue and Christian assembly (see Pss. 93.1–2; 97.1; 99.1), as is the connection between God's rule and God's commitment to bring justice, righting all that is amiss in the earthly sphere (Pss. 96.10, 13; 97.2; 98.9; 99.4). The latter is, of course, a (if not *the*) fundamental theme of Revelation, and John reinforces the connection between God's governance and justice throughout the drama (see, e.g., Rev. 11.16–18; 19.1–2, 6).

The absence of human characteristics in John's description of God, unlike descriptions of the same in other apocalyptic writings, is noteworthy. 'John's reserve maintains a sense of God's transcendence so that he is not construed as a human being writ large' (Koester 2014: 368).[7] Instead, John speaks merely of One who projects an aura resembling nothing on earth except its most precious gems and frightening natural phenomena (4.3, 5). An *iris* surrounds the throne, which many readers interpret as a 'rainbow' recalling the covenant God made with Noah, that God would not destroy the earth again with a flood (though Revelation will show that God has kept many other options open for the next time!).[8] Against such a connection is the fact that this *iris* is of a single colour – that of emerald – and that the very word *iris* is never used in the Greek translation of the Old Testament current in John's time to refer to the rainbow, which is God's 'bow' (*toxon*). John's hearers would more likely visualize a green halo around the throne, even as they will be asked to visualize another such halo (*iris*) around the head of an angel in Revelation 10.1.

From the initial focus on God enthroned, John pans outward, as it were, to direct his audience's mental gaze to the expanding circles of otherworldly attendants who focus their adoration on the One who properly occupies the centre of the cosmos. During the second and third centuries, Christians interpreted elements of John's visions – especially these heavenly beings who surround God's throne – as figurative representations of more familiar realities of more immediate concern to them. Thus Irenaeus (*Haer.* 3.11.8) explained the four living beings sporting the faces of lion, ox, human being and eagle as representations of the four Gospels, each of which presents a different face of the one Jesus, an interpretation that became quite popular.[9] John's vision provided Irenaeus with a warrant for embracing a fourfold Gospel canon in

---

7   See also Friesen 2001: 169–70.

8   Aune 1997: 285; Hansen 2014: 77.

9   See also Origen, *Comm. Jo.* 5.6; Victorinus, *In Apoc.* 4.4; Augustine, *Tract. Ev. Jo.* 36.5.2.

opposition to contemporaries who promoted a single, conflated harmony of the four Gospels. The considerable variety among the church fathers when it came to which 'face' matched up with which Gospel (e.g. was Matthew represented by the living being with the human form, since Matthew opened with Jesus' human genealogy, or by the living being with the lion's form, since he presented Jesus as coming from the tribe of Judah?) suggests the subjectivity of the enterprise as a whole.[10] The 24 elders were taken to represent the symbolic authorities of the Old and New Testaments – the 12 patriarchs of Israel and the 12 apostles of the Lord (Origen, *Comm. Jo.* 5.6; Tyconius, *Exposition of the Apocalypse* 2.4.4) – or the 24 books of the Law and the Prophets themselves (Victorinus, *In Apoc.* 4.3; Weinrich 2011b: 7).

While some of John's images are rightly 'decoded', since John himself gives indications of this (Rev. 17.9, 18), others of John's images may not represent anything beyond themselves. Here, it is likely that John believes himself to be describing the supernatural personnel of God's heavenly throne room, the aim of John's precursors from Isaiah on.[11] An angelic order of 'thrones' surrounds God in the *Testament of Levi* and seems to be indicated in Colossians 1.16. John's audiences may have understood the 24 elders seated upon their thrones as a more detailed representation of this angelic order. Some have suggested that this order represents a survival of the 'star gods' of Ancient Near Eastern lore, in which case 'we see one manifestation of a theme that will be found throughout Revelation: the humbling of those to whom undue honor has been ascribed', who appear no longer as independent deities but as willing servants in the court of the One God (Morton 2001: 97). Others have suggested that they represent 'resurrected Christ-believers', since they appear in the same basic attire (white robes, wreaths) and are seated upon thrones now as Christians anticipate being seated in the future,[12] though one is left to wonder what to make of John's vision of the faithful in Revelation 7.9–17, whom he explicitly represents *as* the faithful, *alongside* the 24 elders and other figures in the throne vision.

---

10 Koester 2014: 352–3. Joachim of Fiore (d. 1202), by contrast, thought that the four living creatures represented the four senses of Scripture as commonly accepted in medieval exegesis: the literal, the spiritual, the moral and the anagogical (Kovacs and Rowland 2004: 66).

11 The multiplication of angelic and other supernatural powers named or depicted in the New Testament (in addition to Rev. 4 and Jewish apocalyptic works, wherein the notion of ranks is visually depicted, see Rom. 8.38; Eph. 1.21; Col. 1.16) prompted later church leaders to attempt to classify them. Gregory the Great's posited pecking order (discussed in Thomas Aquinas, *Summa Theologiae* Part 1, Question 108) runs thus from highest to lowest in rank: Seraphim, Cherubim, Thrones, Dominions, Principalities, Powers, Virtues, Archangels, Angels. Dante, *Paradiso* 28.97–129, offers an alternative configuration.

12 E.g. Whitaker 2015: 111–14.

It seems more promising to regard the 24 elders as a heavenly archetype for the 24 orders of priests and Levites in the earthly Temple (1 Chron. 24.1–19).[13] In the visions that follow, John will more explicitly describe the divine realm as a cosmic temple in keeping with the fairly widespread notion that the wilderness tabernacle and Jerusalem Temple were essentially models of a heavenly prototype (see Wisd. 9.8 and Heb. 8.1–5, both reflecting a current interpretation of Exod. 25.40).[14] The elders' accoutrements – harps, suggestive of Levitical duties in the Temple, and bowls of incense, suggestive of priestly duties in the Temple (Rev. 5.8) – strengthen the impression of their priestly function. The object of their devotion causes these white-robed and wreathed heavenly priests to stand out in contrast with the white-robed, wreathed priests and worshippers in the cities of the seven churches celebrating, in counterfeit adoration, the emperor and the Greco-Roman pantheon.[15]

The seven lamps, which John himself explains as 'the seven spirits of God', have long and often been taken to represent the one Holy Spirit (Primasius, *Commentary on the Apocalypse* 4.5), motivated no doubt by the propriety – in a Nicene and post-Nicene Christian context – of finding the Trinity represented in this vision of heaven, completed by the appearance of the Lamb in 5.5–6. Writers from the patristic period to the present claim Isaiah 11.2–3, which seems to speak of 'the sevenfold Spirit of God', as a warrant for this identification. John's use of the singular *pneuma* throughout Revelation to refer to the Holy Spirit (2.7, 11, 17, 29; 3.6, 13, 22; 14.13; 22.17) suggests that he intends a different referent for the plural *pneumata* here and elsewhere. The prominence of 'the angels of the Presence' in Jewish angelology – a group to which John himself will shortly give attention ('the seven angels who stand before God', 8.2) – also points in a different direction.[16] In addition to *Testament of Levi* 3.4–6 and Greek *1 Enoch* 20.1–8, the book of Tobit bears witness to such an established group. There the disguised angelic helper reveals himself to be 'Raphael, one of the seven angels who stand ready and enter before the glory of the Lord' (Tob. 12.15 NRSV).[17] 'Angels' and 'spirits' are used interchangeably in other texts (Ps. 104.4 and Heb. 1.7 explicitly equate the two). Not all interpreters have found it necessary to choose *one* referent, however.

---

13 Witherington 2003: 117.

14 See Rev. 6.9–11; 8.1–6; 11.19; 14.15, 17; 15.5–8.

15 Koester 2014: 368–9.

16 John's use of the definite article in Rev. 8.2 may point to these seven as a previously identified group, the only antecedent for which would be 'the seven spirits who are before his throne' (1.4), the 'seven lampstands burning before the throne, which are the seven spirits of God' (4.5).

17 See also Aune 1997: 34–5; Witherington 2003: 75.

The sixth-century theologian Andrew of Caesarea was happy to entertain both options simultaneously.[18]

The four 'living creatures' or 'living beings' in tight orbit around the throne closely resemble the seraphim of Isaiah 6.2–3 in the enumeration of their six wings and the words of their song of adoration. Their faces recall the other-worldly attendants of God's throne in Ezekiel 1.5–11 (though, where *each* of Ezekiel's four 'living creatures' had the four faces of lion, ox, human and eagle, John's 'living creatures' each have a single face). Koester (2014: 364, 369) suggests that these figures are representatives of creation, though the absence of any representation of sea life is striking, all the more as John shows an explicit interest in the creatures that live in the sea elsewhere (Rev. 8.8–9; 10.6; 16.3). Once again, it may be best not to seek to find hidden meanings in the descriptions of these beings and allow the different orders of God's entourage to make an impact on us in all their strangeness. The 'glass sea like crystal' (4.6), also a feature of Ezekiel's vision (Ezek. 1.22, 26), may be a relic of the Ancient Israelite cosmology in which two solid layers ('firmaments') created a space for life by separating the primaeval waters into waters 'below' and waters 'above' (Gen. 1.6–8; Ps. 148.4).[19]

Once the cast of heavenly characters is introduced, the drama that follows is worship. The living creatures offer praise 'day and night without rest' (4.8), another feature with precedent in the tradition,[20] to 'the One who lives into the ages of ages' (4.9). As this description of God is repeated verbatim in the immediately following verse, it seems to be significant, perhaps because this God is thus distinguished from 'dead' idols 'which are able neither to see nor to hear nor to walk about' (9.20), perhaps because the genuine God is thus distinguished from mortals who must die before becoming (counterfeit) gods, like the emperors.[21] The elders put their faces to the immaterial ground before God to acknowledge God's significantly greater honour, and place their golden wreaths at God's feet – a gesture familiar from the civic and cultic rituals of the Roman world where one wishes to show one's recognition of another's superior power and authority.[22]

---

18 *Comm. in Apoc.* 4.10; Weinrich 2011a: 129.

19 Koester 2014: 363; see also Ps. 104.2–3 on God's house being set above those waters.

20 See *1 Enoch* 39.13: 'My eyes saw all those who do not sleep standing before him and blessing and saying, Blessed are you, and blessed is the name of the Lord for ever and ever!'

21 Vespasian famously quipped in the grip of his final illness, 'Alas! I think I am becoming a god!' (Suetonius, *Vesp.* 23).

22 Koester 2014: 362, 365.

The hymn sung by the elders makes a claim on God's behalf, both explaining the elders' falling down in reverence around God and asserting that this is the response *owed to* God on the part of all who have life and breath:

You are worthy, our Lord and God,
    to receive the glory and the honour and the power,
because you created all things,
    and by your will they were and were created.
(Rev. 4.11)

Benefactors merit gratitude and, among benefactors, God holds the first place, having given to all the gift of existence itself.[23] Greco-Roman ethicists would agree that worship is the proper response to 'the gods' for their gifts,[24] but John makes this claim exclusively on behalf of the one and only God. Gratitude towards the One God necessitates living the life that one received from God in line with God's commandments, which include the prohibition of worshipping any other would-be divinity.[25] The hymns to God (4.11) and, shortly to follow, the Lamb (5.9–10) challenge the legitimacy of the worship that is going on all around the congregations John addresses.

John's vision of God enthroned and of the personnel and activity around God's throne, if imaginatively engaged by his audiences, cannot fail to arouse emotions that are strategic to John's pastoral aims for his communication. A primary emotion here must be awe – an emotional response frequently targeted in the world of John's audiences. The massive temples in their cities with the colossal images of their resident deities (like Artemis, Augustus and Domitian in Ephesus, or Athena, Dionysus, Demeter and Augustus in Pergamum) and the rituals executed in connection with the same (including hymns and acclamations rivalling those in John's heaven)[26] were staged with a view to renewing awe towards the powers upon whose favour a stable life was believed to depend. Falling back into such responses was no doubt an ever-present temptation for 'recovering pagans'.[27] John directs their awe afresh towards the

---

23 See, further, Seneca, *Ben.*; Danker 1982; deSilva 2000: 95–156. On the rationales in the hymns of Revelation 4—5 as enthymemes: Humphrey 2007: 186–7; deSilva 2009: 260–1.

24 See *Rhet. Alex.* 1421b37–1422a2; *Rhet. Her.* 3.3.4; *Eth. nic.* 8.14.4.

25 Compare the near-contemporary *4 Ezra* 7.21–24; 8.59–61.

26 On the role of choirs in the imperial cult, see Tacitus, *Ann.* 14.15 (which recalls adulation offered to Nero 'day and night' by a circle of men dedicated to this task); Kraybill 1996: 61–2 (citing *I. Eph.* 18d.11–14); Friesen 2001: 105–13.

27 The Letter of Jeremiah suggests that the pomp and circumstance of Gentile religion might even lead Jews resident in Gentile lands to feel 'awe' before their gods, a feeling from which the author of that

Creator God and the Redeemer Lamb, the genuine Saviour and Son of the Divine, offering an antidote to similar emotions evoked in settings of imperial cult and Greco-Roman religion that will expose them as counterfeit.[28] The vision of the adoration of God and the Lamb trumps all the pretensions especially of human rulers and their pomp.

The commissioning of the Lamb

The ceaseless adoration of the One seated upon the throne recedes into the background as John focuses his audiences' attention on a decisive event in the heavenly court – an episode that shows the Lamb to have attained a truly *unique* dignity through his death. The story of a universal search for one who was 'worthy' to receive the divine commission represented by the scroll in God's hand, the initial failure to find *anyone* worthy (resulting in a tense disappointment) and the dramatic resolution as the slaughtered-but-standing Lamb is revealed makes a claim on behalf of the Christian Messiah familiar from standard eulogistic practice: showing someone to have been the first or only person to succeed in a particular venture or achieve a particular end.[29]

The focal point of attention has shifted from the One seated upon the throne to a scroll at his right hand. That the scroll bears writing on both front and back recalls the scroll seen by Ezekiel (Ezek. 2.9–10), sustaining the resonances between Revelation and this prophetic predecessor. That it has been sealed with seven seals – and we should imagine these seven seals all lined up in a row at the single seam that prevents the scroll from being opened – underscores the gravity of the document. Though seven seals might seem excessive, it is not without precedent (though admittedly very rare) in actual practice.[30]

What is this scroll at the centre of so much to-do? Early church fathers tended to connect it with the Scriptures, and the opening of the scroll to the interpretation of Scripture. Primasius regarded the writing on the outside of the scroll as representing the Jewish Scriptures or Old Testament, and the writing on the inside the writings of the New Testament, for the New Testament 'lay hidden within the Old' (*Commentary on the Apocalypse* 5.1). Similarly, Victorinus reads this scene as an affirmation that the meaning of the Old Testament remains sealed up unless it is read in the light of the Lamb, that is, in

---

text seeks to insulate his audiences (see deSilva 2002b: 234–7).

28 Schüssler Fiorenza 1985: 123; Morton 2007: 105.

29 See Aristotle, *Rhet.* 1.9.38; 2.7.2; Quintilian, *Inst.* 3.7.16.

30 Koester 2014: 383.

the light of the life, death and resurrection of Jesus, for only in Christ is the veil removed from the reading of the Old Testament (*In Apoc.* 5.2, appealing to 2 Cor. 3.15–16). Origen essentially concurs, also finding here a reference to the two senses of Scripture – the literal sense that everyone can read (on the outside), and the spiritual sense that must be revealed in Christ (the inside; *Comm. Jo.* 5.6).[31]

While these readings accurately reflect the interpreters' interests, John gives signals that the scroll is perhaps to be understood differently. As the narrative progresses, the opening of the seals preventing the scroll from being read sets in motion the eschatological judgements that cycle down throughout Revelation, giving the book its distinctive outline in its series of seven seals, trumpets and bowls. It seems highly likely that the open scroll that John sees in Revelation 10 – also written on both sides – represents the same scroll that the Lamb had been opening throughout Revelation 6. John's digestion of that scroll will provide him with the prophetic message that, one might presume, he commits to written form in the remainder of Revelation. The handling and contents of this scroll form the basis for what the scroll of Revelation itself contains. At the same time, the process of opening the scroll brings this age and all that belongs to it to an end, and over this process – and thus this age itself – the Lamb holds ultimate authority. The scene of the scroll securely at God's right hand, transferred solely and securely to God's Messiah for execution of its contents, speaks less to questions about biblical interpretation (as in Primasius) and more to questions about who ultimately exercises sovereign control over the world – questions that must have been pressing for John 'with Jerusalem destroyed, fellow Christians slaughtered at Rome, and John himself apparently in trouble with imperial authorities' (Kraybill 2010: 97).

The drama of the scene is heightened first by a strong angel's challenge, implicitly directed to all in heaven, upon the earth and under the earth, calling for one who is worthy to step forward to take the scroll and peer into its contents, and then by the failure of anyone to step forward (Rev. 5.2–3). Passing over other potential (and, in John's world, prominent) saviour figures here is silent eloquence: 'No human being, no angel, no Caesar can open that scroll. By that simple sentence John reminds the church of the limitations of the emperor's power' (Boesak 1987: 53).[32] It is the crucified-and-resurrected Messi-

---

31 References and quotations are from Weinrich 2005: 69–70, 76.

32 The absence of Rome's deified emperors and their deified family members from John's heaven may strike his audiences as significant, standing in stark contrast to public discourse and iconography about the apotheosis and assumption of numerous members of the Julio-Claudian and Flavian

ah, Jesus, who steps forward into that open space, who alone has proven worthy of this singular honour, this singular role in the unfolding drama of God's extension of God's kingdom into every region of the cosmos, over every pocket of resistance. The hearers might get the impression that the time frame of this episode is the immediate sequel to Christ's Ascension, which would mean, for them, that the sequence of events marking God's breaking in upon those pockets of rebellion had already begun some 50 years prior to Domitian's accession. The wheels had already been set in motion long before John writes.

An angel introduces this figure with familiar messianic titles. The 'Lion from the tribe of Judah' recalls Jacob's deathbed words to Judah, calling him 'a lion's whelp' and promising that rule and pre-eminence would not depart from his tribe (Gen. 49.9 NRSV). The Aramaic paraphrases of the Pentateuch, called *targumim*, bear witness to the messianic interpretation given this passage:

How beauteous is the King Meshiha, who is to arise from the house of Jehuda. Binding his loins, and going forth to war against them that hate him, he will slay kings with princes, and make the rivers red with the blood of their slain, and his hills white with the fat of their mighty ones; his garments will be dipped in blood, and he himself be like the juice of the winepress.[33]

The 'Root of David' (Isa. 11.1, 10) had similarly taken on messianic overtones, with the designations 'Root' and 'Branch' of David serving as messianic titles in the Dead Sea Scrolls, for example.[34]

Interpreters make much of the fact that a Lion is announced but a Lamb is seen, sometimes even claiming that the same figure had been described as both a Lion and a Lamb (Moyise 1995: 128). Eugene Boring considers this

---

households into heaven by this point. Marcus Manilius, a near contemporary of Jesus, wrote of Augustus as a star that fell from heaven to rule the earth, bringing order to this realm, then returning to heaven with his deification (*Astronomica* 1.799–800). The starry heaven grows brighter as more members of the imperial family ascend as gods themselves (*Astronomica* 4.933–5). Statius, a poet writing under Domitian, speaks of Vespasian ruling the cosmos from heaven with one son (Titus) in heaven and another (Domitian) on earth as his viceroys (*Silv.* 3.3.138–9). Domitian's own penchant for deifying his deceased family members has created 'a Flavian heaven' (*Silv.* 4.4.18–19; for a fuller discussion of these and other references, see Yeates 2017: 45–9). John, however, assigns a very different place in the cosmos to these imperial figures – all sharing a common fate in the lake of fire, being joined together into one monstrous, seven-headed prodigy.

33 *Targum Pseudo-Jonathan* Gen. 49.10–11 (tr. from Etheridge 1862–5). The introduction of details from Isa. 63.1–3 into the depiction of the Messiah's appearance and activity both here and in Revelation (e.g. Rev 19.11–16) is noteworthy.

34 Koester 2014: 375–6; Bauckham 1993a: 180–1. The promise in Isa. 11.4 (LXX) that this Root 'will strike the earth with the word of his mouth' contributes also to the picture in Rev. 19.11–16.

juxtaposition of images to be 'mind-wrenching' (1989: 108). But there is a difference between being *named* and being *described*. Jesus is *named* the 'Lion of Judah' but *described* as a slaughtered-but-standing Lamb. The description reinterprets the title even as the title interprets the figure described. It is true that many Jews around the turn of the era nurtured expectations that their messianic hopes would be fulfilled by a military conqueror who would throw off the yoke of Gentile oppression (and, indeed, such hopes helped to fuel the two disastrous revolts against Roman rule in 66–70 and 132–5 CE). It is also true that Jesus presented a very different model for how God's messianic promises would come to pass. But it is hardly true that John's Christian audiences would find Revelation 5.5–6 shocking or even surprising in any way. They are not expecting to see a roaring Lion and not surprised to see a slaughtered-but-standing Lamb. They already know the surprising manner in which God's Anointed redeemed them and accomplished his God-given mission. They already know the frustrated expectations of Jesus' first circle of followers and the stories of how they had to come to terms with a messiah whom no one anticipated. They have already accepted as fact the conviction that 'the sacrificial death of Christ [was] the fulfillment of Jewish hopes of the messianic conqueror' (Bauckham 1993a: 184). They will naturally assent when 'the slaughtered victim is declared conqueror' (Whitaker 2015: 155), which is essential to their acceptance of the point John does hope to drive home to all of them: that costly obedience and witness on their own part is their path to 'conquering' in the Lamb and enjoying the prizes thereof.[35]

The Lamb, though slaughtered, is not sheepish. His seven horns represent perfect power and authority.[36] His seven eyes, the 'seven spirits of God sent into all the earth' (5.6), ascribe to the Lamb the omniscience of the Almighty,[37] affirming him indeed to be 'the one who searches mind and heart' (2.23), whose scrutiny becomes a major motivator to watchfulness over oneself in every situation.[38] As Richard Bauckham observes, 'the Lamb really does conquer, though not by force of arms, and his followers really do share his victory, though not by violence'. The landscape of John's world is indeed a battlefield, but the war is 'fought and won by sacrificial death' (1993a: 229–30). The way of the Lamb is not the way of weakness. The Lamb is also the glorified

---

35 See Rev. 2.8, 10b; 3.21; 11.7–13; 12.11; 15.2–4.

36 Such is the most regular connotation of this symbol in John's tradition. See 1 Sam. 2.10; 2 Sam. 22.3; Pss. 17.3; 75.10; 89.17, 24; 92.10; 112.9; 132.17; 148.14; Sir. 47.5, 7, 11; 49.5.

37 The image recalls Zech. 4.2, 10, where seven lamps (on a single lampstand) represent the eyes of God that see all things, before whom no creature is hidden.

38 Maier 2002: 70–4; see also Boesak 1987: 57–8; Blount 2009: 116–17; Whitaker 2015: 156–7.

Christ, a resplendent and powerful figure (Rev. 1.12–16), described in language recalling – and combining – the Danielic 'Ancient of Days' and 'Son of Man', the inheritor of the kingdoms of the world (Dan. 7.9–14), as indeed Christ is destined to be (Rev. 11.18). The post-mortem, post-resurrection Jesus – the slaughtered-but-standing Lamb – is notably more glorious, powerful and impressive than the earthly Jesus, which is surely significant in a text promoting the sacrifice of this life in order to attain the life beyond death. He becomes a potent symbol both of life beyond death, and of the way to attain such life. And he will *yet* ride against his enemies at the head of the armies of heaven (Rev. 19.11–16).

The four living creatures and 24 elders resume their worship, now focused on the Lamb. They hold kitharas, instruments familiar from the worship life of Israel as represented, for example, throughout the Psalms, and the shallow bowls used in ritual – ubiquitously in Greco-Roman ritual! – to pour out offerings of incense, wine or grain over altar fires. The identification of the incense with 'the prayer of the saints' (5.8) recalls the observance of the evening incense offering in the Jerusalem Temple as the hour for prayer (see, e.g., Ps. 141.2; Luke 1.10) and provides a powerful image of John's audiences' connection with the One seated upon the throne (see also Rev. 8.2–5). These heavenly beings 'recite a new song' (5.9), recalling the summons that appears frequently in the Psalms to sing a new song to God (33.3; 40.3; 96.1; 98.1; 144.9; 149.1). These are often invitations to reflect afresh on God's well-known character and deeds, though in some instances they summon worshippers to acknowledge some new act of God performed on the psalmist's or the people's behalf (see especially 40.1–3; 144.7–10; possibly 98.1–4). The latter appears to be the case here: a new song breaks forth from the heavenly court to acknowledge the recent and singular achievement of the Lamb that has brought him unparalleled worthiness.

The elders' and living beings' acclamation of Christ follows the pattern of their earlier acclamation of God (4.8), namely a claim followed by a supporting rationale:[39]

> You are worthy to take the scroll and to open its seals,
> *because* you were slain and you bought back for God with
>   your blood
> out of every tribe and language group and people and
>   nation

---

39 Schüssler Fiorenza 1991: 61–2.

and made them a kingdom and priests for our God,
and they will reign over the earth.
(Rev. 5.9–10)

The Lamb has won the right to take the book and open its seals – that is, to initiate judgement upon 'the kingdoms of this world' (11.15) and subdue them under God's rule – *because* the Lamb gave up his own life to buy back for God the people who would constitute God's kingdom on earth. The Lamb's selfless actions rescued people from a situation of significant distress, as is implied by the language of 'redeeming' or 'ransoming', and have won for him incomparable honour thereby, as befits so great a benefactor. The language specifically recalls God's actions on behalf of God's people in the exodus, redeeming them from slavery in Egypt to make them 'a kingdom of priests' for the one and only God (Exod. 19.6; 20.2–3), announcing again (see Rev. 1.5–6) the motif of a new exodus event that will run throughout Revelation.[40] Here, however, as in early Christian thought generally, it is not a matter of God's acting on behalf of a single, distinct people group (the Hebrews); rather, he acts on behalf of people who would be drawn together from across every line that differentiates them – 'out of every tribe and language group and people and nation'.

Beneficence and selfless action undergird the Lamb's dominion; the same rhetoric was prominent in the legitimation of Augustus's dominion. The latter is exemplified particularly well in the *Res Gestae Divi Augusti*, a list of Augustus's achievements and benefactions drawn up by the emperor himself shortly before his death and prominently inscribed in public spaces (including the temples of Rome and Augustus in Pisidian Antioch and Ancyra). Here in the heavenly court, it is the Lamb who is acclaimed for genuine beneficence (having given his very life to bring benefit to many) and unique achievement, presenting an alternative and superior picture of the perfect benefactor serving the divine design for humanity and empire.

At the close of chapter 5, John completes the circles of adoration centred on God's throne, extending these first to 'ten thousand ten thousands and a thousand thousands'[41] of angels joining in the acclamation of the slaughtered Lamb (5.11–12) and thence to 'every creature' occupying every region of creation – heaven, earth, underworld and sea – ascribing 'blessing and honour and

---

40   The focal image of the Lamb may also recall the Passover lamb of Exodus (Bauckham 1993a: 184), though the Passover lambs were not offered in connection with sins, as was John's Lamb (see Rev. 1.5).

41   John recalls similar images of 'a thousand thousand . . . and ten thousand times ten thousand' serving the enthroned Deity in older visions (Dan. 7.10 NRSV; cf. also *1 Enoch* 1.9).

glory and power to the One sitting upon the throne and to the Lamb for ever and ever' (5.13). Since God has benefited *all* with God's creative and life-sustaining activity (4.11), *all* properly stand before God in awe and gratitude.[42] Augustus had claimed his power to be legitimate on the basis of being granted primacy 'by universal consent' (*Res Gestae* 34). The scene with which John closes this vision of heavenly worship, however, shows a far more genuinely *universal* consent upholding the reign of the God of Israel and this God's Messiah, and on the basis of far more fundamental benefits.[43]

The larger picture and audience perspective

In these scenes of worship, John presents his audiences with a model of a cosmos that is ordered rightly – a universe in which all created beings in every region of that multi-tiered universe orient themselves towards this one centre, the throne of God and of the Lamb, in grateful adoration. It is not merely *descriptive*, however, but also highly *prescriptive* since, at the time of John's writing, not every part of the created order falls in line with the vision for *universal* worship that, in John's opinion, belongs to God and to the Lamb by right. This tension between what ought to be and what is can be seen already in John's narrative: on the one hand he sees 'every creature in heaven and on earth and under the earth' falling in place around God and the Lamb in adoration (5.13); on the other, the acclamation of the Lamb itself speaks of a division of humanity into two camps as the Lamb ransoms some portion of humanity '*out from* every tribe and language and people and nation' (5.9), leaving an unredeemed remainder *in* those groupings to find solidarity together in a rival kingdom, that of the monster and the dragon who empowers him (see 11.9; 13.7–8; 17.15). The people in the latter group gather themselves around alternative centres in adoration, constituting little circles of disorder obstinately resisting the universal consensus of the cosmos in their commitment not to 'repent of the works of their hands, so as not to worship the demons and the idols of gold and silver and bronze and stone and wood, which can neither see nor hear nor walk' (Rev. 9.20–21).

---

42 The theme of all creation owing, and therefore being summoned to give, honour and praise to God is also prominent in the worship texts of Israel (see especially Ps. 148; Song of the Three Young Men).

43 So also Barnett 1989: 115. John will challenge public discourse about 'universal consent' again in Rev. 13.3–4: it is not the emperors' beneficence, but their military power and their use of violence to unify multiple peoples, languages, nations and tribes into 'empire', that created the 'universal consent' they allege supports their rule.

John effects a stunning coup with these visions. The vast majority of the people living in the cities in which John's audiences resided gathered in worship around the traditional Greco-Roman and local deities, including the Roman emperors and the goddess Roma (the deification of the city at the centre of *their* maps), while the Christians gathered in small circles in the corners and margins of their cities. The latter could feel like an insignificant pocket of deviance even without their neighbours loudly proclaiming the fact. In John's vision – potentially received as divinely authorized and thus being truer to reality than that which could be observed by the audiences every day with their own eyes – the *many* are the deviant minority. Angels, archangels and all the company of heaven know whither to direct their worship, gratitude and loyalty, and John's Christian audiences are rightly aligned with the universal consensus. As Revelation continues to unfold, they will learn how all that is presently out of order will be brought in line with God's order – or be eliminated from God's renewed ordering of the cosmos!

Revelation and worship

The scenes of worship in Revelation do not merely reassure John's audiences that they are worshipping rightly. They also invite his audiences into worship of a kind that changes their everyday experience of their world. As Nelson Kraybill has put it so well, 'Revelation is *a book of worship*, not a book about worship' (2010: 36–7).[44] John's vivid portrayal of the throne room of the invisible God gives his audiences the opportunity to imaginatively experience the God whom they worship and to whom they are to give exclusive allegiance, opening them up to an epiphanic encounter with 'a God who might otherwise appear to be absent both spatially and temporally' (Whitaker 2015: 34–5). The hymns sung in that heavenly space speak of those external acts that rightly shape human lives and properly determine their trajectory: their creation for God's good pleasure and their redemption to live under God's rule. Such worship is a political act, the creation of a space where God is sovereign in the midst of the present political order, 'a territorial outpost claimed and ordered by a foreign and future imperial center' (Hansen 2014: 46). Worship sustains hope that the inevitable will *indeed* happen, when 'the kingdom of this world has become the kingdom of our Lord and of his Anointed' (Rev. 11.15).[45]

---

44 See also Humphrey 2007: 155.
45 Kraybill 2010: 106.

Revelation has continued to have an impact on Christian worship through the centuries, particularly in the music of the Church. The great chorus 'Worthy Is the Lamb' forms the climax of George Frederick Handel's oratorio, *Messiah* (1742), its lyrics drawn from Revelation 5.9, 12–13; the *informal* climax of the same oratorio, the 'Hallelujah' chorus, also takes its lyrics principally from the hymnic acclamations of Revelation (Rev. 11.15; 19.6, 16). Composers both of hymns and contemporary praise songs are consistently drawn to the acclamations and images of Revelation as they create new expressions of worship for successive generations. The most enduring of these is probably 'Holy, Holy, Holy, Lord God Almighty' by Reginald Heber (1783–1826), the second stanza of which directly recalls the scene in Revelation 4:

Holy, holy, holy! All the saints adore thee,
casting down their golden crowns around the glassy sea;
cherubim and seraphim falling down before thee,
which wert, and art, and evermore shalt be.

Worship has continued to serve the indispensable functions in successive generations that it did for John's first audiences. For those who face conditions not far different from theirs – or potentially far more hostile conditions – it provides the re-centring and the assurance of God's reality, presence and power that sustain faithfulness under pressure. For those in modern, secular democracies where religious freedom is prized, but religious affiliation is essentially irrelevant to and marginalized in public discourse, worship provides a connection with the God whose confessors in every age and every nation constitute a political entity that dwarfs any single nation in any age. For those tempted to regard religion as a form of therapy that makes the rest of their lives more manageable, it provides the regular reminder that they do not summon Christ into their congregations to help them cope with life's burdens,[46] but they are summoned to join with angels, archangels and all the company of heaven in using the life God has given them to serve *God's* good pleasure.

---

46 Kraybill 2010: 38.

8
Seals, trumpets and plagues: Revelation as cosmic exodus (Revelation 6—9, 10—11, 15—16)

The focus of Revelation's dramatic movement falls on how the forces of the divine centre seen in chapters 4—5 break into and overrun the world in which the seven congregations live and move. In the future that John narrates, everything that is out of order in regard to the divine centre of the cosmos is either eliminated or set back in order with respect to the centrality of God and the Lamb and their just requirements. The earth is a passive sphere. It, along with its inhabitants, is the object of divine action as the Lamb opens the seals (6.1–8) or as angels unleash the disasters that play a role in God's resolution of the disorder in God's cosmos, dismantling the present order (7.1–3; 8.7—9.19; etc.). Real power, represented in part by the vast, supernatural forces aligned alongside God, belongs to God and the Lamb and not to those pretenders who are seen at last merely to 'strut and fret their hour upon the stage' as players in the dragon's long-standing and long-failing rebellion against the Almighty. 'The kings of the earth and the magnates and the generals and the rich and the strong' are helpless before the coming of God and the Lamb, unable even to face them (6.12–17). The beast's throne (16.10–11), proud Babylon (16.17–21; 18.21–24) and all their assembled forces (19.17–21; 20.7–10) are helpless before God's fury. Though they might wield power temporarily over God's faithful ones (2.10; 11.7–8; 12.17; 13.7, 15–17), they are helpless before the Christians' divine Ally, whose vindication of his saints draws inexorably nearer.

Linear plot and/or recapitulation?

Interpreters differ as to whether the seals, trumpets and bowls outline a completely linear plot or whether John is circling back at some points to an earlier moment. Two factors have led some to favour the second view. The first is the arrival of what appears to be 'the end' at multiple points throughout Revelation. John seems to bring Christ's second coming (and its accompanying events) before our eyes at no fewer than four places (see 1.7; 6.12–17; 14.14–20; 19.11—20.15)! The second is the similarity of certain of the visitations of judgement, for example the correspondences between the first four trumpets and the first four bowls. The latter observation led Victorinus to assert as early as the third century: 'Whatever he said rather briefly by way of the trumpets he said more completely by way of the bowls' (*In Apoc.* 8.2; Weinrich 2011b: 12). A number of modern interpreters have adopted an even more extreme version of this view. Nelson Kraybill (2010: 119), for example, understands the seals, trumpets and bowls to 'portray the same events, each showing the end-time trauma with images that are increasingly more graphic and comprehensive'. Louis Brighton (1999: 150–4) similarly considers each of the three cycles to 'cover the same time period' and carry '*the same message*', each calling more forcefully for repentance. Joseph Mede (1586–1638) took a related approach in his *Clavis apocalyptica*, positing that synchronisms were the key to the book. There was but one period of three and a half years, or 42 months, or 1,260 days, and all the passages speaking of such a period were speaking about the same period of time (see Kovacs and Rowland 2004: 22–3).[1]

On the one hand, it must be admitted that the seals, trumpets and bowls are not entirely sequential, as the opening of the sixth seal already provides John with a vision of 'the great day of the wrath' of God and the Lamb (6.17), including the utter dissolution of the present cosmos (6.12–14). On the other hand, John gives us several clear indications that he is not merely telling the same story three times with different imagery. There is a high degree of non-overlap between each cycle. The fourth horseman's ride, the fourth trumpet's plague and the fourth bowl's consequences are not identical. There is also unambiguous escalation in intensity and effect that ought not to be overlooked. The fourth horseman presages the slaughter of a quarter of earth's inhabitants (6.8); the first four trumpets announce the destruction of one third of the earth and its creatures (8.7–12); the bowls summon total devastation of the remaining elements (16.3–4). The 'symptoms' of theophany increase incrementally as well in 4.3; 8.5; 11.19; 16.18, 21, as if God is drawing closer and closer

---

1 The stretch of time variously measured as 42 months and 1,260 days (11.2, 3) has often played an important role in calculations of the end. Joachim of Fiore took it to represent the span of time from Christ to the end – 42 generations of 30 years each, mirroring the 42 generations from Abraham to Christ in Matthew's genealogy (Kovacs and Rowland 2004: 124). Several interpreters have taken the 1,260 days as an indication that the papacy (as the reign of Antichrist) would last 1,260 years (Koester 2014: 438–9). Of course, they can also be taken literally as half of the final seven-year period of tribulation in dispensationalist timelines.

in visitation and judgement at each juncture between cycles. The introduction of the seven bowls, moreover, specifically guides the hearer to think of these as the last in a sequence of such visitations of divine wrath: 'I saw another great and awe-inspiring sign, seven angels holding seven plagues – the *last* ones, for with *these* God's wrath was fully expressed' (15.1).

Revelation's plot reveals a lack of linearity from other angles as well. For example, the important scene of sealing the 144,000 (7.1–8) *cannot* follow the event portrayed in the sixth seal (6.12–17), for there are no further plagues from which to be sealed for protection after 'the day of the wrath of God and the Lamb'. Similarly, the seventh trumpet with its announcement that 'the kingdom of this world has become that of our Lord and of his Anointed' (11.15) cannot precede the events of chapter 12, which take us back to the dragon's rebellion in heaven and his attempt to swallow up the Anointed One during his Incarnation (a moment of 'recapitulation' – or, at least, of circling back – noted by Bede, *Exp.* 11.18; see also Barr 2003c: 18).

Breaking the seals

John's description of the actions accompanying the opening of the first four seals provides one of the most enduring images of Revelation – the four horsemen of the Apocalypse.[2] Their grisly gallop has been the frequent subject of art, as in Albrecht Dürer's iconic woodcut, which has become so iconic as to spawn parodies, as in the depiction of four Nazi cavalrymen riding in the air above Nazi tanks and aircraft.[3] They have also made frequent appearances in popular culture, from the naming of four pre-Second World War football players as 'the four horsemen of Notre Dame', to heavy metal songs about 'The Four Horsemen' by Judas Priest and Metallica and the heavily intertextual 'The Man Comes Around' by Johnny Cash, to the allies of the Marvel Avengers' nemesis, Apocalypse.

The group lends itself to being interpreted as a relay team of menacing figures presaging unparalleled destruction, though early interpretations tended to set the first rider apart from the other three. Irenaeus (*Haer.* 4.21.3) and Victorinus (*Comm.* 6.1) identified the first rider with Christ and the conquering advance of the gospel through its preachers, while the remaining three

---

2 The events that accompany the opening of the seals are probably not to be understood as the *content* of the scroll (Bauckham 1993a: 250), which does not stand open until 10.2, 9–10 when it is handed to John by the 'strong angel' that has brought it down from heaven (10.1). Its contents become John's prophetic word, once he has digested its message (10.8–11).

3 The latter can be seen in Wainwright 1993 (pl. 8, facing p. 193).

represented 'the famine, wars, and pestilences that the Lord foretold in the Gospel' (Victorinus, *In Apoc.* 6.1; Weinrich 2011b: 10), aligning the seals with the signs of 'the end' in Jesus' Apocalyptic Discourse.[4] Bede read the first four seals as a forecast of the first several centuries of church history. The first is the ancient Church, still pure under the rule of the Lord; the second represents persecution of the Christians; the third 'the troop of false brothers who have the balance of right confession but harm their friends through works of darkness'; the fourth the heretics (Bede, *Exp.* 6.1–8; Weinrich 2011b: 128–30).[5] In the thirteenth century, Joachim of Fiore extended this reading to his own time, which he located at the cusp of the breaking of the sixth seal (Gumerlock 2009: 18–20, 55–60). In this, Joachim was driven more by a conviction that he lived near the end of the present era than by clear correspondences between the seals and the events to which Joachim related them.

The pattern of conquest, bloodshed, famine and pestilence is so basic, however, that many writers could find in these images a reflection of their own times. Samuel Taylor Coleridge found the horsemen to be riding through the French Revolution, and Adolf Deissman through the horrors of the First World War (Kovacs and Rowland 2004: 87–8).[6] Indeed, John and his immediate audiences would have had occasion to do the same, which raises the question: where does John place his audiences – or where might they have placed themselves – in this sequence? Would they suspect that the Lamb's opening of the seals belonged to their future?

John's presentation of the scene in chapter 5 might suggest that the Lamb took possession of the scroll immediately upon 'conquering' in his death, resurrection and Ascension. John's audiences might well relate the opening of the first four seals to their own history between Jesus' Ascension and their present moment. The intervening decades would have supplied ample experience and report of Rome's military expansionist policies, 'going forth conquering and to conquer' (6.2) and its consequences, starting with the devastating civil wars of 68–9 CE and the suppression of uprisings and revolts throughout the empire (the suppression of the Jewish Revolt of 66–73 CE being no doubt foremost on the minds of John and other Jewish Christians). Famine and death by sword, famine and disease followed as a matter of course (not to mention outbreaks of famine due to the unequal distribution of goods ensured by the parasitic

4   Luke 21.10–11 must be in mind, for Jesus makes no mention of 'pestilence' in the parallel passages in Mark or Matthew.

5   A similar reading is found in Anselm of Havelberg; see McGinn 1979: 114–15.

6   Of course, some interpreters postpone the ride of the horsemen to a future time (as do Scofield, Lindsey and LaHaye, in keeping with their strict futurist readings of Revelation).

Roman economy). Schüssler Fiorenza may correctly surmise that John's audience would have understood 'the first four riders . . . to articulate symbolically a sociopolitical critique of imperial rule' (1991: 63), particularly of the official propaganda concerning peace, security and prosperity (see also 1 Thess. 5.3).[7]

It also seems quite plausible that John's audience would hear about the scene that accompanies the fifth seal and think about Christian martyrs already crying out for vindication – the first generation of apostles, the Christians brutalized in Nero's Rome, the few local martyrs who bring the horror home – rather than suppose John to be looking to some future body of martyrs yet to come. The opening of the sixth seal – with its unmistakable description of the Day of the Lord (already!) – may take John's audience quite by surprise. Indeed, the only thing that the seals tell John's audiences for sure about the time between Christ's conquering and taking the scroll and 'the end' (the Day of the Lord revealed in the breaking of the sixth seal) is that there are more martyrdoms to come (6.10–11) – and thus the implicit summons to continued faithful witness to be lived out in the face of whatever degree of hostility is encountered. While John shares with several other Jewish writings the expectation that a certain tally of martyrs or the righteous needs to be reached before the end (see *1 Enoch* 47.1–4; *4 Ezra* 4.35–37; *2 Baruch* 23.4–5; Bauckham 1993a: 48–50), the delay of justice presupposed in Revelation 6.9–11 is not merely the consequence of the predetermination of this number; it is the opportunity for witness that will *increase* and *fulfil* that very number, achieving the full reach of God's kingdom (Bauckham 1993a: 56).

The opening of the sixth seal, the most developed of the images in the series, summons a scene of abject terror in the face of the cosmic disruptions accompanying the sudden coming of God and the Lamb to exact satisfaction ('wrath') from the inhabitants of the earth. Sky, mountains and islands are moved from their places as if they, like earth's inhabitants, cannot face the anger of God and his Anointed.[8] John invites his own hearers to imagine themselves in this scene of terror, which is said to grip not only the rulers and magnates but also '*every* slave and free person' (6.15). They have also, however, had the opportunity to see themselves in the vision of Revelation 5.13, where 'every created being' in heaven, earth and under the earth shouts in worshipful acclamation of God and the Lamb rather than in fear. Such contrasting (and surprisingly universal) visions drive the hearers to experience both and, thereby,

---

7 Kraybill and Boesak also both connect the four horsemen not to divine action but to 'human greed and violence' (Kraybill 2010: 102) or 'the lust for power and domination' (Boesak 1987: 67).

8 Details from the cosmic upheaval of the sixth seal figure prominently in African-American spirituals like 'My Lord, What a Morning'.

confirm themselves in the path of remaining centred on God and the Lamb in all their actions so as to encounter them with celebration, rather than terror, at their forthcoming intervention. This will be reinforced by the vision shortly to follow in chapter 7. The sixth seal's scene of panic closes poignantly with the rhetorical question with respect to God's appearing: 'Who is able to stand?' (Rev. 6.17; cf. Mal. 3.2). John will shortly show his audience the company – and the *qualifications* – of those who will indeed 'stand before the throne and before the Lamb' in victorious celebration (7.9), whom John hopes his hearers will seek therefore to emulate.

A new Egypt, a new exodus

Like many other Jewish authors and visionaries, John conceptualizes God's future interventions in terms of God's prior ones, among which the exodus event – the foundational event in Israel's history and identity – looms large. The exodus becomes an important framework by means of which John leads his hearers to interpret their situation in Roman Asia Minor, discern the paths of greatest advantage in the midst of that situation, and set their expectations for God's actions on their behalf and on behalf of God's own honour.

Sealing God's people

A pause follows the opening of the sixth seal, breaking the rhythm of chapter 6 and deferring the opening of the seventh seal for a full chapter. Angels with authority over the natural elements that will serve as God's punitive arsenal – a familiar feature of Jewish apocalypses (see *T. Levi* 3.2–3; *1 Enoch* 66.1–2) – are put on 'standby' to allow for a seal to be applied to the foreheads of God's servants. John hears the census of those who are sealed (7.4–8) and then sees an innumerable multitude standing in God's presence, acclaiming God for their deliverance and enjoying the shelter of divine protection from hunger, thirst and every scorching heat (7.9–17). These scenes contrast sharply with the scenes related in the preceding and succeeding chapters, which tell of great multitudes *not* enjoying such protection, but rather the opposite. This is a pause that, in strict chronological terms, *cannot* follow the event announced by the sixth seal (which is already the 'end'). It *can*, however, speak to the situation of costly witness that stretches between the martyrs of the past and the future day of the wrath of God and of the Lamb. By interrupting the sequence of the seven seals, delaying the last and presumably climactic event in the series, this intervening scene – what might rhetorically be called a 'digression', though the connotations of that word in everyday parlance make it somewhat misleading – acquires greater weight and significance for the hearers (Perry 2009: 147, 230). The same will be true of the scenes in chapters 10 and 11, which interrupt the sequence of the seven trumpets (also between the sixth and the seventh).

John's audiences will learn that the marking of God's servants with God's seal upon their foreheads means their protection from God's plagues (see Rev. 9.4; 16.2, 10–11), even as God kept the Ancient Hebrews out of harm's way in regard to the plagues God sent upon the Egyptians in the exodus story. Before the fourth plague, God announced: 'I will make a distinction between my people and your people' (Exod. 8.23 NRSV). Thus there were no flies in Goshen (Exod. 8.22), the Hebrews' livestock remained unharmed (9.4, 7), no hail fell in Goshen (9.26), the Hebrews had light while darkness struck the Egyptians (10.23) and, most famously, the firstborn children of the Hebrews were spared while the first-born of Egypt were struck down (11.7; 12.26–27). Possessing God's seal would thus be seen as highly desirable even as, by contrast, carrying the mark of the beast will prove highly disadvantageous in the long run (even if it brings re-lief from short-term difficulties; 13.15–17; 14.9–11; 16.2). And as worship was a central issue in the exodus (Exod. 4.23; 7.16; 8.1, 20; etc.), so worship emerges as central to the distinction between those who suffer God's judgements (those who refuse to dissociate themselves entirely from idolatrous worship; 9.20–21) and those who are protected in Revelation (those who give their exclusive alle-giance and worship to God and the Lamb).[9]

Questions concerning the precise identity of the 144,000 who are sealed and the innumerable multitude who stand before the throne – particularly concerning their relationship to one another – have met with varying answers throughout the history of interpretation. The formal, even formulaic, pres-entation of the 144,000 emerging in equal instalments of 12,000 from (essen-tially) the 12 tribes of Israel has suggested to many that they represent Jewish Christians.[10] The innumerable multitude from 'every nation and tribe' (7.9), then, would represent either Gentile Christians or the totality of Christians, Jewish and Gentile. Thus Victorinus believed that John showed first the num-ber of 'the Jews who will believe and [then] the great multitude of those from the Gentiles'.[11] The roster of 7.1–8 followed by the vision of the multi-ethnic body of the redeemed in 7.9–17 could be heard to articulate 'the same argument

---

9   This contrastive theme can be traced out throughout Revelation: see deSilva 2009: 259–63, 270–9.

10   Some church fathers would regard them as symbolic of celibate clergy, since they are called 'virgins' when they appear again in 14.4–5; see Methodius of Olympus, *Symp.* 1.5; 6.5.

11   *In Apoc.* 7.1; Weinrich 2011b: 11–12; see also Irenaeus, *Haer.* 5.30.2; Augustine, *Serm.* 248.3.

that we find in Paul's Letters – that Jewish followers of Jesus have a kind of spiritual priority over Gentiles' (Kraybill 2010: 114–15). A similar view persists in modern dispensationalism, which anticipates the conversion of a great number of Jews to faith in Christ during the 'seven last years' of the Great Tribulation that follows the Rapture.

Origen (*Comm. Jo.* 1.2–8), however, regarded the 144,000 as symbolic of the whole Christian Church, the new Israel. Others have regarded them as the elect at the end of the age, often identified with the interpreter's own party or group. For example, Ubertino of Casale (d. 1329) believed them to represent his 'Spiritual Franciscans', while the Jehovah's Witnesses see the elite among their membership reflected in this number.[12] There are indeed some difficulties with limiting the 144,000 to Christians of specifically Jewish origin, most notably the lack of any explanation that might account for the seal of God – and thus protection from God's plagues – to be the prerogative only of a portion of the Christians bearing their costly witness in this world. In the world of Revelation, one has either God's seal or the beast's mark, so the seal, and hence the roster of 7.4–8, most probably pertains to *all* believers (Beale 1999: 425–6).

The innumerable multitude, on the other hand, clearly stand on the other side of the struggles of discipleship in this world. They are seen standing before God's throne and the Lamb in the midst of the heavenly entourage of angels, elders and living creatures. They are clad in white and carrying palm branches, a common symbol of victory. One of the 24 elders makes explicit that this multitude has emerged victorious from 'great affliction' (7.14), following the Lamb's own path to conquering (5.5–10). They enjoy God's personal protection and the Lamb's shepherding where pain and sorrow can no longer touch them (7.15–17). We will learn more as Revelation's visions continue to unfold about the nature of this affliction and what is required to overcome in the face of the same (see, e.g., 12.11; 13.1–18; 15.1–4). In dispensationalist readings, 'great affliction' becomes 'the Great Tribulation', a fixed period of three and a half years during an anticipated final seven years of history, a period of oppression and persecution to be endured by those who come to Christ only during the seven-year period, that is, who had not been genuine Christians and thus 'raptured' prior to the start of those final seven years. In order to sustain such a reading, however, one must overlook the modern reality of millions of Christians worldwide who have already passed or are passing even now into the great multitude 'out of great affliction' in Africa, the Levant, the Indian subcontinent, North Korea, and many other settings hostile to Christian faith.

---

12   Koester 2014: 355.

The most essential distinction between the two groups, then, may not be found in their ethnic constituency, but in their situation. The 144,000 require sealing in order to be protected from the plagues that are about to fall upon the inhabitants of the earth. They are still in the thick of history and adversity. The form of the roster in 7.4–8 recalls the censuses taken to determine the military capacity of Israel (see Num. 1.1–14; 26.1–64; 31.1–6), which may be in mind here since the 144,000 will appear again mustered as an army to fight alongside the Lamb (Rev. 14.1–5; see Bauckham 1993a: 217–29; Pattemore 2004: 194). But the vision of the innumerable multitude in 7.9–17 shows us God's holy ones in victory before the throne of God, enjoying the rest, protection and eschatological blessings of eternity (note the correlations between 7.15–17 and 21.1—22.5). We may find here, then, the first clear visions of the Church Militant and the Church Triumphant – a vision of the 'complete church in its eschatological state' (Brighton 1999: 191, 199). Revelation 7.4–8 (together with 14.1–5) speaks of the situation of the Church as it faces the challenges of faithful witness in the increasingly hostile Roman world. The scene in 7.9–17 provides the answer to the anguished question of the inhabitants of the earth as they face the wrath of God and the Lamb: 'Who is able to stand?' (6.17). The movement of the chapter suggests that there is only one path to safety on that fearsome day: to prove oneself in the interim to be of such a sort that receives and retains God's seal of ownership, whatever the costs such allegiance incurs in the face of this world's powers.

John's portrait of 'who is on the Lord's side' (cf. Exod. 32.26) – a tremendous, indeed *innumerable*, crowd of those redeemed by the Lamb, who have been steadfast towards God and the Lamb – may also serve to embolden an unempowered minority group scattered throughout the cities under the authority of Babylon, the beast and ultimately the dragon. It is a portrait of the vastness of God's design and the Lamb's work in regard to the redemption of a people to be 'a kingdom and priests for God' (1.5–6; 5.9–10). On the one hand, it offers them a more realistic measure of what 'soon' and 'quickly' must mean as regards the end since the Christians in Ephesus, Smyrna and the rest can quickly figure out that the Christian movement had not yet nearly embraced such numbers. The image may also reinforce the call for witness that is issued throughout Revelation, for it is only unflagging witness and energetic evangelism that will close the distance between the reality of the small congregations meeting in a few homes in the cities of Asia and the 'innumerable multitude' that can swallow up 144,000 as a mere 'first fruits' (14.4) of a greater harvest (14.14–16). But it will also encourage them that they are part of a kingdom far more vast than they can currently fathom.

The situation of the Church Militant and Church Triumphant may appear from a different angle in the vision of measuring the 'temple'. In the midst of another digression, this one interrupting the series of trumpets between the first six (8.1—9.21) and the seventh (11.15-19), John is given a measuring rod and these instructions:

> Rise and measure God's temple and the altar and those worshipping there and leave out the outer court of the temple and don't measure it, because it is given to the nations and they will trample the holy city for 42 months. (Rev. 11.1–2)

Some read this as a reference to the Jerusalem Temple and reason that John either wrote his Revelation before the Temple fell (Gentry 1998: 165–92) or weaves into his work an earlier oracle from before that event (Aune 1998a: 593–8).[13] Alternatively, others read this (in connection with 2 Thess. 2.1–11) as an indication that the Temple will be rebuilt in Jerusalem in the end time as a theatre for the antichrist's self-deification. This view emerged as early as Irenaeus (*Haer.* 5.30.4) and Hippolytus (*Antichr.* 6; 63–4) and continues to be a feature of dispensationalist schemes of the end times (e.g. LaHaye 1999: 183–5).

Against such a reading is the fact that *all* other references to temple precincts and paraphernalia in Revelation have in view the heavenly temple, the place of God's dwelling in heaven (6.9-11; 7.15; 8.2-5; 11.19; 13.6; 14.15, 17; 15.5-8; 16.1, 7, 17; cf. 3.12). The notion that the desert tabernacle and Jerusalem Temple were physical models of God's unseen realm, the home of God's eternal temple, is well attested in the Second Temple (and post-Second Temple) period (see Wisd. 9.8; Heb. 8.5; *2 Baruch* 4.1-7). Some Jewish writers saw in the layout of the tabernacle and Temple a map of the cosmos, as it were. Josephus regarded the court and the first tent to represent the realms accessible to human beings ('land and sea') while the second, inner tent represented the heaven accessible only to God and God's angels (*Ant.* 3.123, 181). The security of the sanctuary and those worshipping therein could readily be understood by John and his hearers as a reference to the martyrs under the altar (6.9-11)

---

13 A related question concerns the identity of 'the great city' in Rev. 11.8 and whether this city, in addition to being symbolically identified as 'Egypt' and 'Sodom', is symbolically (Mounce 1997: 220-1; Court 1979: 102; Bauckham 1993a: 282-3) or geographically (Charles 1920: 1.289-90; Beagley 1987: 66) identified as 'where also their Lord was crucified'. Given the identification of 'the great city' as 'Babylon' (quite likely a *nom de guerre* for Rome) in 17.18; 18.10, 16, 18, 19, it is not at all as clear as some think (e.g. Gentry 1998: 175) that 'where their Lord was crucified' is meant as a geographical clue.

or the multitude worshipping before God's throne and serving God in his temple (7.13–17). Having passed through the 'great trial' that encounters the faithful in this realm, the Church Triumphant enjoys protection. The Church Militant, however, remains vulnerable to the hostility of – and trampling by – the inhabitants of the earth. The faithful Christ-followers on *this* shore represent the earthly manifestation of the 'holy city' (11.2) that will later descend in all its glory after God's visitation (21.2, 10).[14]

Trumpets and bowls as exponential exodus

The plagues that God sent upon Egypt return with a vengeance as the angels sound their seven trumpets and pour out their seven bowls. John's visions of God's future visitations of judgement upon the oppressors of God's people and ravagers of God's earth (11.18) are inspired by particular exodus plagues at many points, a correspondence already noticed by Bede (*Exp.* 16.21): sores (Exod. 9.10; Rev. 16.2); water transformed into blood (Exod. 7.20–21; Rev. 8.8; 16.3–4); darkness (Exod. 10.21; Rev. 8.12; 16.10); locusts (Exod. 10.12; Rev. 9.1–11; cf. also Joel 2.4–5, 10); frogs (Exod. 8.2–3; Rev. 16.13); hailstones mixed with fire (Exod. 9.23–25; Rev. 8.7; 16.21); water made bitter (not a plague against Egypt, but still a prominent echo of the exodus event, Exod. 15.23; cf. Rev. 8.11); and the unprecedented amplitude of God's judgements (Exod. 9.18; 10.6; 11.6; Rev. 16.18; cf. also Dan. 12.1; Mark 13.19). The response of those thus afflicted, namely hardening against God rather than repentance, also re-enacts the exodus story (Exod. 7.22; 8.15, 19, 32; 9.7, 12, 34–35; etc.; Rev. 16.9, 11, 21).[15]

Interpreters have tended to read the trumpets and the bowls as a symbolic unfolding of events or figures throughout the history and future experience of the Church, whether a series of heretics and their symbolic effects (e.g. making bitter the water of life or obscuring the light of the truth), or traumatic events already past or yet to unfold (e.g. barbarian invasions).[16] During the Reformation period, it was popular to find one's rivals, whether Protestant or Catholic, in the plagues initiated by the trumpet blasts. Dispensationalist interpreters can look for the fairly literal fulfilment of these plagues in

---

14 So Giblin 1984: 438; Bauckham 1993a: 272; Brighton 1999: 287; Koester 2014: 438; Yeates 2017: 39–40.

15 There are other important precedents for some of the specific plagues. For example, Har-Magedon (16.16) may recall the battle between the true God and Baal on nearby Mount Carmel (1 Kings 18.19–46; Beale 1999: 839–40), which would further resonate with 'Jezebel' and the Elijah-like signs performed by the two witnesses. Megiddo is itself the site of many disastrous and decisive battles and an appropriate location for history to repeat itself (Judg. 4.5; 5.19; 7.1; 1 Sam. 31.1–6; 2 Kings 9.27–28; 23.29–30; Ezek. 38—39; Zech. 12.11).

16 See especially Bede, *Exp.* 8.2 in Weinrich 2011b: 137; Kovacs and Rowland 2004: 109–15.

the future, sometimes linking some of them to disasters in the recent past or contemporary scene (e.g. the scorching of the earth in the aerial bombings of the Second World War or the poisoning of water as a result of the Chernobyl meltdown; Koester 2014: 438–9). There may be a hint of condescension where interpreters think to see now more clearly the squadrons of attack helicopters and tanks armed with flamethrowers that John could only approximate from his pre-industrial location as demonic locusts and fire-spewing horses (Lindsey 1975: 123–4, 126–7).

The two woes narrated in chapter 9 contain perhaps the most fantastic images of Revelation. However, identifying the instruments of God's punishment as Parthians or Goths (or, with Lindsey 1975: 124–7, the army of Communist China!) may represent a misguided attempt at demythologization. John's goal may be, rather, to affirm that God will punish those who have opposed him with fearsome instruments beyond our imagination, capable of inflicting such pain as makes death a wished-for escape. What God *could* have done in the exodus and conquest of Canaan (Wisd. 11.17–19), God *now* does, sending 'newly-created unknown beasts full of rage, or such as breathe out fiery breath, or belch forth a thick pall of smoke, or flash terrible sparks from their eyes' (Wisd. 11.18 NRSV) upon the inhabitants of the earth lacking God's seal (9.7–10, 17–19). Given the emergence of these locust-like scourges from the abyss, however, John's audiences might justifiably regard these beings not as creaturely aberrations but as demonic hordes, restrained from ravaging humankind until this moment (9.1–3, 11). This would introduce the irony that the earth-dwellers refuse to cease worshipping the very forces that seek to harm rather than bless them (9.20–21). These fear-evoking images serve chiefly to underscore the value of the seal of God as the means of safety from these imminent experiences of harm (Rev. 9.4; Stewart 2017: 232–7). They also challenge the integrity of Rome's borders and the impressiveness of Rome's military power. The Euphrates, featured in both the sixth trumpet and sixth bowl (9.14; 16.12), is an important boundary marker on both Jewish and Roman conceptual maps. It had set the eastern boundary of Israel's inheritance (Gen. 15.18; Exod. 23.31; Deut. 11.24; Josh. 1.4); it set the approximate eastern boundary of the Roman Empire until Trajan's victory over the Parthians in 114–16 CE (Caird 1966: 122). But there are 'all-powerful hostile force[s] beyond Rome's borders that [are] about to act', even as 'there is a safe territory for those who conquer through death' (Yeates 2017: 51). And the inhuman cavalry of 200 million awaiting the command of the true God on the throne makes a mockery of the might of Rome, whose armies were a paltry 250,000 strong at their zenith in the first century.

The significance of these chapters may not lie in discovering any one-to-one correspondences between the plagues and events in past or future history, but in their overall impact, particularly the impact of setting John's audiences within the framework of the exodus story. It is significant that worship was a key concern both in the historic exodus and John's Revelation. God's word to Pharaoh was: 'Let my people go, so that they may worship me in the wilderness' (Exod. 7.16 NRSV). John's summons to his congregations is to come out and/or keep standing aloof from the idolatrous worship that pervaded the structures and systems of the Roman Empire and worship God and the Lamb exclusively (deSilva 1998). 'Each plague is God's challenge to the power of the Caesar. Each trumpet blast is a ringing command from the Liberator God: "Let my people go!"' (Boesak 1987: 76). But each plague is also John's reminder to his own congregations: it is far more advantageous to live so as to preserve God's seal upon your foreheads than exchange it for the mark of the beast given to those who have consented to participate in the behaviours that legitimate and cooperate with Roman imperialism (see esp. 9.4, 20–21; 16.2, 10). The exodus frame itself denies any legitimacy to the Roman promises of peace, protection and prosperity: God's people live in an oppressive situation and their hope must be placed in God's liberation rather than accommodating to bondage. The unfolding narrative, however, also unmasks the powerlessness of the Roman oppressors and the emptiness of their gods before the wrath of *real* Deity. The trumpets and bowls do not lay out a playbook for the end times but narrate the systematic deconstruction of Caesar's world – and the order allegedly upheld by Caesar's gods – as the one true God makes room for God's kingdom (Hansen 2014: 66).

A new song of Moses on the shore of a new sea

As the seven angels entrusted with the seven last plagues that complete God's wrath step forward (15.1), John sees a vision of the victorious people of God, standing beside a crystalline sea in heaven and singing 'the song of Moses, the slave of God, and the song of the Lamb' (15.2–3). Their victory consists in their successful resistance to the pressures to conform to the worship of the beast and its image and, thus, their steadfast fidelity to the One God and his Anointed. Though this meant victimization from an earthly perspective (11.7; 13.7, 15–17), in God's realm they are celebrated – and celebrate – as conquerors (Bauckham 1993a: 235). Such people gathered beside a sea and singing the 'song of Moses' cannot fail to recall the celebration of the Hebrews on the eastern shore of the Red Sea (Exod. 15.1–18). Here the redeemed proclaim their answer to the (rhetorical) question at the heart of the original song of Moses: 'Who is like you among the gods, O Lord?' (Exod. 15.11).[17]

Every line of this new song echoes an earlier declaration about God's character, God's commitment to justice, and the inevitability of all people coming to recognize the power and justice of the one true God (see especially Deut. 32.4; Pss. 86.8–10; 111.2; Tob. 12.22). The echo of Jeremiah 10.7 is particularly significant, since Jeremiah 10.1–10 is itself a hymn contrasting the God of Israel with the empty gods of the nations, highlighting the folly of worshipping the latter (Bauckham 1993a: 303). Placing this new song on the lips of those on the farther shore who have already overcome, and have thus experienced God's power and faithfulness, helps to impress upon John's congregations that the old songs about God – about God's power, justice and truth manifesting themselves on behalf of God's people – will prove reliable and thus be renewed in the future (deSilva 2009: 300–5).[18] The truth of these premises, at the same time, renders necessary (or, at least, plausible) the consequences that John will shortly portray where Rome's crimes are concerned. Guilty of the same crimes as historic Babylon – a judgement John shares with his contemporaries, the authors of *4 Ezra* and *2 Baruch* – Rome will come under the same judgement, since God's commitment to justice and opposition to injustice, greed and self-glorification remain constant and reliable.

A number of other liturgical aspects surrounding the volleys of trumpets and bowls merit attention. The breaking of the seventh seal introduces the angels charged with the seven trumpets in a highly liturgical scene. Silence in heaven (8.1) makes room for 'the prayers of the suffering saints on earth [to] be heard before the throne of God' (Charles 1920: 1.153). Another angel burns incense at the heavenly altar 'for the prayers of all the saints' (8.3).[19] The smoke from the incense ascends, carrying these prayers before God (8.4), after which the angel takes fire from the altar and throws it down to earth in the very censer used to offer the prayers (8.5). The action recalls Ezekiel 10.2, 6, where an angel similarly casts fire from heaven down to Jerusalem as a sign of impending judgement (a scene that also immediately follows 'the marking of the righteous on the forehead for protection', Ezek. 9.4; cf. Rev. 7.3) (Bauckham 1993a: 82).

---

17 See Bauckham 1993a: 297–306 for a careful study of the relationship between this verse and the Old Testament texts John has incorporated into the song of Rev. 15.3–4.

18 A liturgical exchange that accompanies the pouring out of the third bowl further affirms the reliability of God's commitment to justice and to vindicate God's faithful ones (16.5–7; cf. 6.9–11).

19 'The early Jewish belief that the angels bring human beings' prayers to God (Tob 12:12, 15; *1 Enoch* 47:1–2; 99:3; &c.) is here dramatized in terms of the liturgy of the heavenly temple' (Bauckham 1993a: 81).

This liturgical drama expresses the conviction that the prayers of God's right-eous ones for justice (the martyrs being located under this very altar, 6.9) rise before God and are effective in calling down justice upon the perpetrators of injustice. The angels bearing the seven trumpets go forth also in response to this scene of effective prayer, and the martyrs speak again to confirm God's justice as the bowls are emptied (16.5–7; Yarbro Collins 1980: 190; Withering-ton 2003: 139). The dignity of the liturgical processions of both groups of angels charged with unleashing the series of plagues amplifies the hearers' sense of God's control over the cosmos and its fate (8.1–6; 15.5–8).

Worship erupts not only at the outset of the pouring out of the seven bowls but also at the climax – or perhaps *as* the climax – of the sounding of the seven trumpets. Within a lengthy interlude intruding between the sixth and seventh trumpets (the second and third 'woes'), a resplendent angel des-cends from heaven to announce that there would be 'no more delay, but in the days of the sounding of the seventh angel, whenever he is about to sound the trumpet, the mystery of God was fulfilled' (10.6–7). Apart from the irony of announcing 'no more delay' in the midst of a lengthy delay in the sequence of plagues, it is far from clear in what sense 'the mystery of God' is fulfilled or brought to completion when the seventh trumpet finally sounds in 11.15–19. What the trumpet does clearly usher in, however, is a scene of worship in which heavenly voices celebrate the victory of God and the Lamb. God is at this point no longer called 'the One who is and the "he was" and the One who is coming', but only 'the One who is and the "he was"', for God *has* come by this point and has begun to express his wrath (11.18), his indignation at human beings' disregard of God's commands and beneficence and at their mistreatment of God's faithful clients.[20]

Such scenes as 11.15–19 and 15.2–4 suggest that, for John at least, an impor-tant function of worship is 'to transport participants forward in time to God's final victory – or to bring the future into the present' (Kraybill 2010: 171). Cele-bration of the assured victory of God and the Lamb here at what is only the midpoint of Revelation is an expression of faith's assurance that 'it is only a matter of time until God defeats every abusive power and restores creation' (Kraybill 2010: 106). The importance of worship for sustaining both hope and faithful witness remains clear to those who have themselves persevered in situ-ations of oppression, as for example Allan Boesak protesting apartheid South Africa (and deriving and sharing strength from Revelation in that setting):

---

20 God's anger is referred to at Rev. 6.16, 17; 11.18; 14.10, 19; 15.1, 7; 16.1, 19; 19.15.

The joy of the oppressed is a source of fear for the oppressor. But we sing because we believe, we sing because we hope. We sing because we know that it is only a little while, and the tyrant shall cease to exist.
(Boesak 1987: 61)

Repentance or recalcitrance?

Does John believe that there is any hope for unredeemed humanity? Or is the die cast for 'the inhabitants of the earth' (13.8)? John emphasizes at several points the failure of the plagues to evoke repentance (9.20–21; 16.9, 11, 21). By pointing out that repentance did *not* result from the experience of these punitive interventions, John seems to imply that repentance *ought* to have resulted.[21] The goal of motivating, or at least making room for, repentance may lie behind the proportional relationship between the trumpets and the bowls. The catastrophes accompanying the first four trumpets and the first four bowls are almost identical save in their scope. The trumpets call forth the destruction of one third of their targets; the bowls signal total devastation. John's visions present in narrative form the conviction expressed elsewhere in Jewish literature, as for example in Wisdom of Solomon in regard to God's driving out of the Canaanites: 'judging them little by little you gave them an opportunity to repent' (Wisd. 12.10 NRSV). While this goal is frustrated in Revelation (as it was in regard to the Canaanites, according to Wisd. 12.10), it does not follow that God has made *no* provision within Revelation's visionary world by means of which the goal might yet be attained.

This brings us once again to the very important 'digression' in chapters 10—11 and the events presented in the hiatus between the sixth trumpet blast (and its notice of non-repentance in 9.20–21) and the seventh. The digression consists essentially of two scenes – a recommissioning of the prophet John directly reminiscent of the commissioning of Ezekiel (compare Rev. 10.8–11 with Ezek. 2.8—3.7) and a narrative of the career of two witnesses who proclaim God's righteous demands upon humankind while God works alongside them through wonders (including both plagues and the miracle of the witnesses' resurrection).

Discussion concerning the significance of the story of the two witnesses has tended to focus on solving the problem of their identity. Early church fathers

---

21 Beale (1998: 207–8), however, believes that the goal of the plagues was to harden the idolaters' hearts, in keeping with the effects of the plagues in the exodus story that provides such important background.

debated whether they might represent Enoch and Elijah (as two figures who were whisked off to heaven alive),[22] Elijah and Moses *redivivus*, or perhaps Elijah and Jeremiah, whose calling to be a 'prophet to the nations' (Jer. 1.5 NRSV) was not fulfilled during his lifetime (thus Victorinus, *In Apoc.* 11.3). One can also observe a tendency to identify them with figures in contemporary history, as in the case of the proto-Reformers Jan Hus (d. 1415) and Jerome of Prague (d. 1416), both of whom were burned at the stake, or, in sixteenth-century Münster, the rebel leaders Melchior Hoffmann and Jan Matthijs (Koester 2014: 439–40). Others regarded the two witnesses as representative of groups. Bede understood them very broadly as symbolic of 'the church, united from two peoples', Jew and Gentile (*Exp.* 11.3; Weinrich 2011b: 146), with the two olive trees representing the two testaments – the oil that flows into the Church's lampstand to make its witness burn brightly (*Exp.* 11.4). Joachim of Fiore understood them more narrowly as the monastic orders of the Dominicans and Franciscans, fountainheads of reform in the twelfth and thirteenth centuries (Petersen 1993: 32–8). The two witnesses have also been identified as the two testaments of Scripture (Beatus of Liébana, *Commentary on the Apocalypse* 367–406), a reading that survives in Seventh-day Adventist interpretation (E. G. White 1911: 267; Mueller 2002: 34–40).

The anonymity of these witnesses, however, may not be a mystery to be solved but rather a rhetorical potentiality, 'a point of orientation for the hearers', who 'aspired to being God's witnesses, to giving testimony about God's cause in the world' (Yarbro Collins 1984: 151; see also Bauckham 1993a: 285). The story of the witnesses is less a prediction of events involving two specific people (or, even less likely, the Scriptures themselves), but constitutes rather an appeal to emulation. Bauckham (1993a: 274) helpfully suggests that the story be read as 'a parable which dramatizes the nature and result of the church's prophetic witness to the nations . . . It can be taken less as a straightforward prediction than as a call to the churches to play the role which God intends for them.'

The hearers have already been exposed to several laudable figures worthy of emulation who were specifically connected with faithful witness, including Jesus (1.5), Antipas (2.13), John himself (1.2, 9), and the martyrs (6.9–11) who appear again reigning with Christ (20.4). The two witnesses themselves stand in the revered – and divinely empowered – traditions of Elijah and Moses (Rev. 11.5–6; cf. 1 Kings 17.1; 2 Kings 1.10). Their career follows Christ's

---

22 Hippolytus, *Antichr.* 43; Tertullian, *An.* 1.5; Augustine, *Ep.* 193.3–5.

pattern that is consistently held up for praise and emulation in Christian culture. They suffer disgrace and martyrdom for their witness but are vindicated by God through resurrection and ascension in the sight of their enemies. Their story therefore has great potential to excite emulation, emboldening John's congregations to faithful witness (deSilva 2009: 222–5; Perry 2009: 209). Their namelessness invites the hearers more easily to supply their own faces to the picture.[23]

Of particular importance is the fact that witness is portrayed as effective, even if its effects are not realized until after the witnesses' deaths. Revelation 11 offers the only picture of people turning to the living God in reverent fear, responding in the way that the angel of 14.6–7 summons humanity. What visitations of judgement, however spectacular, cannot achieve is accomplished through obedient and empowered witness. Faithful witness in the power of God, leading ultimately to being slain by the powers of the kingdom of this world, is 'the way in which the nations will be brought to repentance and faith, and the sovereignty over them transferred from the beast to the kingdom of God' following the example of the Lamb who also attained victory 'by his faithful witness, death and vindication'. In this way, the followers of the Lamb will share in his victory and 'give the victory universal effect' (Bauckham 1993a: 283).

A number of interpreters have suggested that, among its many other plot complexities, Revelation plays out 'alternative endings' (Maier 2002: 79) or 'alternative futures' (Koester 2014: 227). The stories of the two witnesses and the seventh bowl (including, then, the close-up of the judgement of and lament over Babylon in 17.1—19.4) are not part of a single story, but alternative stories concerning 'the great city', whose fate was not determined when John wrote down his visions. As it happened, the faithful witness of the Church in the face of increasing hostility led to the empire's story resembling more the outcome of 11.3–13 than 16.17–21 and 18.1–24. The testimony of the martyrs, authenticated by their obedience unto death, brought about conversion on massive scales, though ongoing developments within the empire and throughout the world would eventually bring about the fall even of Christian Rome. These same alternative futures, however, still loom before every system of domination, even as the same call to witness issues forth to every follower of the Lamb. The 'kings of the earth' may gather under Satan's banner against the beloved

---

23 There are *two* witnesses in keeping with 'the well-known biblical requirement that evidence be acceptable only on the testimony of two witnesses (Num 35:30; Deut 17:6; 19:15; cf. Matt 18:16; John 5:31; 8:17; 15:26–27; Acts 5:32; 2 Cor 13:1; Heb 10:28; 1 Tim 5:19)' (Bauckham 1993a: 274).

city (20.7–9), but they may also follow a different course that will allow them to bring the glory of the nations into the new Jerusalem (21.24–26; Maier 2002: 150–2). John's hearers are invited to see themselves cowering in terror at the coming of God and the Lamb alongside their idolatrous neighbours (6.12–17) or standing in confidence before them as the consequence of their faithfulness (7.9–17). Those who are unrighteous are invited to remain unrighteous (22.11), but they are also invited to wash their robes with a view to attaining the tree of life (22.14–15) and to 'come' and 'drink the water of life' (22.17). By means of presenting these alternative endings, John's Revelation places all of its weight not on the future (ironically the focus of so many of the book's interpreters), as if it communicated fixed predictions of destruction or redemption, but on the present moment wherein one faces 'the decision either to choose a life of costly testimony or to refuse it' (Maier 2002: 151–2), to walk after the beast or to follow the Lamb wherever he leads, to live now so as to be welcome in the new Jerusalem or so as to be shut out (see also Mathewson 2003: 164–75; Koester 2014: 227).

9

Roman power and propaganda in perspective (Revelation 12—14)

Those listening to Revelation as it was being read aloud to them (1.3) would probably not have heard any major break at the artificial chapter division between 11.19 and 12.1. God's temple 'in heaven' is opened and the ark 'appeared'; 'a great sign', the woman clothed with the sun, 'appeared in heaven' (12.1); 'another sign', a great, red dragon, 'appeared in heaven' (12.3).[1] They would, however, have had to navigate a temporal break in the narrative, for the action of 12.1–6 quite clearly refers, however briefly, to the Incarnation and Ascension of Jesus, the messianic figure who 'is to shepherd all the nations with an iron rod' (12.5, referring to Ps. 2.9, a text frequently read as messianic). This takes the listeners back behind the events of Revelation 5, for example, where the Lamb is already standing in heaven after his Ascension. The dragon's decision to pursue the woman's 'other children' – those who 'keep God's commandments and hold on to Jesus' testimony' (12.17) – refers to an activity also already well in progress by this point in the narrative.

In the visionary experience that John relates, he is himself taken from an anticipatory celebration of the final achievement of God's interventions (11.15–18) back into the situation of Satan's rebellion and his evolving strategies for resisting God's agenda that led to the circumstances that John and his audience were facing in their cities. The story of that rebellion and those strategies, however, profoundly influences John's view of the situation in late first-century Asia Minor – the view he hopes to inculcate among his congregations – and clarifies for them what responses within that situation are ultimately advantageous or disadvantageous for them to pursue.

---

1 These two protagonists in the sky may be inspired by the constellations Virgo and Draco (van Henten 2006: 191).

Rewriting the myths of Roman rule

As we saw in Chapter 4, Roman rule was promoted throughout the Mediterranean as the gift of a benign 'Providence'. Rome's rulers were the instruments by which the gods sought to assure the well-being of the many inhabitants of the lands around the Mediterranean and bring unprecedented good to the region and its peoples. John radically transforms this myth of origins, painting a very different picture of the spiritual forces at work behind the rise of the emperors and the aims those forces sought to achieve. To accomplish this, John, like the supporters of Roman imperial rule, moves in the realm of myth, both parodying Greco-Roman myths that would have been familiar to many in his congregations and recasting them in the light of the mythic figures of his own tradition. I use the language of 'myth' here not to deny any historical value to the stories (for example, concerning the birth and even the Ascension of Jesus or the opposition of a demonic arch-antagonist) but to acknowledge the highly figurative and even archetypal nature of the way in which John tells this story. Jesus was indeed born, but not from 'a woman clothed with the sun, with the moon beneath her feet' (12.1).

John opens this review of the forces at work behind the scenes and on the scene wherein his congregations must navigate their way with a retelling of a familiar myth – the birth of a divine child to a mother and the threat posed by a monster.[2] Many members of John's audience would have been familiar with this story in a different form. Python, a great serpent, was an oracle at Parnassus. He knew that he would be killed by a child born of Leto. Learning that Jupiter had impregnated Leto, Python hunted her down in order to kill her before she could bear a child, but she was saved by the North Wind (called Aquilo). She bore the twins, Apollo and Artemis. Just a few days after his birth, Apollo hunted down Python, first wounding and finally killing the monster at Delphi with his bow (Edwards 2018: 531).

The imperial house was frequently aligned with Apollo, and thus would be seen as represented in the 'hero' of this myth. Augustus was hailed as Apollo by Virgil (*Ecl.* 4.10) and Nero was lauded by his Augustiani as Apollo, Pythios and Pythian Victor, the latter two titles celebrating Apollo's defeat of Python (Dio Cassius, *Hist. Rom.* 62.20.5; Cuss 1974: 77–80; van Henten 2006:

---

2   The classic study of these myths and their import for Revelation remains Yarbro Collins 1976: 57–100. See also Aune 1998a: 667–76; van Henten 2006. Balch 2006 documents the pervasive use of the Leto–Apollo–Python myth in the domestic art of the period. As John's hearers encountered these representations, they might begin to view it quite subversively as a reminder of Christ's ascendancy and of the monstrous power behind Roman rule.

192). This background highlights further the subversive effect of John's myth-ic narrative in Revelation 12.1–18, which will align the imperial house (the heads of the beast from the sea in Rev. 13.1–8) with the dragon figure instead of the divine child.[3]

In John's narrative, the conflict begins in the heavens as the dragon lies in wait to devour the male child shortly to be born from the heavenly woman. He is thwarted in his primary goal, as the child is safely snatched up to God's throne and the woman, now earthbound, flees into the desert (12.1–6). The ac-tion shifts to a battle in heaven between the archangel Michael and his forces and the dragon and his forces in which the dragon proves the loser. He is at this point clearly identified – 'the great dragon, the ancient serpent, the one called Accuser and Satan who leads the whole world astray' (12.9), titles that at once connect the dragon with the serpent of the garden of Eden (Gen. 3.1–19; cf. Wisd. 2.24), the court prosecutor of heaven (Job 1—2), and the enemy of Christ and his Church (e.g. Matt. 4.1–11; 2 Cor. 2.11; 11.14–15; Eph. 6.11; 1 Pet. 5.8–9). The dual means of the arch-enemy's defeat is of central import-ance: God's angels cast him down from heaven to the earth, while the fol-lowers of Christ conquer him 'on account of the blood of the Lamb and on account of the word of their testimony' and because 'they loved not their lives as far as death' (12.11).[4] The dragon, finding himself cast down to the earth, sets after the woman to do her harm; but she is protected by the earth, and the rest of her children become the thrice-thwarted dragon's new targets (12.13–17). Heavenly voices make clear, however, that his fury is itself a sign that he recognizes how short a time is left to him (12.12). It is a sign of his desperation and the proximity of his end, the death throes of the enemy; it is a sign that the 'salvation and the power and the kingdom of our God and the authority of his Messiah' (12.10 NRSV) have triumphed.[5] It is at this point that the dragon

---

3   John subverts symbolism relevant to Apollo throughout Revelation. The angel of the abyss is named 'Apollyon' ('Destroyer') in Greek, which may involve 'derogatory wordplay' on Apollo (Schüssler Fiorenza 1991: 71). The locust was one of Apollo's symbols (Aeschylus, *Ag.* 1080–6; Witherington 2003: 154), making the name more deliciously subversive: John finds a place for Apollo in his cos-mos as the infernal leader of these demonic locusts (in keeping with the tendency among Jews to equate idol worship with the worship of demons, as in 9.20–21). The emperors' association with Apollo would, through the lens of Revelation, connect them with the leader of these demonic hordes (Schüssler Fiorenza 1991: 72).

4   There is a certain temporal paradox here, since enduring persecution is both the 'necessary *result* of the conquest of Satan' and 'the means to his defeat' in the earthly realm (Humphrey 2003: 86).

5   Andrew of Caesarea (*Comm. in Apoc.* 12.34; Weinrich 2011a: 157–8) regarded the war in heaven as referring to both the primaeval casting out of Satan for his pride and the defeat of Satan by Christ in his Passion (see John 12.31). In his *Paradise Lost* (1674), John Milton would popularize the interpre-tation of this battle as an event prior to the creation of Adam and Eve, explaining Satan's presence in the garden of Eden and his hostile intent towards God's creatures.

summons the beast from the sea and empowers it as his proxy in his persecution of the remaining children of the heavenly woman, the siblings of the exalted Christ (13.1–10).[6]

The parallels between the myth of Leto, Apollo and Typhon, on the one hand, and the story of Revelation 12 are immediately clear (Yarbro Collins 1976: 72; Satake 2008: 278–9). A dragon has it in for a woman and her imminently-to-be-delivered offspring but is thwarted in his intent by that same offspring. The differences are equally noteworthy. The cast of characters is greatly expanded by the intervening scene in 12.7–12; the scenes alternate between heaven and earth; and this moment of conflict is but the prelude to a much longer tale of conflict that is not to be resolved until the final judgement.

As this longer tale unfolds, John's polemical perspective becomes much clearer. The imperial house is now aligned with the character who plays the role of Python – Satan, the Dragon-Snake who is the power behind and doppelgänger of the Principate,[7] the collective incumbents of the offices that made Augustus and his successors the 'emperors' that they were. Even this twist was not without parallel in near-contemporary critics of specific emperors. Seneca, for example, likened Nero to the dragon figure in the myth (*Octavia* 237–41), while Dio Chrysostom did the same for Domitian (*Or.* 1.67–84; Maier 2002: 243). And the purpose that drives the emperors is not at all what the public discourse claims it to be, namely ruling on behalf of benign deities (as in Ovid, *Metam.* 15.858–70; Statius, *Silv.* 4.3.128–30). Rather, they extend the dragon's – Satan's – rebellion against God, deception of humankind and repression of God's faithful servants. But their very presence and activity in John's world are themselves consequences of God's triumph over Satan in the heavenly realm and the latter's final desperation. Even at this point, John is overturning public discourse about imperial rule. From Virgil's fourth Eclogue to the Priene Inscription (see discussion on pp. 46–8), the promoters of imperial rule presented the emergence of the emperors, particularly Augustus, as the beginning of a new epoch – indeed, as the inauguration of the long-awaited return of the 'golden age'. John, however, places the emergence of the Principate not at the beginning of the new age but at the end of the old age, the final period of decline before God's kingdom breaks in to supplant it.

---

6 Thus Bauckham (1993a: 285) is correct to suggest that 'chapters 12–14 add to the account in 11.3–13 . . . a much fuller exposition of the conflict between the forces of evil and the witnessing church, to which 11.7 briefly alludes'.

7 The best explanation for the dragon's sporting seven heads may be simply that the monster from the sea must emerge as his reflection, and the monster from the sea must have seven heads (the sum of the heads of Daniel's four beasts, conveniently also the sum of the hills on which Rome sits).

While John explicitly identifies the dragon in his narrative,[8] he has left the identity of the 'woman clothed with the sun' (12.1) rather open. Interpreters through the centuries have favoured four possibilities. It has been popular to view the woman in some sense as Mary, the mother of Jesus, and to read the chapter essentially as an allegory of Matthew 1—2 (Oecumenius, *Comm.* 6; Weinrich 2011a: 51-2). The vision of the woman clothed with the sun has exercised considerable influence on Mariology and particularly the iconography and artistic representation of Mary through the centuries.[9] Many interpreters, however, have regarded the woman as symbolic of a larger group and not a single individual both on analogy with the great prostitute of chapter 17 and in line with the prophetic traditions of portraying Israel or the people of God as a woman, whether pregnant and in the pains of labour or a mother longing for her children who have been separated from her (see, e.g., Isa. 26.17-18; 66.7-11; Bar. 4.9-16, 30-37; 5.5-6). Thus the woman has been taken as representative of Israel (with the 12 stars of her crown perhaps indicating the 12 patriarchs or their tribes) or as the Church, labouring to bring Christ to birth in each believer (as in Gal. 4.19; Methodius of Olympus, *Symp.* 8-9) or to bring forth Christ in the world through its witness in the face of the world's hostility (Hippolytus, *Antichr.* 61; Koester 2014: 35; Kovacs and Rowland 2004: 144-5). Neither one seems adequate to capture the woman's parentage of both the Messiah (which certainly points to historic Israel) and the rest of those who keep God's commandments and Jesus' testimony, which certainly suggests something more akin to 'the Jerusalem above, who is mother' to Christians of all backgrounds (Gal. 4.26), than to a particular ethnic body.[10] Hence Victorinus may have been on the right track when he regarded the woman as the people of God throughout history (before and since Jesus).

The emperor's new genus

The book of Daniel's influence on John's visions is evident at many points, but perhaps nowhere is it clearer than in John's re-visioning of the Roman heads

---

8 This has not, however, prevented interpreters from moving in their own directions. For example, Methodius and Andrew of Caesarea regarded the dragon as symbolic of the sin and evil in general that the faithful must resist by fleeing to virtue (Koester 2014: 526).

9 See Drury 2002: 170-5 on paintings of Mary by Francisco Pacheco (d. 1644) and Diego Velázquez (d. 1660).

10 Dispensationalists, with their particular interest in Israel and its role in the 'end times', tend to favour viewing the woman as ethnic Israel nevertheless, limiting 'the rest of her children' (12.17) to Jewish Christians who fled to Pella before the destruction of Jerusalem around 70 CE (Koester 2014: 527) or to Jews who would convert to Christianity during the tribulation of the last seven years of this age.

of state. In Daniel 7 we can read of a succession of global empires ('global' by Hellenistic-era standards at least) depicted as monstrous beasts – a lion (the Babylonian Empire), a bear (the Persian Empire), a four-headed leopard (the empire of Alexander the Great, quickly divided into four among his generals) and a prodigious ten-horned beast unlike anything in nature (the empire of Seleucus, one of Alexander's successors, and his descendants). John presents the collective of the emperors as a many-headed monster that clearly stands in some genetic and generic relationship to the four beasts representing a succession of foreign empires in Daniel 7 (the family resemblance is unmistakable).[11]

The 'beast from the sea' is not, however, simply to be equated with the fourth of Daniel's beasts, as the near-contemporary apocalypse, *4 Ezra*, claims (12.11–12; see also Josephus, *Ant.* 10.276). Rather, it is an unholy hybrid of all four. Part leopard, part bear and part lion, its seven heads and ten horns are the sum total of the heads and horns of Daniel's four beasts. Even as the Roman Empire has taken into itself all the territories, might and wealth of preceding empires, John would aver, so it has also taken into itself all that was 'beastly' about those earlier domination systems. This finds a parallel in the way John blends elements of God's prophets' denunciations of earlier seats of empire like Tyre, Babylon, and even Jerusalem, in his denunciation of 'Great Babylon' (Rev. 18.1–24). If the popularly promoted view of the emperors suppressed their humanness in the direction of divinizing, John moves in the opposite direction towards dehumanizing. In so doing, John also suppresses any possibly legitimate claim on the emperor's part to the loyalty and gratitude of John's audiences. This is especially significant, given the fact that their neighbours and civic leaders celebrated the emperor's patronage so enthusiastically.

Where Augustus and his successors were popularly viewed as the embodiments of piety, John characterizes this beast and its activity as a blasphemous affront to God (13.1, 5–6). The titles ascribed to the emperor – 'god' and 'son of a god' in inscription after inscription;[12] 'lord and god' (Suetonius, *Dom.* 13.2; Martial, *Epigrams* 5.8.1); 'saviour' (Philo, *Flacc.* 74; Josephus, *J.W.* 7.71; Aune 1998a: 734; Cuss 1974: 53–74) – were all 'blasphemous names' (13.1), arrogating what belonged to the One God and God's Anointed for the pawn of Satan. The closest analogue in the world of John's hearers to the ubiquitous worship offered to the beast was the imperial cult and general attitude towards

---

11 Compare Rev. 13.1 with Dan. 7.2–3, 7; Rev. 13.2 with Dan. 7.3–6; Rev. 13.4 with Dan. 7.6, 12; Rev. 13.5–6 with Dan. 7.8, 25; Rev. 13.7 with Dan. 7.14, 21 (Bauckham 1993a: 424–5).

12 While Latin distinguishes between a being that was always divine (a *deus* or *dea*) and a being that was elevated to deity (a *divus* or *diva*), Greek made no such distinction, such that both Domitian and Christ could be acclaimed *huios theou*, 'son of god'.

the emperors. John's visions exhibit how such worship draws 'the whole earth' into the worship of the dragon, God's cosmic enemy (13.3–4), thereby revealing the names of such people not to be among those 'written in the Scroll of Life of the Lamb slain from the founding of the cosmos' (13.8).[13]

One source of the world's admiration and a further impetus to worship was the beast's recovery from its 'mortal wound' – a wound inflicted in some sense both on one of its heads and on the monster as a whole (13.3, 12, 14). While this could be heard to refer to the assassination of Julius Caesar and the rise of Augustus (with Andrew of Caesarea, *In Apoc.* 13.36; Weinrich 2011a: 160), it seems more likely to be heard be an allusion to Nero's suicide, a wound that left the empire itself vulnerable to imploding in the midst of the civil wars of the rivals Galba, Otho, Vitellius and Vespasian until the last of these successfully consolidated his power and restored stability to the empire (see discussion in Chapter 3 above).[14]

Another source is the military power of the beast. The rhetorical question, 'Who is able to make war against him?' (13.4), will prove ironic as the narrative unfolds and the beast is unceremoniously deposited in the lake of fire (19.20), eventually to be joined by his already-defeated patron, the dragon. For the short run, however, Rome appears to the majority to assure peace through deterrence of aggression or through active conquest or reconquest. A particularly instructive edifice in this regard is the promenade connecting the principal forum of the city of Aphrodisias to its Temple of Augustus and Roma (this city sat a few days' walk from Laodicea). This promenade was lavishly decorated with near-life-size friezes visually depicting facets of Roman imperial ideology, whether foundational myths of the Julio-Claudian line (myths connected to Aeneas and to Venus, the two mythic progenitors of the line), the triumphs of various emperors over various provinces (like Claudius subduing Britannia or Nero Armenia), or simply scenes showing various emperors crowned by Roma, Victory or other figures, or standing beside trophies erected over bound captives (Smith 1987). Military power – the ability to wage war – was the principal means by which the beast's dominion attained its global dimensions

---

13 Speaking of Roman domination as extending over 'the whole earth' (13.3) is common in John's world (as in Luke 2.1; see Chapter 4 above). There is some question as to whether John presents the Lamb as 'having been slain from the founding of the earth' or certain names as having been written in the Scroll of Life before the founding of the earth in 13.8. In Rev. 17.8, the latter is clearly meant.

14 See, further, Bauckham 1993a: 441–3; Gentry 1998: 308–16. This tumultuous period is an important feature of the (same) monster's story in the contemporary apocalypse, *4 Ezra* (=2 Esdras 3—14): 'As for your hearing a voice that spoke, coming not from the eagle's heads but from the midst of its body, this is the interpretation: In the midst of the time of that kingdom great struggles shall arise, and it shall be in danger of falling; nevertheless it shall not fall then, but shall regain its former power' (2 Esd. 12.17–18 NRSV).

(13.7–8). The so-called *pax Romana* is shown also to be a time of 'making war with the saints' (13.7) and with the witnesses of Jesus, conquering and killing them (11.7; see also 2.13; 6.9–11; 16.5–7; 17.6; 18.23). Rome's rule is the rule of violence, ultimately responsible for the blood of 'all those who had been slain upon the earth' (18.24). The fact of this conflict is, indeed, 'part of the revelation' and 'not necessarily an obvious component of the social situation of the seven churches' (Johns 2003: 182).

John makes extensive use of parody in order to guide his hearers in their assessment of their everyday realities, particularly where their connections with the Roman emperor and (later) the Roman economy are concerned (O'Leary 1993: 388). Parody is 'the perfect tool for revealing imperial pretensions' (Carey 1999: 154). Parody raises awareness of counterfeit, and this is nowhere more apparent than in John's presentation of the beasts. The 'beast from the sea' has a mortal wound (13.1, 3a), a monstrous reflection of the slaughtered-but-standing Lamb (5.6). The worship offered to the beast, and to the dragon that gave the beast its throne (13.4), is a dark reflection of the proper worship centred on the Lamb and on the throne of God (4.1—5.14). The beast is the object of such worship because of its miraculous recovery (13.3b–4) and reign over 'every tribe and people and language and nation' (13.7b–8), as is the Lamb in regard to his resurrection and his creation of a kingdom for God by ransoming people 'from every tribe and language and people and nation' (5.9–10).[15] The parody is deepened when the worshippers of the beast ask the question, 'Who is like the beast?' (13.4), a rhetorical question that implies that this great and powerful being has no equal. This very question, however, is stolen from the worship of God, just as the worship given to the beast and the dragon is worship stolen from the God to whom it is uniquely due as Creator of all that is, sharpening the impropriety and injustice of this beast-worship: 'Who is like you among the gods, Lord? Who is like you, glorified among the holy ones?'(Exod. 15.11).[16] Isaiah had portrayed a king of historic Babylon as one who, in his arrogant ambition, sought to rival God: 'I will ascend above the clouds, I will be like unto the Most High' (Isa. 14.14). Now 'the whole earth' uses language appropriate to the praise of God's unique dignity and power to flatter the beast who carries 'Babylon' on its back.

Parody makes 'the contrasts between God and evil . . . clearer in the visionary world than they were in the readers' social world' – thus qualifying the work as a revelation, since it 'gives readers a way of seeing the forces at work

---

15   So Laws 1988: 41–3; Schüssler Fiorenza 1991: 83; Bauckham 1993a: 432.

16   See also Pss. 35.10; 71.19; Bauckham 1993a: 235; Aune 1998a: 741.

in the world', thereby shaping their responses to the same (Koester 2014: 577). This web of echoes underscores the continuing competition between the Lamb and the Monster to draw as many as possible into their opposing camps – and to serve the interests of the Creator God or of the rebel Satan, respectively. In such a context, there is no place for cooperation between followers of the Lamb and supporters of the beast.[17]

Not surprisingly, some Christians living under the Roman Empire's persecutions in the second and third century, like Cyprian and Victorinus, regarded the empire as the vehicle for the activity of the antichrist (Cyprian, *Fort.* pref. 1–2; *Ep.* 58.1–4, 8; Koester 2014: 31–2, 535). Victorinus similarly identified the beast from the sea with the antichrist and with the Roman imperial power, noting especially the connections with Nero in John's description (*In Apoc.* 13.1–3; Weinrich 2011b: 17–18). He expected 'the image of the beast', however, to be erected in a temple in Jerusalem yet to be rebuilt in the future. Others, however, were reluctant to regard Revelation as a critique of Roman imperial rule. Irenaeus suggested that the beast and its regime would arise upon the Roman Empire's collapse, with the antichrist arising from the tribe of Dan, conspicuously absent from the roster of Revelation 7.4–8 (*Haer.* 5.24–30). Tertullian took a similar view, regarding the Roman Empire as the restraining force on evil (*Fug.* 12; *Marc.* 3.25; *Res.* 24–5; cf. 2 Thess. 2.6–8). Tyconius promoted a reading of the beast from the sea quite generally as the collective people under the sway of sin and Satan, perhaps influenced by the more general use of the term 'antichrist' in 1 John 2.18–22 (as Augustine clearly was; see his *Tract. ep. Jo.* 3.4, 8). Hippolytus (*Antichr.* 50) promoted the view that John's visions looked ahead to a revived Roman Empire in the last days. This view has dominated popular dispensationalist interpretations in the modern period, for example Hal Lindsey's suggestion that the European Union would emerge as the venue for the antichrist once it gained its tenth member state (Lindsey 1975: 173–5, 226). This is also likely the interpretative move that facilitated the application of John's denunciation of imperial Rome to papal Rome, both before and after the Protestant Reformation.[18]

As in his presentation of the emperors, John similarly suppresses the humanity of the local voices charged with promoting the imperial cult. They

---

17 See Resseguie 2009: 127–8 on the work of the beast from the land (13.11–15) as a parody of the career of the two witnesses (11.3–13).

18 See the views of Peter Olivi (d. 1298) in Kovacs and Rowland 2004: 19; John Wyclif (d. 1384) and Jan Hus (d. 1405) in Koester 2014: 48; McGinn 1994: 181–2, 187–8; and Martin Luther (d. 1546) in Koester 2014: 537. Luther's German New Testament included woodcuts that showed the beast and the Whore wearing a papal crown (Koester 2014: 49). The Geneva Bible revives the suggestion that 'Lateinos', whose letters tally 666, is the name of the beast and, therefore, an indication of the papacy.

collectively constitute another monster, a 'beast from the land' or 'local monster' that carries out the work of Satan in 'leading people astray' (13.14; compare 12.9; 20.3, 8, 10). It does this chiefly by further diverting worship from the One God, the Creator of heaven and earth, to yet another image of yet another of the gods who 'did not make heaven and earth' (Jer. 10.11). Part of this work of deception involves making the cult of the image of the beast more impressive, and thus making the counterfeit god seem more real, using 'special effects' to manufacture the impression of merit where none exists (see Scherrer 1984; Aune 1998a: 762–4). Where deception and chicanery fail, this second monster uses coercion to exact the local populations' adulation of the emperors (13.15–17), making participation in the lie prerequisite to continued economic and physical well-being. By denying that the worship offered to the emperors was an authentic and free expression of gratitude for their gifts, held to possess such magnitude as to merit the thanks given to the gods, John disavows the public claim that 'grace' undergirds this institution.

While there is widespread agreement that John's audiences would have connected this 'beast from the land' with local promoters and orchestrators of the imperial cult, this figure would have potentially pointed to a number of different – though interconnected – targets. There was, first and highest, the provincial assembly of Asia (the *koinon*), one of whose principal duties was to organize and promote the imperial cult at the provincial level and oversee the provincial temples (Augustus at Pergamum, Tiberius at Smyrna, Domitian at Ephesus).[19] The members of this assembly often served as priests and officials of the cult themselves. But there was also a much wider circle of imperial priests and other promoters of the worship of the emperors and supporters of their temples and rites at the local level in every city of the province drawn from the families of the elite who could financially underwrite the cost of the cult and its activities. These elites, moreover, tended to be the same people who held important offices in civil government and economic guilds, who supported a wide swathe of public life with their generous benefactions, and who expected their households and clients to value what they valued (Friesen 2003: 58; Kraybill 2010: 149).

It is impossible to know exactly where John's hearers' minds would have gone – to the whole cult-promoting machine at all levels (Bauckham 1993a: 446), to those who visibly officiated as imperial priests (Cuss 1974: 96; Beasley-Murray 1978: 216; Aune 1998a: 736) or to some other facet of this web that

---

19 On the *koinon* of Asia and its activities, particularly vis-à-vis the provincial imperial cult, see Price 1984: 128–30; Friesen 1993: 7–28.

'supported the imperial vision of a peaceful province under Roman control' (Friesen 2003: 62–3). It is highly likely, however, that their minds would have gone *somewhere* in the direction of the network that provided 'the religious . . . justification which the first beast absolutely cannot do without' (Boesak 1987: 104). This network is as much a 'monster' as the beast that dominates the inhabitants of the world because it represents the 'indigenous collaboration' without which 'imperialism cannot survive' (Carey 2008: 166), the decision on the part of local elites to accept their own 'subordination in international affairs' in exchange for securing their power and position locally (Maier 2006: 7).

The mark of the beast (13.16–18) and the seal of the living God (7.2–3) – again the element of parody is clearly present – signify belonging to one party or the other.[20] It is noteworthy that, in John's visions, bearing one precludes receiving the other. One's worship practices mark one as belonging to one's neighbours' party (and that of their larger body, namely the multinational empire of the monster) or to God. Worshipping the beast and its image, hence receiving the beast's stamp of approval, provides access to participation in the Roman economy and the enjoyment of physical security. Refusal of such worship would bring the opposite.[21] The coercive measures described in 13.15–17 are not yet in place as John writes, but are projected for the near future as an extension of the pressures John and his audiences have already experienced in their local contexts (Bauckham 1993a: 447).

While some have regarded the number 666 as symbolic of humankind in general, which falls short of perfection (symbolized by the number seven), John quite clearly explains the number as 'the number of a person' (13.18), and more particularly as 'the number of [the beast's] name' (13.17). This directs the hearers to play the well-attested game of **gematria** (Cullmann 1956: 80–2; Bauckham 1993a: 386–8). Since the letters of the alphabet also had numerical values in Greek, Latin and Hebrew, one might refer to a person by a telltale number if one wished to be discreet, mysterious or just playful. Thus a bit of graffiti in Pompeii reads 'I love her whose number is 545', leaving the reader to start adding up the numbers in the names of the ladies he or she knew to try to figure out the object of the author's affections (Deissman 1910: 276). The authors of *Sibylline Oracles* identify successive emperors by the number of their first initial (*Sib. Or.* 5.12–51) and Jesus by the number 888, the sum of the letters of his name in Greek (*Sib. Or.* 1.141–5). A slur that circulated after

---

20 Precedents include Ezek. 9.4 and *Pss. Sol.* 15.6–9, both of which speak of marks on the righteous for salvation and marks on the wicked for destruction. Compare also Ignatius, *Magn.* 5.2, written perhaps two decades after Revelation.

21 On the intersecting webs of cult and commerce in the Roman world, see Kraybill 1996.

the suspicious death of Agrippina involved gematria: 'A new calculation: Nero killed his own mother' (Suetonius, *Nero* 39.2). In Greek, both the letters of Nero's name and the letters in the phrase 'he killed his own mother' add up to the same number: 1005.

Many suggestions for the solution to John's numerical riddle have been proposed throughout the centuries. Irenaeus discussed a number of possibilities, reluctant to land upon a particular name (*Haer.* 5.30.1–4). One of his favourites – *Lateinos* (a 'Latin', i.e. a Roman) – resurfaced in the Reformation as a symbol for the Latin Church. During Emperor Frederick II's struggle with Pope Innocent IV, it was happily discovered that the letters in *Innocencius papa* could be made to yield a sum of 666. Ubertino of Casale (d. 1329) decried Pope Benedict XI (d. 1304), an opponent of the Franciscan order, as the antichrist, as *Benediktos* also adds up to 666 in Greek (Koester 2014: 46; Kovacs and Rowland 2004: 158–9). The game persists into the modern era: even Hitler can be made to yield a sum of 666 (if one adds 100 to the value of each letter, the value being determined by order in the English alphabet; Koester 2014: 539).

The solution that seems the most compelling to the most authors is 'Nero Caesar'. Written in Hebrew letters (which are only consonantal), the name reads *nrwn qsr* and totals 666 (n=50; r=200; w=6; n=50; q=100; s=60; r=200). This solution is particularly attractive as it also accounts for the early textual variant that presents '616' as the sum of the name, a sum at which one can arrive using the Hebrew transliteration of the *Latin* form of Nero's name (*Nero*) rather than its *Greek* form (*Nerōn*).[22] John uses Nero as a kind of symbol to characterize the Principate: he invites his hearers to see in Nero the true character of the Principate, bare, exposed in all its ugliness. While the 'mortal wound' affects the beast as a whole and not merely one of its heads (13.3, 12, 14), the sword-blow to one of its heads cannot help but recall Nero's suicide. The idea that an 'eighth' ruler will arise from among the seven that preceded is perhaps the clearest echo of the 'Nero *redux*' or 'Nero *redivivus*' legend in the book (17.11). But Nero is not merely one aberrant head among others: he gives the beast its character. John might well have thought of this as a mathematical certainty, for the Greek word for beast, *thērion*, transliterated into Hebrew as

---

22 For a thorough discussion of 666 and 616 as pointing to Nero, with answers to multiple objections, see Gentry 1998: 193–212 (Irenaeus, *Haer.* 5.30.1–4, is a witness to the early variant '616'). The fifth-century *Liber genealogus* also connects the 'number of the beast' with Nero, though by a different process of calculation (see Gumerlock 2006). Victorinus of Pettau also connected the beast from the sea most closely with Nero, understanding the expression in 17.11 to refer to the expectation of Nero's return from the east (*In Apoc.* 13/17.2–3; Weinrich 2011b: 17–18).

thrywn adds up to 666 as well (tau=400; resh=200; yodh=10; waw=6; nun=50; Bauckham 1993a: 389).

John selects the practice of emperor worship as 'the defining activity that separates those who are condemned from those who belong to God' (Friesen 2001: 147), drawing a battle line there from which there can be no retreat on the part of his congregations, if they are to maintain their loyalty to God's commandments and their testimony to Jesus. Local manifestations of the imperial cult sought to nurture continuing awe and gratitude towards the emperor and Rome. John seeks to replace these feelings with indignation and enmity in order to advance his goal of nurturing critical witness against the crimes of Roman imperialism – with Christians allocating no room for idols, no room for participating in the mechanisms of imperial legitimation. John's visions also serve to arouse critical awareness and enquiry on the part of John's hearers, who will be disposed to test a broad range of practices for their potential to transfer the beast's mark on to them. The (hyper-)vigilance that he awakens is itself a tremendous gain for John's vision for Christian identity, group boundaries and lifestyle witness, for he will have moved his hearers in the direction of being as intensely interested and internally motivated in preserving these things themselves as he is.

The other column in the ledger

Throughout Revelation, John has been brutally honest about the costs of remaining faithful disciples of the Lamb, as John understands the requirements of fidelity (see, e.g., 2.8–11; 6.9–11; 11.3–13; 13.15–17). In Revelation 14, he pays greater attention to the costs of *not* remaining faithful disciples. The importance of juxtaposition as a strategy in John's narration of his visions emerges again as he shifts his hearers' attention from the 'lamb-like' beast and those who gather around it (13.11–18) to the true Lamb surrounded by his followers on Mount Zion (14.1–5). Parody is also at work in high gear. The former join in worship around a lifeless statue, artificially enhanced by means of special effects (13.13–15); the latter sing hymns before the throne of God in the company of the host of heaven (14.3). The former receive the mark of the beast (13.16) that seals them for disaster (as 14.9–11; 16.1–11 make clear); the latter have the name of God upon their foreheads that protects them from God's punitive judgements (14.1; cf. 7.1–3; 9.4). Indeed, the same figures who are the victims of violent repression in chapter 13 are likely to be seen among those who stand alongside the victorious Lamb in 14.1–5 (Pattemore 2004: 195). The latter vision provides a different perspective on witness and its this-worldly costs: what leads to marginalization in Roman Asia confers high privilege in the sight of God.

John may evoke here a transformed image of holy war, depicting the Messiah and his army gathered on Mount Zion (cf. *4 Ezra* 13). This army, however, already celebrates a victory, singing a 'new song' that marks a new victory, a new act of deliverance worthy of being commemorated (compare Pss. 98.1–3; 144.9; Isa. 42.10–13; Judith 16.2–3; Bauckham 1993a: 230). If John is indeed invoking the framework of holy war, this might help explain why he depicts this group – which symbolizes martyrs of both genders and all ages – as composed (implicitly) of males who avoid the pollution of intercourse with women (Deut. 23.9–14; 1 Sam. 21.5; 2 Sam. 11.9–13; Bauckham 1993a: 230–1). This description has occasioned significant difficulty. Does John truly set virginity (or, at least, abstinence) as a Christian ideal? Is John displaying his own misogynistic presuppositions when he speaks of women as sources of defilement and limits the company of the 144,000 to males (Pippin 1992: 70)?

Elisabeth Schüssler Fiorenza (1985: 190–1) helpfully suggests that this statement be read within the context of the sexual imagery that pervades Revelation and that works at a purely figurative level to caution against inappropriate degrees of accommodation to, or interaction with, the non-Christian society and its practices – as it does throughout the Hebrew prophets. Holding up the 144,000 'who have not defiled themselves with women' as exemplary and specially privileged serves to dispose John's hearers – male *and* female – to avoid entanglements with 'Jezebel' (the Christian prophet who seeks to legitimatize accommodation) and with 'Babylon, the mother of harlots', the economic, political and religious system that has otherwise ensnared the known world. In this context, John's choice of the image of 'virgins' to characterize the redeemed brilliantly nurtures 'either/or' thinking in regard to fidelity towards Jesus versus participation in local religious, economic and social practices – once again rending asunder what 'Jezebel', for example, would join (so also Duff 2001: 76; Pattemore 2004: 185–7).

These exemplary figures 'follow the Lamb wherever he goes' (14.4b), an image that suggests walking after the example of Christ, maintaining his witness and obedience to God in the face of the world's hostility and rejection, even to the point of death, as did he (Bauckham 1993a: 231). The Lamb's path to conquering remains that of his disciples as well: 'we look in vain for another way through, for a story which gets to the sky without the cross. There is none' (Pattemore 2004: 195). The fact that 'no lie was found in their mouth' (14.5) calls attention to the importance of speech, especially not letting any words escape one's lips that might reinforce the deceptions perpetrated by the forces advancing Satan's cause on earth – even if only to pay lip service for the sake of temporary advantages.[23]

John then relates the messages of three angels spoken 'to those sitting on the earth, even to every nation and tribe and language and people' (14.6). These bring together three of the principal points John wishes to impress upon the hearers from beginning to end – a kind of summary statement of John's arguments particularly where forcing a choice between the worship of God and the worship of the beast, alliance with the Lamb and alliance with Babylon, is concerned (deSilva 1998; Aune 1998a: 848). Each reinforces the wisdom of standing on Mount Zion alongside the Lamb that was slain and withstanding the beasts' coercive measures and Babylon's enticements. Either choice brings a price, but it is John's aim to bring his congregations face to face with the larger stakes that he believes to be at play in their situation, forcing them to look beyond short-term solutions for short-term losses and demonstrating that the exclusive worship of the living God is ultimately the most advantageous course by far (see Smith 2002).

The first angel's announcement calls the inhabitants of the earth to 'revere God and give God honour' and to 'worship God' (14.7). The angel offers two rationales in support of this summons. The first is explicit: the time has arrived for God's intervention to judge those who have failed to honour God as God merited and to walk in obedience to God as was fitting for the creatures God had given life in the first place. The second is implicit in the description of God as 'the One who made heaven and earth and sea and springs of water'. God is frequently identified as 'the one who made heaven and earth' not just to recall God's acts of creation but also to distinguish this God from the counterfeit gods worshipped by other nations (see, e.g., 2 Kings 19.15; Neh. 9.6; Isa. 37.16; Jer. 10.11). As the Creator of the cosmos (Gen. 1.1—2.4; Jer. 10.1–10), God – and God *alone* – merits the honour and grateful service of all who have received the gift of life and enjoy creation's bounty (cf. 4.11; deSilva 1998: 90). The angel's 'eternal gospel' represents the call that has always gone out to all the nations of the world – 'to worship the one true God who is coming to judge the world and to establish his universal rule' (Bauckham 1993a: 288; cf. Ps. 96.5–10).

The second angel asserts the fate of the city at the heart of a world empire: 'She fell, she fell, Babylon the Great, who gave all the nations a drink from the

---

23   John highlights the problem of deceptive speech both globally, in the work of the dragon, the land beast and Babylon (12.9; 13.14; 18.23; 19.20; 20.3, 8, 10), and locally, in the work of false apostles and prophets (2.2, 9, 14, 20; 3.17; Schüssler Fiorenza 1985: 190–1).

wine of the passion of her fornication' (Rev. 14.8). This message looks ahead to the detailed indictment of 'Great Babylon' and depiction of her fate in 17.1—19.6. The thumbnail sketch of her activity here as 'fornication' presents her as a contaminant that must inevitably be purged from a moral universe. John will restate Babylon's 'intercourse' with the nations as the cause for her downfall more explicitly in 18.2–3. John and other Christian prophets (like 'Jezebel') are at odds with one another where partnership with the local manifestations of Roman imperialism is concerned. The second angel's pronouncement, shortly to be explored in close detail, declares the vaunted advantages of such partnership to be short-lived – and the partnership itself inherently polluting.

It is significant that John had already painted the prophetess 'Jezebel' in Babylon's scarlet hues, particularly in regard to 'fornication' (compare 2.20–21; 14.8; 18.2–3). The very word pictures suggest that Jezebel's ministry leads believers into the webs of fornication spun by Babylon (that is, into partnership with Rome; see Carey 1999: 141–9; Duff 2001). As a result, the believers who yield to Jezebel's persuasion will incur a share of responsibility for the injustices of Roman imperialism, in which they have shared for the sake of the temporal benefits such partnership brings (18.4–5). Such believers would stand apart from and in contrast to the 144,000 'who have not defiled themselves with women' (14.4 NRSV) – in this context, most pointedly with 'Babylon'.

Where the first angel called earth's inhabitants to one course of action (the rightful worship of the Creator God), the third angel seeks to dissuade people from an alternative, competing course of action (Bauckham 1993a: 286) by declaring the consequences – and that quite vividly. Smith (2002: 113) rightly stresses that Revelation achieves its effect not by imparting necessarily new *information* about the future, but by stimulating the *imagination* of that future so that it weighs more heavily as a factor in present decision-making. This angel asserts that participating in the imperial cult will expose one to pain and disgrace: endless torment in fire and burning sulphur,[24] with the angels and the Lamb bearing witness to the offenders' degradation (14.9–11). The latter detail has occasioned no small discomfort among interpreters (e.g. Ford 1975: 249; Roloff 1993: 176; Kraybill 2010: 122–3), but John writes within an honour culture wherein *public* disgrace is a greatly feared evil – the prospect of which would have greater dissuasive power (compare *1 Enoch* 62.11–12).

---

24 D. H. Lawrence (1931: 76) is mistaken when he blames John for the invention of a lake of fire and eternal torment, claiming that this 'did not exist before': as many more recent commentators and theologians also forget, the punishment of the wicked with fire is prominent already in Jesus' sayings (see Matt. 5.22; 13.42, 50; 18.8–9; 25.41; Mark 9.43, 48; Luke 16.23–26).

While John does not explain *why* participation in idolatrous cult should result in such consequences, his congregations would readily supply the logic behind the anger of God that brings offenders to this end. Worshipping another as god violates the first and foremost of God's commandments (Exod. 20.2–6; Deut. 5.6–9) – a prohibition that, moreover, runs throughout the scriptural tradition (Exod. 23.34; 34.13; Lev. 26.1; Deut. 8.19; 11.16; 30.17; Josh. 23.16; etc.), extrabiblical Jewish literature (Letter of Jeremiah; Wisd. 13.1—14.31; etc.) and early Christian instruction (Rom. 1.18–32; 1 Cor. 10.14–22; Gal. 5.19–21; 1 Thess. 1.9; 1 Pet. 4.3; 1 John 5.21). Taking the honour that is the Creator God's due and giving it to the pawn of God's arch-enemy enacts the grossest ingratitude towards the Being to whom human beings owe everything. Whether Revelation 14.12 is heard as part of the angel's pronouncement or as John's comment on the angel's message, this statement identifies the knowledge of the cost of violating God's honour as the source of 'the patient endurance of the holy ones, the ones keeping the commandments of God and the faith of Jesus' (or, perhaps better, 'keeping . . . faith *with* Jesus'; Prigent 1988: 57; Murphy 1998: 135). Better by far to run afoul of the expectations of human society where obedience to God's commandments requires it.[25]

A macarism – the second of the seven that punctuate Revelation – follows upon the series of angelic messages, pronouncing 'those who die in the Lord from this point on' to be 'favoured', 'honoured' or otherwise 'privileged' (14.13). The heavenly voice commends all who have lived out the core values of keeping the commandments of God and keeping faith with Jesus (14.12), whether or not this has led to a violent end, even though John does lead his hearers to expect increasingly violent responses to their faithful witness, swelling the number of the martyrs (6.9–11; see also 20.4–6).[26] Dying 'in the Lord' brings the followers of the Lamb 'rest' from the demands of exercising faithful discipleship in this life (such as are implied by 13.15–17). 'Their works follow them' to bear witness on their behalf and assure their enjoyment of blessedness and honour in God's realm beyond this mortal life (20.11–15). The value of 'possessing' such works has been evident throughout Revelation, particularly in the glorified Lord's commendation of individual congregations (2.2, 19, 23; 3.8). The 'righteous deeds' performed by God's holy ones are the warp and woof that weave the 'fine, pure white linen' in which the Lamb's bride will be adorned at her appearing (19.8). John's affirmation of the value of deeds

---

25 For similar logic at play, see 4 Macc. 13.13b–15; Matt. 10.28; Acts 5.29.

26 Thus Harrington 1993: 152; Giesen 1997: 68; Prigent 1988: 230; against Bousset 1906: 386–7; Kraft 1974: 195; and Mounce 1997: 275–6, who link the macarism exclusively to martyrs.

performed in faithful obedience to God, joining the chorus of other New Testament voices affirming the same (e.g. Paul's in Rom. 2.6–11; 2 Cor. 5.9–10), was valued by Catholic theologians in the wake of the Protestant Reformation (for example, at the Council of Trent as reflected in Session VI, chs 10, 16; Koester 2014: 55–6).

John concludes the sequence of Revelation 12.1—14.20 (for the introduction of the next sequence of plagues in 15.1 seems to signal a new act in the drama) with a vision of judgement – the sorting out of humanity and the consequences of this sorting (14.14–20). These scenes reinforce John's agenda of presenting the 'hour of judgement' as the principal challenge facing the hearers (see also 1.7; 6.12–17; 19.11—20.15), the challenge to which they must give their first and best attentions. The scenes continue to be rich with scriptural language and references, beginning with the description of 'one like a son of man upon the cloud' (Rev. 14.14; cf. Dan. 7.13), subtly reminding John's audiences of the authoritative heritage behind John's message.

John presents judgement in three scenes – the harvesting of the earth, the gathering in of the vineyard and the trampling of the wine press. The whole is a narrative expansion of Joel 3.13–14 (NRSV): 'Put in the sickle, for the harvest is ripe. Go in, tread, for the wine press is full . . . Multitudes, multitudes, in the valley of decision! For the day of the LORD is near in the valley of decision.' Joel himself used both a grain harvest and a grape harvest as images of punitive judgement and John *may* have as well. But there are numerous indications that his hearers, at least, would not have heard the passage in this way.[27] They would likely be aware of Jesus' teachings using the image of harvesting to describe both the gathering of the righteous and the judgement of the wicked (e.g. Matt. 13.24–30, 37–43) and be inclined to hear Revelation 14.14–20 in terms of such contrasting images. Presenting the 144,000 as the 'first fruits' in Revelation 14.4 (the offering made prior to the harvest; see Lev. 23.10–14; Deut. 26.1–11), moreover, implies a larger harvest to gather in those similarly, if later, redeemed (Bauckham 1993a: 291–2). John also uses the generally more positive image of 'reaping' (see Mark 4.29; John 4.35–36) and not the images of threshing (Jer. 51.33; Mic. 4.12–13; Hab. 3.12; Matt. 3.12; Luke 3.17) or blowing away or burning the chaff (Pss. 1.4; 35.5; Isa. 17.13; 29.5; Dan. 2.35; Hos. 13.3; Matt. 3.12; Luke 3.17) that commonly express the forthcoming destruction of the wicked (Bauckham 1993a: 293–4).

However they would have processed the images of harvesting the earth, the image of treading 'the great wine press of God's fury' (14.19–20) would have

---

27   See Aune 1998b: 800–3 and Beale 1999: 773–9 for a detailed review of arguments.

left John's hearers in no doubt that Christ's visitation in judgement would have horrific consequences for a great many. Here again the influence of earlier prophetic visions upon John's own is unmistakable, particularly as regards trampling a wine press as the exercise of divine wrath and the violent consequences of the same for the human beings that had provoked such wrath (compare Rev. 14.19–20 with Isa. 63.2–6). John's elaboration of the volume of blood spilled is also reminiscent of earlier traditions concerning God's execution of judgement (specifically, *1 Enoch* 100.3–4). The bundle of allusions to Daniel, Joel, Isaiah and *1 Enoch* serve to remind the hearers of God's thoroughgoing and historic commitment to tread down the ungodly.

John's vivid depiction of the horrors of the day of God's visitation in judgement disposes his congregations to give greater weight to discovering a strategy for surviving *this* challenge – such as the strategies that John has already relayed to each assembly in the oracles of Revelation 2—3 as well as to the assemblies collectively thus far in the visions – than to following the strategies for avoiding temporary hardship and deprivation such as other teachers like 'Jezebel' and the Nicolaitans are advancing among the same assemblies.

Witness and conquering

John draws back the curtain on these mythic events to reveal for his congregations the cosmic backdrop of their everyday challenges and conflicts. The activity of the monsters in their world – the collective heads of the Roman state and the local mechanisms that promote their worship to the point of coercing the unwilling – is the ultimate expression of the fallen dragon's rebellion against the Creator of heaven and earth. John transfers feelings of enmity against Satan, a well-established enemy, to the more ambiguous figures of the emperors, who are generally regarded favourably by the majority of the population (including, perhaps, some within these churches), not least by stressing their opposition to God through false worship (13.1, 4–6, 8, 11–14) and their commitment to advancing Satan's agenda of making war against the saints and overcoming them (Rev. 13.7, 15–17; cf. 12.17). There is no more the possibility of accommodating to imperial cult practices and propaganda than there is the possibility of forging an alliance with God's arch-enemy – and no more advantage in so doing (Barr 1984: 40). The framing narrative of a cosmic war and the concomitant drawing of battle lines diminishes the attractiveness of accommodation and compromise, for now it is not a neutral matter of survival but a betrayal of one's own 'side'. The cooperation or coexistence urged by John's rivals must yield to a different reckoning of the options: conquering or capitulation.

Stephen Pattemore rightly observes that 'for the most part John simply narrates his visions and the audience must infer from these how they are to live their lives' (2004: 218). John's narrative guides his hearers to identify with 'those who keep God's commandments and hold on to Jesus' testimony' (12.17), that is, with the targets of God's (fallen) enemy rather than with the *allies* of the same, such as we meet in 13.1–18 (Pattemore 2004: 115). He positions them to 'conquer [Satan] by the word of their testimony' even if they have to do so at the cost of their livelihoods and, ultimately, their lives (12.11). They 'follow the Lamb wherever he goes' (14.4), in large measure, by following Jesus in his obedience to God to the point of death, by means of which he has already won the decisive victory against Satan and his agents (Bauckham 1993a: 234; Johns 2003: 175). Their testimony is thus 'not merely about Jesus, but participates in the very nature of his witness', making Jesus' witness in his own obedience unto death continually present and visible in the world (Pattemore 2004: 218).

The military imagery that John employs throughout Revelation (e.g. 'conquering' through witness) arouses some unease among interpreters, though Richard Bauckham (1993a: 234) helpfully defends the propriety of such imagery. Witness such as John's congregations are called to bear 'is as active as any physical warfare and his use of holy war imagery conveys this need for active engagement in the Lamb's war'. Similarly, Steven Moyise affirms that 'there really is a battle for Christians to face, just as there really was a battle for Christ' (1995: 134). The battle is waged, however, through non-violent resistance and witness. This faithful witness through lived obedience to the commandments of God and through 'the word of their testimony' to God's Anointed (12.11), moreover, does not only preserve the disciples' victory over Satan and faithfulness to the Creator God and Redeemer Lamb. It also provides an opportunity for their neighbours round about them to emerge from the deceit that the dragon has spread across the inhabited world through his agents (Bauckham 1993a: 237).

It is vitally important to recognize that from beginning to end John encourages only non-violent protest and resistance on the part of his Christian audiences. As Steven Friesen rightly observes, 'the only humans who make war in Revelation are those who are deceived by the Dragon' (2001: 189). While John 'makes lavish use of holy war *language*', he applies it entirely 'to non-military means of triumph over evil' (Bauckham 1993a: 233). Christians can respond to oppression without violence because of – and as a witness to – their firm conviction that God is just and will bring justice to their own stories and to the story of this world's history. Such non-violent resistance is, nevertheless, profoundly powerful: 'It shakes and shatters the very foundation of political reality because death is . . . the *only* moral and practical sanction of the State' (Stringfellow 1973: 149), whether that state be the Roman Empire or apartheid South Africa, where Allan Boesak found that John's prophetic call to bear witness to God's values and to the situation's injustice provided the necessary courage to unmask 'the power of the world . . . as powerlessness, as mere brute force, and therefore inauthentic' through non-violent resistance (whose practitioners, in turn, suffered *significant* violence from the agents of the beastly regime whose crimes they protested; Boesak 1987: 83).

10
The goddess exposed
(Revelation 17.1—19.10)

The juxtaposition of contrasting images and scenarios has been an important facet of John's persuasive strategy in Revelation and this is nowhere truer than in the final third of his work. Hearers will encounter two female figures, each representing a very different kind of community, a very different way of ordering human society. The first is the prostitute, 'Great Babylon';[1] the second is the bride, 'New Jerusalem'. The two ways of ordering human community, like the feminine images John sets before our eyes, could not be more different, and John will make clear that one cannot both cavort with Babylon, profiting from her favours, and be welcomed by – and as a part of – the bride of the Lamb.[2] The juxtaposition allows John to portray Rome as a counterfeit society, a distorted image, a parody of the divine vision for a community that nurtures justice and wholeness. This allows him to encourage critical distance from Rome and involvements with Roman domination on the part of his hearers, a number of whom, like the many outside the congregations, viewed Rome positively and wanted to be viewed positively by Rome and its partisans in turn. While John was likely aware of the legacy of the teachings of the Pauline and Petrine missions concerning temporal authorities (Rom. 13.1–7; 1 Tim. 2.1–2; 1 Pet. 2.13–17), he also knew that there are lines that the temporal authorities must not cross and, when they do, God's people are called to stand apart and to protest the powers' violation of their divine commission.

---

1   It is common to speak of 'the Whore of Babylon', but to do so is to send false signals concerning John's language. He speaks of 'Babylon the Whore'. The Prostitute *is* 'Great Babylon' (17.5); she does not *belong* to a city but *is* 'the great city which has dominion over the kings of the earth' (17.18).

2   In a landmark study, Barbara Rossing (1999) has shown John's visions of Babylon and New Jerusalem to use the frame of a choice between two women – a commonplace in the ancient world – as a means of presenting the two as mutually exclusive and forcing a choice between the two, contrary to the position of rival prophets in John's situation (Rossing 1999: 18, 37–40, 162). Older examples of the frame of a choice between two consorts include the sage's choice between Lady Wisdom and Dame Folly (Prov. 1—9); Heracles' choice between Virtue and Vice (Xenophon, *Mem.* 2.1.21–2); the choice within each person to pursue Virtue or Pleasure (Philo, *Sacr.* 20–35); and Heracles' similar choice between Kingship and Tyranny (Dio Chrysostom, *Or.* 1.65–84). See the fuller survey in Rossing 1999: 18–37.

In these chapters, John holds Roman imperialism under the lens of the scriptural witness, particularly the critique of domination systems from Tyre to historic Babylon found among the Hebrew prophets. He brings a judicious selection of the old prophetic texts to bear on the Roman domination system in order to name the crimes perpetrated by 'Babylon', forecast the consequences that must follow such crimes, and summon his hearers to divest themselves of all involvement in these crimes so that they might also escape the consequences. John knew long before the modern prophets of postcolonialism that one cannot benefit from the exploitative oppression of imperialism without being guilty also of its injustices. John also begins to display more decisively in this section the consummation of God's own commitment to justice, first in 'putting a stop to the destructive actions of the agents of evil, which begins with the fall of Babylon' in this section and continues in 19.11—20.15, and then in 'the restoration of life for all the faithful who have suffered', which will occupy the closing visions of the book (Koester 2014: 716).

Re-dressing Roma

Revelation presents one of the most memorable (and negative!) portraits of Rome in ancient literature. The image of 'Great Babylon, mother of earth's prostitutes and abominations' (17.5) is meant to be shocking, for nothing less than 'shocking' would allow some of John's hearers to take a fresh look at Rome past the images of Rome that were everywhere to be seen in their cities. Cult statues depicting Roma as an austere and benevolent goddess stood in the temples to Rome and Augustus in Ephesus and Pergamum and in the temple to Dea Roma in Smyrna. The same image appears on the reverse of many first-century Roman coins, including many provincial mintings in Asia featuring specifically the Temple of Augustus and Roma in Pergamum with the two cult statues clearly visible.[3] It is specifically this public image of Rome that he wishes to address – or, better, re-dress. One coin, a bronze sesterce minted by Vespasian, is particularly interesting. It shows the goddess Roma reclining on the seven hills on which the city rests. As if flipping the coin over to reveal its underside, John shows his congregations a prostitute astride a seven-headed monster.[4]

Would John's hearers have made this connection? It is indeed likely that they would have done so, given the clues John provides to guide their interpretation. Authors who are near-contemporary with John frequently use

---

3   See Magie 1950: 2.1613–14 for a list of cult sites of *Roma* and *Roma et Augustus*.

4   Further on the significance of the Dea Roma coin, see Aune 1998b: 920–2.

the label 'Babylon' to designate Rome. This is especially the case after Rome reprises Babylon's historic destruction of Jerusalem and its Temple (*Sib. Or.* 4.158–61; 5.143, 159; *2 Baruch*; *4 Ezra*; 1 Pet. 5.13; Aune 1998b: 829–31), though it was also appropriate before the disasters of 70 CE given the conditions of 'domination and diaspora' under which Jews were already living (Friesen 2001: 138).

John explicitly identifies the seven heads of the monster on which his prostitute sits as 'seven hills' (17.9). Poets commonly referred to Rome as *urbs septicollis*, a 'seven-hilled city' (Virgil, *Georg.* 2.535; *Aen.* 6.782–4; Ovid, *Tristia* 1.4.69; Martial, *Epigrams* 4.64.11; see also Horace, *Carmen saeculare*, ll. 7–8; *Sib. Or.* 2.16–18). A festival called Septimontium may have celebrated the growth of the city to encompass the seventh of these hills (Plutarch, *Quaest. rom.* 69; Varro, *De lingua latina* 6.24). Oecumenius believed this clue to be decisive as far as 'Babylon's' identity was concerned: 'From this it is clearly evident that the passage refers to Rome, for it and no other city is reported to be on seven hills' (*Comm.* 17.9–14; Weinrich 2005: 276). Placing his 'Babylon' on seven hills incidentally tells against the common myth that John wrote in such figurative language in order to hide his meaning from any Roman authorities that might get their hands on his book. Equally telling, John identifies the prostitute as 'the city that has dominion over the kings of the earth' (17.18). If we read this verse from any of the seven cities in which John's congregations resided, we would immediately look to Rome.

Some have suggested that Revelation's Babylon represents Jerusalem, with John indicting the Judean elites for their collusion with the beast (Ford 1975: 285–8; Beagley 1987; Buchanan 1993: 428–31). While it is true that the Hebrew prophets also compared Jerusalem to a wife who was unfaithful to God and even to a prostitute, it is difficult to maintain that this was *John's* purpose given his explicit clues as to his meaning (17.9, 18). His description of the resources of the world being siphoned off to satisfy one city's cravings would also be grossly exaggerated in connection with a peripheral city with under 100,000 inhabitants – as opposed to a seat of empire with over one million.

John does not draw his hearers' attention only to the figure of the prostitute in these chapters. Revelation 17.7–14 focuses them far more directly on the seven-headed monster than on its rider. Readers are given several indications that they are once again seeing the first monster of Revelation 13. It sports the same blasphemous names (17.3; cf. 13.1); those 'inhabitants of the earth' whose names 'are not written in the book of life' marvel after it (17.8; cf. 13.3, 8). Like the beast in 11.7, it comes up from the abyss (17.8). In this vision, he shows his congregations the emperors alongside Roma – which they also saw in tandem in temples and on coins[5] – in a significantly different light. John is told that the seven heads, besides representing the seven hills on which the prostitute sits, represent seven kings – and that the beast itself is 'an eighth, who comes from the seven' before going on to destruction (17.11). The beast's story resonates here with the 'Nero *redivivus*' myth that arose shortly after Nero's (apparent) suicide in 68 CE.

One form of this Roman urban legend speaks of Nero not actually committing suicide, but fleeing beyond Parthia, east of the Euphrates, to bide his time.[6] It tells of the Roman civil wars of 68–9 and the devastation of Judea in 70. In divine retaliation, God would bring Nero back from the east, 'having crossed the Euphrates with many myriads' (*Sib. Or.* 4.119–39; see also *Sib. Or.* 5.28–35, 137–50, 363–9). The legend had a long lifespan. As late as the reign of Marcus Aurelius, an author still anticipates the return of 'the blazing matricidal exile . . . from the ends of the earth' to restore to Asia the wealth hoarded in Rome (*Sib. Or.* 8.68–72). Victorinus (*In Apoc.* 17.2) understood the coming of the eighth king as Nero's return from the east.

The legend took on flesh on several occasions. Two gained a following, in part, based on their physical resemblance to Nero – the first in July 69 (Tacitus, *Hist.* 2.8–9; Dio Cassius, *Hist. Rom.* 63.9.3), the second, whose real name, Terentius Maximus, is known, in 79–80 (Dio Cassius, *Hist. Rom.* 66.19.3). Terentius emerged from Asia and won the support of a contender for the Parthian throne. A third arose in 88/9, now with the support of the Parthian Empire, and proved a credible threat (Suetonius, *Nero* 57.2; Tacitus, *Hist.* 1.2.1; Bauckham 1993a: 413–14; Friesen 2001: 137). The legends concerning Nero's return from the east may also undergird John's understanding that the beast's ten horns represent (eastern) rulers who have not yet received power, but would in the future alongside Nero as he returns against the Rome that had abandoned him (Bauckham 1993a: 429; Koester 2014: 679).

Speaking of the beast itself as something that was, is not, and is about to arise from the abyss and go to perdition (17.8) also resonates with 'the once and future Nero' legend and well suits John's conviction that Nero showed the world the Principate's truest colours.[7] The frame is appropriate to the time be-

---

5 See Price 1984: 40–3; Mellor 1975: 79–82.

6 On the legend of Nero's return in general and its relevance for Revelation in particular, see Bauckham 1993a: 407–31; Gentry 1998: 301–3. The Greek orator Dio Chrysostom, a later contemporary of John, also bears witness in passing to the belief that Nero was still 'out there' somewhere: 'even now everyone wishes he were alive, and most believe that he is' (*Or.* 21.10).

7 It also parodies the identification of the genuine God as 'the One who is, and the "he was", and the One who is coming' (1.4, 8; 4.8).

tween persecutions: 'the tyranny that has reared its head in the past might not be widely visible at present, but it is not gone; the beast's character has not changed' (Koester 2014: 691), and John certainly expects it to rise up against the witnesses of Jesus more forcefully in the imminent future.

As discussed in Chapter 3 above, however, it has proven impossible to connect the seven heads with a particular series of seven emperors.[8] The suggestions have been myriad. The annotation to 17.9 in the Geneva Bible confidently declares the heads to be Nero through Nerva (the seventh who remains but a short time) and the eighth to be Trajan who, as a persecutor of Christians, also 'goes to perdition'. Oecumenius identified the heads with the emperors he presumed to be among the worst persecutors of the Church, namely Nero, Domitian, Trajan, Severus, Decius, Valerian and Diocletian (*Comm.* 9.8–19; Weinrich 2011a: 75), thereby extending the scope of the vision by several centuries. Hal Lindsey extended the scope further by claiming that each head represented not a king, but a kingdom, with the one that 'is' at the time of John's writing being the Roman Empire and the one that is to come being the revived Roman Empire that Lindsey identifies with the European Economic Community (1975: 225). What was important – and quite clear – for John's hearers, however, was the fact that the emperor currently reigning at the time of composition was said to be the sixth in a series of seven (or eight), thus locating them nearer the end and God's decisive intervention (Bauckham 1993a: 406–7).

John, then, presents the city of Rome in the guise of a successful, high-end prostitute and tells a very different story about Rome's mission and destiny from the story heard in Virgil's *Aeneid* or in any other work articulating the official ideology of the empire. Rome does not bring peace; rather, she is inebriated with the blood of those who have dissented against or impeded her practices (17.6). Rome does not bring the rule of law to the Mediterranean, nor does she nurture virtue; rather, she seduces and corrupts the world's elites to join her in promoting their collective self-indulgent practices and in multiplying abominations (17.2–5). As Richard Bauckham observes:

> Rome offered the world unity, security, stability, the conditions of prosperity. But in John's view these benefits are not what they seem: they are the favours of a prostitute, purchased at a high price. The *Pax Romana* is really a system of economic exploitation of the empire.
> (Bauckham 1993a: 347)

---

8 'The inappropriateness of trying to produce lists of emperors from such imagery is clear from its results' (Friesen 2001: 141).

John overlays everyday dealings with Rome with the negative connotations of getting into bed with a prostitute or catering to her corrupt and corrupting whims (17.1, 2, 5; 18.3). This was, indeed, a powerful metaphor for connecting imperial cult (the worship of Roma, who is here exposed), global economy (which becomes the purchase of favours with goods and cash) and international politics (local leaders and elites forging self-serving alliances; so, rightly, Friesen 2001: 205).

It is not Rome's destiny to preside for ever over a new (imagined) golden age. Rather, a dreadful and ironic fate awaits *Roma aeterna*, 'Eternal Rome', a city that will go up in flames and be laid desolate rather than live up to its epithet. The scene of the goddess-revealed-to-be-a-prostitute stripped naked, devoured by her former allies and finally burned (17.16–17) is John's answer *both* to the public and official claims made about Rome's eternal destiny *and* to the public ideology of the conquests that forged Rome's Empire.[9] Rome loved to parade its images of stripped or partially stripped and subjugated women to represent the peoples and provinces it had conquered. In the mall leading to the Temple of Augustus and Roma at Aphrodisias, for example, one could see images of Claudius beating down Britannia, or Nero subjugating Armenia, both provinces portrayed as women with their breasts bared and forced to the ground. This and worse, John claims, will one day be visited upon Roma (Koester 2014: 694).

It is important to remember that a good number of Christians in John's congregations have been profiting from their involvement in Rome's global economy, and a good number of others have been looking for ways to reconcile their faith in the One God with improving their social prospects and intercourse through making some room for their neighbours' – and their own former – religious practices in their lives. John's counter-vision of Rome and the moral tenor of its practices is calculated to persuade all such believers that they are putting their own honour and security in grave danger by seeking or preserving any working alliances with the prostitute on her seven hills. Hearing so much about 'fornication' in regard to Rome's activity and the moral significance of involvement in Rome's domination (14.8; 17.2, 4; 18.3, 9) could not help but recall the language in the seven oracles about certain teachers making room for 'committing fornication' in connection with 'social idolatry' (2.14, 20–21).

---

9 The image is not itself without precedent. Ezekiel had spoken of Jerusalem personified as a woman stripped naked, with the survivors of Jerusalem being burned to death (23.25–29; Aune 1998a: 956–7).

Does Revelation promote misogyny?

A number of readers have called attention to John's use of gendered language as highly problematic for women readers and for women in general. We have already encountered this in regard to the picture of an ideal Christian group as a particular 144,000 'who have not defiled themselves with women, for they are virgins' (14.4 NRSV). Even though the image can be explained and understood in ways that are situation-specific (avoiding 'intercourse' with Jezebel and Babylon), the image remains inherently problematic because it presents 'women', without any further explicit qualification, as potentially defiling.

The portrayal of the Roman imperial economy and its supporting systems of domination as a prostitute – one, moreover, that is subjected to a brutal and degrading death at the claws and mouths of the beast and its allies – arouses considerably greater indignation on the part of readers sensitive to the portrayal of women in texts and to the implications of the same for women in 'real' life. A pioneer (and rather extreme voice) in this conversation is Tina Pippin (1992), who regards Revelation so tainted by its misogyny as to hold out little or no prospect for the text's continuing ability to speak to the Church, for 'the Apocalypse is not a safe space for women' (1992: 80; see also Stenström 2009: 51). Her protest stems from a deeply personal experience she had while reading Revelation: 'Having studied the evils of Roman imperial policy in the colonies, I find the violent destruction of Babylon very cathartic. But when I looked into the face of Babylon, I saw a woman' (1992: 80). Revelation 17 thus becomes the story of the sexual exploitation of a prostitute and ultimately a voyeuristic episode of the torture and murder of a woman, making 'this story of death and desire . . . the most vividly misogynistic passage in the New Testament' (Pippin 1992: 58).

As other readers have noted, however, a fundamental problem with Pippin's reading is that 'Babylon' is not *a* woman. She is not a 'sex worker', a person with a face whose identity has been shaped by the fantasies of men and who uses these, in turn, to her profit. 'She' is a *city* – the city that sits at the centre of a web of global domination, enforced by military might and legitimated by religious propaganda that makes self-critique impossible (Rossing 1999: 12–15; Schüssler Fiorenza 2007: 133; Friesen 2001: 186; Morton 2014: 125). When we look into the face of *that* 'woman', John would have us see a domination system built upon a slave economy, on military and 'legal' violence, on exploitation of labour and resources at a hitherto unprecedented scale. He makes this explicit so that no one would miss the point – 'the woman whom you saw is the great city that has dominion over the kings of the earth' (17.18; Schüssler

Fiorenza 2007: 134) – after which we no longer see a *woman* at all, but only the *city* going up in smoke (18.1—19.6).[10]

John presents the city of Rome (itself already a symbol of the massive web of domination systems that constitute Roman imperialism) using the symbol of a kind of woman in large measure because he is responding directly to the official and ubiquitous presentation of the city of Rome in female guise, namely as the goddess Roma. He re-presents the same female figure in a different guise to say as clearly and directly as possible to his hearers: 'The goddess Roma is not what she seems; her impact on the world is nothing like what the official propaganda everywhere asserts; look at her with fresh eyes here.' The use of female figures as symbols for international seats of empire and other cities in the tradition of Israel's prophets, particularly characterizing some as prostitutes, further predisposes John in this direction (Schüssler Fiorenza 2007: 135), providing John with an effective overlay for the image of Roma as goddess.[11]

On the one hand, then, within the limits of John's own purposes, the narrative very well expresses an important truth in the quest for liberation and justice: 'Those who seek to dominate others' – and do so with the use of considerable violence – 'will themselves be devoured in the process; it is, as John says, what God has ordained' (Barr 2003a: 104). The reimagining of Rome and the moral significance of partnership with Roman domination is apt to successfully dispose John's hearers to resist, to withdraw, to witness openly to both the injustices of the system and the possibility of another way to be human together.

On the other hand, one must also consider how the objectification and stereotyping of women over the millennia preceding John nurtured the entire tradition of using females as symbols in these particular ways – a tradition in which John stands (and *not* for misogynistic ends!), but a tradition that John also fails to question and critique along the way to questioning and critiquing other facets of domination and oppression in his context (Pippin 1992: 72, 103). When speaking of the one flesh-and-blood woman with whom he does engage – the Christian prophetess in Thyatira – John was also under no compulsion to use sexual stereotypes of the 'bad woman' to talk about her, no matter how vehemently he opposed her teaching. There is therefore not only the

---

10 Note also that the prostitute and the city are described in identical terms in 17.4 and 18.16 (both are 'clothed with purple and scarlet and adorned with gold and precious stone and pearl'), which is just one more indication that the woman is merely a figuration of the city (Bauckham 1993a: 369).

11 See Isa. 1.21 (Jerusalem); Isa. 23.16–17 (Tyre); Nahum 3.4 (Nineveh); Jer. 3.6–10; Ezek. 16.15–22; 23.1–49; Hos. 4.12–13; 5.3 (Israel; Aune 1998a: 929). Similarly, John's use of female figures as positive symbols for God's people (hence the woman clothed with the sun and the bride of the Lamb) derives from the prominent use of such imagery in the Hebrew prophets.

room but also the necessity for modern interpreters to exercise greater circumspection and care in this regard than did John, as well as, perhaps, a more redemptive imagination as far as the symbolizing of both the 'female' and the 'male' (Yarbro Collins 1993: 130; Carey 2008: 174–5). This work seems preferable to exiling him once again – this time as a misogynistic enemy of liberation – and losing John's voice and power where he is critical of systems of violence and exploitation.

John does not give his hearers any warrant to commit violence against any 'real life' women. Even Jezebel's judgement lies in Christ's hands alone. The Christians in Thyatira are summoned only to reject her teaching and to fall in line again with John's vision for Christian witness and critical distance. But it must be admitted that the history of male violence against women reinforces the dangers of John's decision to use a human (female) image for the system of domination that he so fervently opposed (Barr 2003a: 104; Schüssler Fiorenza 2007: 135) – allowing others to use such images to *perpetuate* other forms of domination.[12]

Prophetic precedents and prophetic critique

John's reuse of language from the Hebrew Scriptures is at its thickest in his denunciation of 'Babylon'. John 'weaves together prophetic oracles against [historic] Babylon's arrogance, violence, and idolatry (Jer 50–51; Isa 13; 21; 47) with those condemning Tyre's commercial empire (Ezek 26–28)' (Koester 2014: 713), to which one should add Isaiah 23 and Jeremiah 25.12–38.[13] His goal appears to be to show his congregations what Rome and Roman imperial practice look like from 'inside' the scriptural prophetic tradition – from God's own viewpoint, as it were. The scriptural tradition becomes the interpretative lens through which John invites his audiences to see these practices afresh, peeling away the veneer of the official ideology that celebrates and legitimates Rome's hegemony. John's premise is simple: if God found fault with a particular set of practices that characterized former domination systems like Babylon's and Tyre's, God would also find fault with more recent or contemporary domination systems that perpetrate the same practices with the same consequences for the people under (or outside) their dominion. Thus, for John, the oracles from the Hebrew prophets

---

12 See, further, deSilva 2009: 324–31.
13 Bauckham 1993a: 345. See the detailed discussion in Kraybill 1996: 152–61.

are more than a literary source. They are oracles which, because they applied to Rome's predecessors in evil, apply also to Rome. He sees Rome as the culmination of all the evil empires in history. Just as the beast, as portrayed in Revelation 13:1–2, combines in itself the features of all the beasts which in Daniel's vision symbolized the evil empires before Rome (Dan 7:3–8), so the Babylon of Revelation 17–18 combines in itself the evils of the two great evil cities of the Old Testament prophetic oracles: Babylon and Tyre.
(Bauckham 1993a: 345; see also Fekkes 1994: 86–8)

John gives new life to the sacred traditions of Israel and channels their word of protest, as it were, against the new empire that has dominated their descendants along with 'peoples and multitudes and nations and language groups' (Rev. 17.15; deSilva 2009: 174; Maier 2002: 105).

A major focus of John's indictment of 'Babylon' is the exploitative nature of its global economy, structured to secure the near-endless consumption of resources from every province and beyond by the population at the centre and, of course, the local provincial elites who support the system. John's interest in this facet of Roman imperialism first emerges in his attention to the prostitute Babylon's luxurious clothing ('purple and scarlet'), adornment ('gold and precious stones and pearls') and luxury goods (the 'golden cup', Rev. 17.4). It emerges again in his denunciation of Rome for 'luxuriating' (18.3) and 'indulging in excesses' (18.5). It emerges perhaps most forcefully in his portrait of her partners in the system of global exploitation lamenting her fall (18.9–19). John crafts a verbal picture of goods and resources flowing from every corner of the world towards and into the city at the centre of its networks of trade and power:

The merchants of the earth will wail and lament over [Rome] because no one can be found any longer to buy their wares – wares of gold and silver and precious stone and pearls and linen and purple and silk and scarlet and every scented wood and every ivory vessel and every vessel made from costly wood, and from bronze, and from iron, and from marble, and cinnamon and spice and incense and myrrh and frankincense and wine and oil and fine flour and wheat and livestock and sheep and horses and chariots and bodies, even human lives.
(Rev. 18.11–13)

One might helpfully recall the description of Rome's global trade network by Aelius Aristides, discussed in Chapter 4 above, in which he boasts on Rome's behalf that the people in the provinces 'must come here to beg for their own goods whenever they need anything' because their own lands have been stripped bare to supply the demand of the empire's capital (*To Rome* 11–13, LCL). Aristides, a member of the elite, might have been woefully oblivious to the downside of the scale and sweep of the economy that he sees as a token of Rome's greatness, namely the deforestation of countries for their wood and produce. The bitter irony of provincials being forced to come to Rome to 'beg' for the produce of their own lands, however, is not at all lost on John, who sees what is left over for the provincial non-elites and the results of the Roman imperial economy for the quality of life of those whom its supply chains are not concerned to satisfy.

John's cargo list shows substantial overlap with Ezekiel's list of 40 items on Tyre's cargo manifest (Ezek. 27.12–24), updated and revised to reflect maritime trade in the first century CE and to highlight Roman luxury (Bauckham 1993a: 350–1). John does not show any interest in where all these goods are coming from, only in the destination towards which they are flowing. The *Periplus Maris Erythraei*, however, a catalogue of ports and goods related to each port composed by a first-century trader, provides a highly detailed window into the stunning scale of trade beyond the Mediterranean basin – along the east coast of Africa, around the Arabian peninsula and around the Indian subcontinent – that made the amassing of such an assortment of goods possible.[14]

While John gives significant space to luxury items, the list of cargoes also includes 'wine and olive oil and fine flour and grain' (18.13), the staples of the diet shared by all peoples around the Mediterranean. Injustice and exploitation were built into the system even where the more mundane cargoes in the shipping lanes were concerned. Rome ensured the grain supply, transported chiefly from North Africa, Egypt, Syria and the Black Sea region as tribute or at fixed, low prices, for the citizens resident in the capital first. Indeed, some 200,000 families in Rome received a daily portion of free grain and were always able to purchase the remainder that they needed at reasonable prices. This amounts to a parasitic luxury, however, when 'provincials paid high prices for grain and sometimes had none' on account of the demand at the centre (Kraybill 1996: 107–8). In regard to the consumption of olive oil, a 35-metre-high (115 ft) mountain made from the discarded amphorae and other clay vessels used (chiefly) to bring olive oil to Rome from Spain and North Africa – Monte

---

14 Casson 1989 is the most up-to-date critical edition. See also the discussion of the global trade represented in Rev. 18.12–13 in Bauckham 1993a: 352–66.

Testaccio – stands as an ironic monument to the massive amounts of supplies brought into the city (Claridge 2010: 402).

At the final and, thereby, climactic position in John's global cargo manifest stands 'bodies, even human lives (or souls)'. The language is striking, but John uses the correct terminology: slaves were spoken of as 'bodies' in the Greco-Roman world and slave traders were *somatemporoi*, 'merchants of bodies'. John corrects the nomenclature, however, by reminding readers that these 'bodies' are also 'human souls' and that slavery traffics in 'human lives'. Estimates of the number of enslaved people in the Roman Empire vary widely from a fifth to a quarter of the population, but wherever the true tally falls within that spectrum, it remains an economic system built upon the backs of slaves. John draws attention here to 'the inhuman brutality, the contempt for human life, on which the whole of Rome's prosperity and luxury rests' (Bauckham 1993a: 370–1; see also Boesak 1987: 120–1).

John depicts three classes of people lamenting Babylon's demise (while standing at a safe distance, of course), namely 'the kings of the earth' who shared in the enjoyment of luxury as a result of their dalliance with Babylon (18.9), and 'the merchants of the earth' and 'every pilot and . . . everyone ploughing the sea' (18.11, 17; compare Ezek. 27.25–32). These groups are not innocent of Babylon's economic exploitation and its global consequences, for they have facilitated and fed the same. Imperialism requires the cooperation of indigenous elites willing to allow the subjugation and, to some extent at least, exploitation of their territories. The 'kings of the earth' give such consent to Babylon for the sake of the benefits that accrue to them personally. Seduction is an apt metaphor for the strategy of offering local elites luxury goods, entertainment and special privileges in exchange for their partnership. The Roman historian Tacitus bears witness to such 'seduction' or 'enchantment' as he gives voice to the Batavian chieftain Civilis: 'Away with those pleasures which give the Romans more power over their subjects than their arms bestow!' (*Hist.* 4.64.3).[15] Rome's seductive power – indeed, the metaphor of sorcery emerges here as even more apt – runs broader and deeper, however, as it was able to supply enough of a share in the rewards to deceive even the majority into viewing empire as a good thing.

Of course, it was the merchants, the pilots and their crews who made the goods themselves flow. A late first-century mausoleum outside the northern gate of Hierapolis personalizes the class of merchants and transportation moguls to whom John refers. The tomb belonged to Titus Flavius Zeuxis, a

---

15 Cited in Howard-Brook and Gwyther 1999: 96. See also Plutarch, *Sert.* 13–14.

merchant who boasted of having made 72 successful sea voyages from Asia Minor to Italy. There is no record of what goods Zeuxis transported, though his connection with Hierapolis might suggest that he was involved in shipping the textile products for which his native city and its neighbours, Colossae and Laodicea, were well known.

John's depiction of the Roman economy works against any feelings of gratitude towards Rome that his hearers might have by drawing attention to the pervasive self-interest and parasitic practices that underlie Roman rule. His emphasis on luxury and excess works to arouse indignation as his hearers are confronted with Rome's consumption of more of the world's goods than is the proper share of any one city to the detriment of the provinces under her exploitative rule. He gives no notice to those interventions that Roman propaganda would highlight – the resources Rome brought to bear to relieve famine, to rebuild cities after earthquakes in Asia Minor, or to all but eliminate piracy and brigandage from the Mediterranean basin – perhaps because John would view all such 'beneficence' as ultimately motivated by Rome's desire to ensure and safeguard her continuing supply in the lands of production and in transit to her lap.

A second focus of John's indictment is Rome's extensive use of violence as the fundamental means of ensuring (and increasing!) this flow of goods, silencing dissent and preventing any people group from 'opting out' of the system. 'Babylon' appears on the scene 'drunk with the blood of the holy ones and with the blood of Jesus' witnesses' (Rev. 17.6; see also 18.23b–24). John thereby reminds his hearers once again of Rome's and Rome's allies' violence against other followers of Jesus (see 2.13; 6.9–11; 16.5–7), amplifying the heinousness of this violence with the image of Babylon's drinking blood to the point of intoxication. This strange blending of 'blood' with the intoxicating effects of wine suggests that Babylon committed this violence for the sake of 'getting a rush', as it were, from doing injury to God's faithful servants – an image that well suits the persecution of Christians in Rome under Nero following the great fire of 64 CE that left only four of the city's 14 districts intact (Tacitus, *Ann.* 15.40, 44).

But 'Christians were only a small minority among countless victims of the great imperial beast', and John is able to step back to 'take a panoramic view of the carnage' (Kraybill 1996: 200) when he indicts Rome for being guilty not only of 'the blood of prophets and of saints' but also 'of all the slain upon the earth' (18.23–24). No one in the Mediterranean was allowed to forget the fate of the province of Judea when its residents sought to opt out of the empire. The victorious generals-turned-emperors, Vespasian and his son Titus, kept their reconquest before everyone's eyes with dozens of mintings of coins of all denominations celebrating *Judea capta*, the retaking of Judea. Keeping Judea in the family of the 'Father of the fatherland', as the emperors were all called, had cost hundreds of thousands of Galilean and Judean lives (whether to slaughter or enslavement).[16] And, of course, the empire had been forged and continued to be expanded, in large measure, through bloody conquest, as the many coin mintings celebrating the 'taking' of this or that region, or the 'victory' over this or that people group, attest. All of this violence, moreover, served primarily commercial and consumerist ends, namely to sustain and expand the Roman imperial economic structure.

Third, John indicts Rome for the arrogance of those who articulated its mythic ideology. John draws attention to this problem in the speech he places in Babylon's mouth – speech drawn, in turn, from an older prophetic denunciation of the arrogance of historic Babylon, a city that had made similar boasts that history proved empty: 'I sit a queen; I am no widow and will surely never see grief' (Rev. 18.7; compare Isa. 47.7-9).[17] The image projected for Rome was that of an 'eternal city' (Ovid, *Fast.* 3.72; *Sib. Or.* 3.46-56; Koester 2014: 612). A graffito in one of the upscale town houses in downtown Ephesus reads, 'Rome, queen over all, your power will never end' (Kraybill 1996: 57). Whether this was meant as an affirmation or remark of despair, the message is the same. Such rhetoric, however, reveals that Rome's spokespersons refused to apply the most basic lesson of history – namely that there has never been a kingdom that has failed to fall from its height into obscurity and subjugation to others – to its own story. They refused to embrace the humility that might have led to a more humane rule. John's own sense of this lesson would likely have been shaped by the book of Daniel, with which he otherwise shows such great familiarity: God 'changes times and seasons, deposes kings and sets up kings' (Dan. 2.21 nrsv); 'the Most High has sovereignty over the kingdom of mortals and gives it to whom he will' (Dan. 4.32 nrsv).[18] Of course, nothing is stronger evidence that Rome exercises its rule unmindful of its accountability to the God who establishes kingdoms and plucks them up again than the promotion of the cult of Dea Roma across the Mediterranean.

While John's depiction of Roman imperial rule is certainly one-sided, it is just as certainly not idiosyncratic. Nor was it, if multiple witness can establish

---

16   Josephus (*J.W.* 6.420) gives the numbers of casualties as 1.1 million slain and 97,000 reduced to slavery, though his numbers are almost universally regarded as exaggerated.

17   See also *Sib. Or.* 4.168-78.

18   See also Dan. 2.36-45; 4.17, 25-27; 5.18-28.

truth, unfair. The authors of the Jewish *Sibylline Oracles* criticized Roman luxury and longed for the time when the wealth siphoned off from Asia would be restored and the servant–master relationship of province to capital reversed (3.350–80; 4.145–8; 5.155–78; Bauckham 1993a: 382; Maier 2002: 244).[19] Roman ethicists also criticized the spirit of the age that the Roman imperial economy had fostered and, in turn, by which it was driven. Seneca, for example, censured Romans' 'insatiable present hungers for every luxury and excess of food, clothing, and shelter, which stand against the simplicity of earlier times and the little that is required for Nature's need (*Helv.* 10.3–11.4)' (Rapske 2012: 336), as did Juvenal, more colourfully (e.g. *Sat.* 6.290–300, 457–9, 501–9). Many of the items on John's cargo list were also specifically cited by the more austere Romans as evidence for their fellow elite citizens' irrational and 'un-Roman' craving for luxury.[20] A number of other Jewish authors also protest against Rome's violence, destruction of fruitful communities for the sake of its imperialist expansion, insolent self-glorification, economic oppression, and suppression of those who dare to call its practices into question. Particularly noteworthy are *4 Ezra* and *2 Baruch* (especially *4 Ezra* 11.39—12.1; 12.23–25) and *Sibylline Oracles* (especially 3.311–13, 350–2; 4.137–9, 145–8, 168–78). But even the Roman historian Tacitus, a privileged member of the dominant culture, knows how Roman domination looks from the margins: 'Robbery, savagery, and rape they call "government"; they make a desert and call it "peace"' (*Agr.* 30).

Based on the human cost of Rome's maintaining its empire and the benefits of empire for its elite, and on the One God's historically demonstrated commitment to remove the perpetrators of systemic injustice, John forecasts Rome's demise: 'Her sins have piled up as high as heaven and God remembered her unjust deeds' (18.5). Allan Boesak reminds us that 'as John writes there is no sign whatsoever of the imminent fall of Rome' (1987: 119). Why should his hearers accept his vision as not only possible, but also sufficiently plausible to stake their own well-being and futures upon it?

By calling Rome 'Babylon' John is subtly invoking a historical precedent on the basis of which to predict the outcome of an analogous case. When the angel asserts, 'She fell, she fell, great Babylon!' (14.8; 18.2), incorporating elements of phrases from Isaiah 21.9 and Jeremiah 25.7–8, the claim is already historically

---

19 It is noteworthy that the author of the late-first-century fourth *Sibylline Oracle* looks for this reversal in connection with the return of Nero (*Sib. Or.* 4.137–9).

20 Pliny the Elder is an outspoken example (see *Nat.* 8.7; 9.105, 112–14, 117–22, 127, 137; 12.82–4; 13.20–2, 91, 95, 102; 16.232; 33.146; 34.1, 6–8, 36; 36.2–8, 48–51, 110, 115, 125; 37.14–17); Bauckham 1993a: 366.

true in one sense. Babylon, the capital of the eastern empire that flourished under Nebuchadnezzar, did indeed lie in ruins. John blends the horizons of historic Babylon's practices and fate and Rome's practices and, therefore, its prospects. Since Rome has committed many of the same crimes as Babylon (and Tyre), Rome must certainly fall under the same judgement of the same God, for God's character, and particularly God's commitment to justice, remains constant (a theme celebrated in Rev. 15.3–4; 16.5–7). Rome's arrogance, violence, idolatries and economic rapine, which reinscribe upon the face of the world the practices of Babylonian and Tyrian domination, cry out for the inevitable intervention and judgement of a just God.

John's forecast of Rome's fate potentially changes his congregation's attitude towards Rome and towards alignment with Rome. The way of witness, lived out by means of reserving worship exclusively and forthrightly for the One God and God's Anointed, will lead to greater tension with Rome's partisans and to greater costs being exacted more broadly from the dissenters. But it is possible to see Rome no longer as the ultimate power and to discover, thereby, the freedom to live out a higher allegiance. It is the same possibility that the Church in South Africa discovered in the later days of apartheid:

> When they see guns and more guns, they see power. The church sees a growing powerlessness: 'it goes to perdition' (17.11). They scrutinize a new law that gives even more frightening powers to the Minister of Law and Order and to his 'security forces'. They see power. The church knows: 'it goes to perdition'. They look at the long lists of names of detainees . . . and they see power. The church prays for these people, calls their names before the throne of God, and knows that 'it goes to perdition', this beast.
> (Boesak 1987: 115)

The verdict has already been rendered and the sentence passed. The execution thereof hangs imminently over Rome's head and the heads of all who remain in partnership with Roman domination. Thus an angel delivers the summons that John most wishes to convey to his congregations and see them take to heart:

> Come out from her, my people,
> in order that you may not share in her sins,
> and in order that you may not receive [a share] of her
>   punishments.

Because her sins have piled up as far as heaven
and God remembered her crimes.
(Rev. 18.4–5; cf. Jer. 51.6–7, 45)

Continued partnership with and profiting from Roman imperialism means continued participation in its systemic injustices, both towards human beings who are exploited, excluded or victimized and against God whose unique claim on human allegiance is denied. Thus, continued partnership exposes one to the same judgement that hangs over Rome. The angel's summons calls 'those who could share in her profits to side with her victims and become victims themselves' (Bauckham 1993a: 378).

The angel issues a second exhortation to the group whose members will hear themselves addressed as part of 'my people':

Give back to her as she gave back
and double the double measure according to her deeds;
in the cup she mixed, mix up for her a double portion.
As much as she glorified herself and luxuriated,
give her that much torment and mourning.
(Rev. 18.6–7)

Many have found this summons, apparently calling human beings to take vengeance – and that by violence and out of proportion ('double') – ethically problematic. But there is no corroboration elsewhere in Revelation for hearing this as a genuine call to violent retaliation, which remains everywhere else securely in God's hands and the hands of God's heavenly forces who execute judgement on behalf of God's servants. This solitary exhortation cannot be heard, then, as a call to Christians to act in a sub-Christian manner. Rather, calling for double the punishment for Rome's crimes against humanity may be heard more as a device intended to heighten indignation against Rome, which is John's immediate aim here in support of his pastoral goal, namely to motivate divestment and distance. Indeed, many among John's hearers appeared willing to forget, as they sought some modus vivendi with the imperial power, that Rome ever spilled so much Christian blood. John needs to revive their indignation so that they will cease to entertain notions of coexistence, even cooperation, and bear the witness to injustice that is the duty of survivors.

To the extent that he has successfully established his forecast of Rome's destiny, John has also shown that such an alliance would not be advantageous, but would in fact be ultimately inexpedient. The hearers would find themselves ranged against God in partnership with a system doomed to fall by decree of divine justice. Partnership with Rome offers not security but rather the danger of incurring the wrath of God as Rome's clients are led to participate in Rome's sins against God. John's hearers must indeed 'work out what it means to disengage from these practices in the contexts in which they live' (Koester 2014: 715), but John's renewal of the prophets' critique of such systems has given them significant motivation for the task of discernment.

Saintly joy or schadenfreude?

The lament over Babylon on the part of the kings, merchants and seafarers in league with the city (18.9–19) is actually spoken by the heavenly voice that utters God's summons to God's people (18.4–8), and this heavenly voice concludes its speech by calling heaven and holy ones and apostles and prophets to 'rejoice' over Babylon's fall, 'because God has exacted judgement on your behalf from her' (18.20). Revelation 19.1–10 both fulfils this summons to rejoice and effects a transition to the anticipation of the 'marriage supper of the Lamb' and the manifestation of his bride – another city, 'New Jerusalem'. The image of a wedding was commonly used to speak of God's entering into a covenant with Israel (Isa. 54.5; 62.5; Jer. 31.32; Ezek. 16.8) and God's renewing of the covenant with an unfaithful Israel (Hos. 2.19–20). Wedding and marriage both came to be used in the early Church to speak of Christ's relationship to the body of his disciples as a whole (2 Cor. 11.2; Eph. 5.28–32; Koester 2014: 729). Depicting the arrival of the kingdom of God as a great banquet is also well attested. John blends these strands together into the image of the 'marriage feast of the Lamb' (19.9).

John has been subjected to significant criticism for calling anyone to rejoice at the downfall of another. What was behind this apparent delight in the downfall of a magnificent city? D. H. Lawrence, an unsparing critic of Revelation, believed that the answer was envy:

> How the late apocalyptists love mouthing out all about the gold and silver and cinnamon of evil Babylon! How they *want* them all! How they *envy* Babylon her splendor, envy, envy! How they love destroying it all! The harlot sits magnificent with her golden cup of wine of sensual pleasure in her hand. How the apocalyptists would have loved to drink out of her cup! And since they couldn't: how they loved smashing it!
> (Lawrence 1931: 88)

It is 'endless envy' that he hears 'screeching through this song of triumph' (i.e. 19.1–10; Lawrence 1931: 118–19).

Other readers, particularly those from social locations more akin to John's own, hear something quite different in John's expressions of joy at the prospect of the removal of the powers that oppress and marginalize him and the populations with whom he identifies (namely, Judeans and Christians). Writing from late-apartheid South Africa, Allan Boesak suggests that:

> Those who do not know this suffering through oppression, who do not struggle together with God's people for the sake of the gospel, and who do not feel in their own bodies the meaning of oppression and the freedom and joy of fighting against it shall have grave difficulty understanding this letter from Patmos.
> (Boesak 1987: 38; see also Klassen 1966: 303, 310; Schüssler Fiorenza 1985: 198)

Indeed, he challenges the right of 'Christians who enjoy the fruits of injustice without a murmur, who remain silent as the defenseless are slaughtered' to 'become indignant when the suffering people of God echo the prayers of the psalms and pray for deliverance and judgment' since 'in the midst of indescribable pain and appalling indifference, this prayer – and the certainty of God's loving response – has become our sustenance' (1987: 72–3).

To rejoice at the prospect of Rome's overthrow is not to gloat or to taunt as those who have been victorious and now add insult to injury. Rather, it is to anticipate the experience of relief enjoyed as those who have been victimized by the brutality of a repressive regime or who live in fear of the same (6.9–11; 16.5–7; 17.6; 18.23–24; 19.1–2). It is significant that John's visions of such 'rejoicing' belong to a future as yet unrealized for John and his audiences. John is thus not actually urging rejoicing or gloating over a fallen victim (against Yarbro Collins 1980: 203) but seeking to arouse indignation against the continuing and as-yet unpunished crimes perpetrated by the Roman systems of domination.

Some readers have criticized John, in regard to his vision of the judgement of Rome, for showing no sense of the tragedy, the human loss, connected with the events he describes: 'there is nothing in Revelation 18 to conceal John's glee over the catastrophe' (Carey 1999: 156–7). Other noteworthy critics, however, hear remarks expressive of pity and regret over Babylon's fall, particularly in regard to 18.21–23a (e.g. Beckwith 1919: 285; Lilje 1957: 237; Caird 1966: 227). Even as he anticipates the relief that will come with the collapse of a global domination system, John acknowledges the personal tragedies that will result as collateral damage: the weddings that would not happen, the songs of joy that would not be sung, the fruitful crafts that would no longer be practised. These verses might indeed arouse pity for the *people* in Babylon destined to be caught up in its downfall, perhaps in turn motivating the witness and evangelism that some believe to be critical to John's larger agenda, namely to bring about the conversion of the nations (e.g. Schüssler Fiorenza 1991: 79; Bauckham 1993b: 103).

Continuing encounters with Babylon

Many interpreters have sought Babylon beyond the context in which John and his congregations lived and moved. Some de-politicized the figure of Babylon and applied it as a moral warning against luxury and ostentatious apparel (Tertullian, *Cor.* 13; Cyprian, *Hab. virg.* 12; Koester 2014: 32). It has been far more common to re-politicize the figure. Babylon has frequently been used as a figure by means of which to criticize the papacy, first by voices from within the Catholic Church. Dante, unsparing in his criticism of the practices of certain contemporary popes, addresses one of them thus in his *Inferno*:

> The Evangelist was looking at you 'shepherds'
> when she who sits upon the waters
> whoring with kings was shown to him.
> (19.106–8, translation mine)

Such an interpretation (or application) became very popular during the Reformation and its aftermath (as in the Geneva Bible and the illustrations in the Luther Bible) and remains so among some Protestant circles (e.g. those receptive to LaHaye 1999: 168–71). Parties have continued to cast those whom they regard as their opponents in the figure of Babylon, whether in political contexts (as among the various parties in the English civil war of the late seventeenth century; Kovacs and Rowland 2004: 186–7) or religious (e.g. 'apostate' Christianity (Brighton 1999: 483) or liberal, ecumenical Christianity (LaHaye 1999: 271–2)).

Another approach has been to see in Babylon all the kingdoms of the world, which hold sway until Antichrist arises and is defeated (Andrew of Caesarea, *Comm. in Apoc.* 18.53; Weinrich 2011a: 176), viewed under one image: the 'city of the devil' – the city 'which Cain founded upon the blood of his brother' – in opposition to the 'city of God' (Tyconius 2017: 170; cf. Augustine, *Civ.*). Or, as Robert Witham, an eighteenth-century Catholic interpreter, understands the image:

> by the great city of Babylon is signified all wicked great Cities in the World, all the multitude of the wicked in all nations, their short and Vain Happiness; their Persecutions and oppressions of the good and faithful Servants of God, who live piously in this world, and who are call'd to be Citizens of the Celestial Jerusalem in the Kingdom of God.
> (*Annotations* 2.510–11; Newport 2000: 86)

On the one hand, such an approach may seem to generalize the image (and, thus, John's critique and call in regard to Babylon) so broadly as to blunt any impact that it might have. On the other hand, this approach orients interpreters to the political, economic, religious and other ideological realities in their contexts in a potentially more fruitful way. It does not call readers and faith communities to the closed-ended task of deciphering, of trying to determine which nation or other corporate entity *is* Babylon. Rather, it calls readers to do, in their present contexts, precisely what John sought to do in his own: to discern what is Babylonish about the domination systems in the midst of which they live and of which they themselves may be a part; and then to discover the ways in which they can both divest themselves of participating in and bear prophetic witness against the same.[21]

---

21 Stimulating examples of this approach can be found in Stringfellow 1973; Boesak 1987; and Howard-Brook and Gwyther 1999.

11
Making all things new (Revelation 19.11—22.5)

In Revelation 10.6, an angel had announced that there would be no more delay. Then, in 11.18, the 24 elders announced that the time had arrived 'for the dead to be judged, and to give the reward to [God's] servants, the prophets and the holy ones and those fearing God's name, the small and the great, and to destroy those who are destroying the earth'. This began to be fulfilled in 17.1—19.10 with God's visitation of judgement upon Babylon and continues to be fulfilled here in 19.11—22.5 as God and God's Anointed defeat all those forces that had rebelled – and would ever rebel! – against God's just rule and institute that rule first in a thousand-year reign of Christ with his holy ones over this creation and then in the endless reign of God and the Lamb in the new creation.

The narrative tension between the announcement that 'there will surely be no more delay' and the passing of another ten chapters before we can begin to say that the promised time had arrived mirrors the tension in the life experience of John's congregations and congregations in every period since. Nevertheless, John's visions of the end continue to remind audiences in every generation not only of the hope towards which they press, but also of the importance of right allegiances and right actions in the 'meanwhile' of waiting (Maier 2002: 132).

The return of the King

The vision of rejoicing over the removal of Babylon's corrupting influence from the human scene closes with the expectation of the marriage of the Lamb to his bride, a familiar figure for the Messiah's deliverance, gathering and establishment of his people under the secure aegis of his rule. Now the bridegroom appears, but not in the manner of a man approaching his wedding. Rather he appears riding through the sky upon a white horse followed by the armies of heaven similarly mounted, hastening to do battle with the forces of the beast and false prophet, whom we encounter already gathered for the fray in 19.19 (perhaps still waiting from the scene in 16.12–16!).

While the rider is not explicitly named, the hearer is given every clue to identify him as the returning Lord Jesus. He is described in a manner that explicitly recalls the opening vision of the glorified Christ, with eyes like fiery flame (19.12; cf. 1.14; 2.18) and a sharp sword proceeding from his mouth (19.15; cf. 1.16). Naming the figure 'the Word of God' may call to mind the tradition about Jesus as the Word-made-flesh celebrated in John 1.1–14. The expectation that he will 'shepherd [the nations] with an iron rod' reflects a clearly messianic image taken from Psalm 2.9 (though such authority is also promised to those who conquer with the Lamb in 2.26–27). Perhaps most telling, he is identified as 'king of kings and lord of lords' (19.16), a title ascribed to the Lamb in 17.14. These titles associate him closely with God in a manner reserved elsewhere only for Jesus.[1] The connection with the content of 17.12–14 goes beyond the appearance of this title. There, the beast gathers his allies and their armies to make war against the Lamb and suffer defeat. Revelation 19.11–21 is likely to be heard to offer a fuller picture of the event anticipated in the angel's earlier monologue.

John sees Christ returning with a blood-spattered robe. Some readers believe the blood to be that of Christ's enemies. 'If his cloak is spattered with blood, it is the blood of his enemies, the destroyers of the earth and of his children' (Boesak 1987: 124). The vision itself takes us back to the image of the treading of 'the wine press of the fury of the wrath of God' encountered in 14.18–20. Those hearers who are acquainted with Isaiah 63.1–3, whence the images of treading this wine press and a blood-bespattered robe derive, might indeed understand the blood here also to be the result of the divine agent's action against the enemies of God's people. On the other hand, other readers note that the robe is bloodied prior to the action of the scene, to which one could add that the figure is identified here as the one who *will* tread the wine press (19.15), not the one who *has* trodden the same (Isa. 63.3, 6), suggesting that, in this late passage, we are once again approaching the events of Revelation 14.18–20 by way of recapitulation. This has led readers as early as Origen to conclude that the blood-stained robe is a figure of Christ's Incarnation and Passion, hence an image of Christ's earlier redemptive activity (cf. 5.9–10).[2]

---

1 See Deut. 10.17, where God is called 'God of gods and Lord of lords'; 2 Macc. 13.4 where God is called 'King of kings' (NRSV).

2 Origen, *Exhortation to Martyrdom* 50. See also Andrew of Caesarea, *Comm. in Apoc.* 20.58; Bede, *Exp.* 19.13; Maier 2002: 187–8; Koester 2014: 755–6.

Christ defeats his enemies with his word (19.15), the power and effects of which are dramatically depicted as a sword proceeding from his mouth (cf. 2 Thess. 2.7–8; Heb. 4.12–13). The power of divine speech, manifested first in God's speaking creation into existence (Gen. 1.1—2.4), is often portrayed as a weapon of mass destruction in the prophetic corpus and its literary heirs (see, e.g., Isa. 11.4; Hos. 6.5; *1 Enoch* 62.2). The armies that accompany him do nothing save witness his victory.[3] Prior to the battle, an angel dramatically invites all the carrion birds of the air to 'the great supper of God' (19.17–18 NRSV), a grisly counterpart to the invitation to 'the supper of the Wedding of the Lamb' (19.9). After the defeat of the beast, false prophet and their armies, 'all the birds ate their fill of their bodies' (19.21). John has appropriated the image from Ezekiel 39.17–20, in which Ezekiel is commanded to issue a similar invitation to the birds and wild animals to 'eat the flesh of the mighty, and drink the blood of the princes of the earth' (Ezek. 39.18 NRSV) after God defeats the ungodly armies – led by Gog from Magog – that have assembled against Israel after its resettlement of the land. As Revelation 19.11–15 takes the hearer back to 14.18–20, 19.17–18 may recall to mind the scene in 6.12–17. The 'kings', 'generals' and 'every free person and slave' who appear on the menu for the carrion birds here (19.18) appeared in the scene of panic at the arrival of 'the great day of the wrath' of God and the Lamb (6.15, 17). Ezekiel contributes the horses and their riders (Ezek. 39.20). These connections reinforce the impression gained otherwise that 6.12–17; 14.14–20; and 19.11–21 look forward to the same intervention on the part of God and the Lamb.

The purpose of the scene in Revelation may be essentially the same as God's purposes for the battle in Ezekiel, namely to make known God's reality and God's power to all the nations that had hitherto failed to acknowledge and honour God, their maker (Ezek. 38.16, 23; 39.6–7, 21–22). At several points in Revelation, such acknowledgement appears to be a primary goal of the action, though too often thwarted by human stubbornness (9.20–21; 11.13; 14.6–7; 16.9, 11). At the same time, the effortless victory that Christ wins over the beast, the false prophet and their forces cannot fail to engender feelings of confidence among John's hearers, helping them master their fear of the Roman authorities and their agents since they have now aligned themselves with a far

---

3   It is unclear who constitutes these armies. On the one hand, an angelic army accompanying the divine Warrior is a staple of the Jewish Scriptures and Second Temple literature. On the other, these acolytes are clothed in 'fine linen', which may recall the attire of the bride in 19.8. Similarly, those who are with the Lamb in the battle predicted in 17.12–14 are 'called and chosen and faithful' (17.14 NRSV), a description better suited to the Lamb's human followers.

more powerful Ally who will not fail to vindicate his own honour, with which their honour is inextricably linked (11.11–13; 16.5–7; deSilva 1998: 98).

Visions of violence and vengeance

The visions of the slaying and serving up of armies of enemies to the carrion birds (19.11–21) – together with the visions of the enemies of the Lamb suffering the punishment of eternal fire while the Lamb and his angels look on (14.9–11), of the treading of the wine press of God's wrath, pressing a veritable sea of blood from the condemned (14.18–20), and of the judgement and desolation of Babylon (18.1–24) – have evoked not only revulsion at the images but also stern condemnation of their author. Carl Jung described Revelation as 'a veritable orgy of hatred, wrath, vindictiveness, and blind destructive fury' that 'overwhelms a world which Christ had just endeavored to restore' (1960: 125). Less sensationally, Greg Carey suggests that, while 'Revelation exposes the extreme violence of the Empire . . . it sometimes seems to cultivate the desire for violence, even to celebrate it (6:9–11; 15:1–8; 16:6–7)' (2008: 174).

Once again the proximity or distance between John's situation and the modern reader's situation emerges as critically important. On the one hand, it would be highly questionable for those in a situation of power, stability and abundance, who are living at peace with the sociopolitical system that sustains them, to use Revelation to justify indulging in fantasies of judgement and destruction upon their enemies, national or otherwise.[4] On the other hand, it would also be presumptuous for 'modern readers who live comfortably in a stable democracy . . . to dismiss John's vision as sub-Christian' (Kraybill 2010: 136) – or to similarly dismiss the desire for justice and vindication voiced by the oppressed. Allan Boesak gives poignant expression to the kind of situation that resonates with John's own, wherein John's rhetoric still finds a natural home:

> From the earliest days of colonial rule, whole communities have been slaughtered to secure the continuation of white power; and in our time there have been Sharpeville in 1960, Soweto 1976, Cape Town 1980, Langa 1984. During recent years there has hardly been a place where the police

---

4 'The kingdom that God establishes through Jesus Christ, however, stands outside and reverses the operations of the systems that govern the world humans have made. In Christ, God no longer identifies with a nation or accommodates nationalist or monarchical objectives' (Hawk 2019: 205–6). Hawk 2019 provides a thoroughly insightful analysis of the violence of, or attributed to, God in the Old Testament and how 'followers of the Prince of Peace' might process these narratives.

and the army have not wantonly murdered our children, piling atrocity upon atrocity for the sake of the preservation of apartheid and white privilege. And as they go from funeral to funeral, burying yet another victim of law and order or yet another killed by government-protected death squads, the cry continues to rise to heaven: 'How long, Lord?' How long before this illegitimate power is removed? How long before the blood of our children is avenged? It is a cry, a longing for justice, for comfort, for the final revelation of the truth, clear and undeniable: 'The Lord reigns!'
(Boesak 1987: 69–70)

One might helpfully recall Psalm 137 with its highly problematic climax: 'O daughter Babylon, you devastator! Happy shall they be who pay you back what you have done to us! Happy shall they be who take your little ones and dash them against the rock!' (Ps. 137.8–9 NRSV). In the immediate wake of the destruction of Jerusalem and the displacement and degradation brought about by the deportation to Babylon, there was room for 'people whose homes or lives [were] destroyed by war or injustice . . . to cry out to God with vehement language', to seek 'catharsis' by unloading 'deep pain or anger on God, who can make all things new' (Kraybill 2010: 123).

While John certainly gives expression to the cathartic desire for justice and vindication on the part of those who have experienced violence and oppression – and certainly nurtures feelings of enmity towards Roman domination (deSilva 2009: 198–215) – he does not nurture a response of violent action on the part of his Christian hearers.[5] Rather, the visions of justice granted and vindication accomplished empower non-violent witness, both in the form of divestment from the economical practices and religious settings that sustain Roman domination and in the form of imitating the Lamb's manner of conquering and kingdom-building by speaking the word of truth and enduring to the point of death.[6]

The millennium across the millennia

John's vision of the millennium – the thousand-year reign that a group of 'holy ones' share with Christ – has been understood in a bewildering variety

---

5 For a stark contrast, see *1 Enoch* 98.12, where it is said to those who practise iniquity: 'you will be given into the hand of the righteous, and they will cut your throats and kill you and will not have mercy on you.'

6 See also Friesen 2001: 189–90; Johns 2003: 187; Kraybill 2010: 103.

of ways over the millennia. Given the paucity of space that the scene occupies in Revelation itself (a mere three verses!), it might be fairly said that it has been given disproportionate attention vis-à-vis other facets of John's vision. What an interpreter does with these three verses can become a litmus test that lands him or her in one of several major interpretative camps like 'Premillennial', 'Postmillennial' and 'Amillennial'. John's vision itself raises several subsidiary questions that receive a variety of answers: who is included in this 'first resurrection', thereby enjoying a share in this thousand-year-long privilege? Where are these people when they reign with Christ (on earth? in heaven?)? What is the temporal relationship of this thousand-year period to other events recounted in Revelation, for example the return of Christ at the head of his heavenly armies or the descent of the new Jerusalem? What significance does the binding and loosing of Satan on either side of the millennium hold for this thousand-year period? In this section, we will first explore the ways in which the millennium has been principally understood and then return to consider the impact of John's vision upon his congregations in their particular setting.

Christians in the second and third centuries tended to regard the millennium as a future time of great abundance that the faithful disciples of Jesus would enjoy on earth. Writers such as Papias of Hierapolis (according to Irenaeus, *Haer.* 5.33.3–4) fleshed out the picture of this thousand-year period using imagery found, not in Revelation, but in other Jewish apocalypses (notably *2 Baruch* 29.5–7). Justin Martyr (*Dial.* 80–1) regarded the millennium as God's fulfilment of God's prophecies concerning the future restoration and exaltation of Jerusalem (e.g. Ezek. 40—48; Isa. 54.11–12; 60.1–3, 11) – a theme that persists in some form to the present day. It was a period that would follow the end of normal history, the seventh 'day' of creation, as it were, following upon the six 'days' (six millennia) of history (Ps. 90.4; *Barn.* 15.1–5; Irenaeus, *Haer.* 5.28.3). As an earthly kingdom of Christ and his saints, it represented God's redemption of creation before bringing the new heavens and new earth into being (Irenaeus, *Haer.* 5.32.1; 5.33.3). This was not the *only* understanding of the millennium in the Church's first centuries. Origen, for example, objected to a materialist understanding of the millennium, seeing in it a figure of the hope of heaven that those who died in the Lord would enjoy (*Princ.* 2.11.2–3). Nevertheless, during the centuries of greatest persecution the most prominent understanding of the millennium was an assurance of an actual thousand-year reign on earth in which all would enjoy the abundance of the earth's produce in peace (Wainwright 1993: 21–31).

This line of interpretation survives in readings that are generally labelled 'premillennial'. The term itself refers to the belief that Christ will return prior to the inauguration of a millennial kingdom, specifically on earth. This may represent, quantitatively speaking, the most widely embraced understanding of the millennium, a view that began to grow in prominence again in the seventh century through the modern period, erupting quite spectacularly in the group that formed around William Miller (which came to be known as Seventh-day Adventists), and made popular throughout the last 150 years as a component of dispensational theology by such writers as Cyrus I. Scofield, John Walvoord, Hal Lindsey and Tim LaHaye (see Wainwright 1993: 83–6; Lindsey 1975: 256–68). Such a reading allows interpreters to affirm that prophetic announcements in the Old Testament regarding Jerusalem's glorious future under an heir to David's throne (see, e.g., Isa. 11.1–9; Amos 9.11–15), apparently left unfulfilled, will find literal fulfilment at last. Indeed, John's interest in making room for a millennium before an eternity may derive from his own concern that such a hope (which persisted into the first century, as *Pss. Sol.* 17.21–32 and Acts 1.6 demonstrate) not go forever unfulfilled (Aune 1998b: 1104–8; Koester 2014: 748).[7]

Constantine's conversion and decrees of toleration towards the Church – indeed the surprising elevation of Christianity as the religion of the empire and its emperor – evoked a very different reading of the millennium. With the disappearance of the beast and Babylon in the form of the Roman imperial machine as persecutor of the Church and self-glorifying alternative to faith in God, the possibility of the saints reigning with Christ upon the earth seemed no longer merely a future hope, but a present reality. Towards the end of the fourth century, Tyconius would speak of the millennium not as the period that would follow Christ's return, but as the period *between* Christ's first coming – during which Satan had been bound (Matt. 12.29) – and second coming (*Book of Rules* 3.4; Kovacs and Rowland 2004: 17, 206). This view would become highly influential after it was embraced by Augustine (see *Civ.* 20.9), the figurative length of the thousand years – a 'perfect number' – being chosen to indicate the 'fullness of time' (*Civ.* 20.7; Weinrich 2005: 322). This view would be adopted by Bede in England (*Exp.* 20.5), and by Oecumenius (*Comm.* 20.4.8) and Andrew of Caesarea (*Comm. in Apoc.* 20.60) in the east.

In such a view, the 'first resurrection' happens whenever one comes to faith and is raised with Christ in baptism (Augustine, *Civ.* 20.9), in line with Paul's teaching about baptism as the means of being 'raised to life' with Christ (Rom. 6.4; Col. 3.1–4). The first resurrection is thus for the saints; all take part in

---

7 John was not alone in this regard. For other temporary messianic kingdoms, see *1 Enoch* 93.3–10; 91.11–17; *4 Ezra* 7.26–30; *2 Baruch* 29.3—30.1.

the second resurrection – the resurrection of the body that precedes the Last Judgement (*Civ.* 20.6). Satan, bound during Christ's earthly ministry, is kept from deceiving those who are destined to come to faith (Augustine, *Civ.* 20.7–8; Bede, *Exp.* 20.2). His influence continues to be felt 'like a Mafia boss who continues to run the family business from behind bars' (Mangina 2010: 228), but those who are to be saved are sheltered from the full force of his power to deceive. The pit into which Satan is cast is the hearts of the wicked and the persecutors of the faithful, over whom he now has the greater hold (Augustine, *Civ.* 20.7; Bede, *Exp.* 20.3).[8]

The view espoused by Tyconius and Augustine persists in modern interpretations that are often labelled 'postmillennial' and 'amillennial'. The former term refers to the location of the millennium *prior to* the second coming of Christ. The millennium need not be understood as a thousand calendar years any more than statements in Scripture that speak of 'God's ownership of the cattle on a thousand hills (Ps. 50:10)' or that measure 'God's love to a thousand generations (Deut. 7:9)' seek to present precise tallies or measurements (Gentry 1999: 52). Thus it can continue to be understood as the period of Christ's reign through his saints in heaven and his Church on earth, however long that period lasts. 'Amillennial' is the label applied to views of the millennium as purely symbolic or figurative (see Strimple 1999), though the term itself is somewhat problematic. Even a figurative interpretation takes the millennium seriously rather than *denying* it (Wainwright 1993: 36).

Another major view of the millennium that belongs more to the late-medieval and modern periods was that it represented a perfected order on earth that would come about through human action. The new Jerusalem was understood in the same way. Some, like the Taborites (the followers of Jan Hus, who was killed in 1415), believed they would bring in this new social order by violent action (Koester 2014: 745). The revolutionaries in the city of Münster (1534–5) similarly declared themselves to be establishing the new Jerusalem, calling like-minded Anabaptists into their city and movement (Kovacs and Rowland 2004: 226–7).

More often, the inauguration of the millennium was sought through steady progress in evangelism and related social reform. This was the view of Jonathan Edwards and Charles Finney (Wainwright 1993: 77–81; Koester 2014:

---

8 As the world neared first the year 1000 CE (for those who assigned the beginning of the millennium to Christ's earthly ministry) and, then, the year 1300 CE or so (for those who assigned its beginning to Constantine's conversion), this view of the millennium fed expectations that the antichrist would soon arise and the end dawn. See, for example, the writings of Alexander the Minorite (Wainwright 1993: 53–5; Kovacs and Rowland 2004: 210) and Peter Olivi (Koester 2014: 745).

746–7). Edwards regarded the Great Awakening to be a sign that God was beginning to fashion 'a new world in a spiritual respect, when he creates the new heavens and new earth' (Kovacs and Rowland 2004: 227). John's visions of the millennial reign and the new Jerusalem were read as a utopian ideal – one to be realized in human history. It is captured rather poetically in William Blake's vision for his native land, 'Jerusalem':

> I will not cease from mental strife,
> Nor shall the sword sleep in my hand
> Till we have built Jerusalem
> In England's green and pleasant land.

Such optimism in the possibilities for human society in the present age, however, ran afoul of the events of the twentieth century into the early twenty-first century – the First World War (ironically 'the war to end all wars'), the Second World War and the unspeakable evils of the Holocaust in Germany and equal slaughter under Stalinist Russia, the proliferation of nuclear arms and the threat of global annihilation of the Cold War, and the global violence inflicted by militant Islamist movements like Al-Qaeda, ISIS and Boko Haram. While the commitment of the Church to witness and to work for the common welfare has survived these tremendous evils, its belief that it can move history forward towards a global order of peace with justice has not.

The difference between Irenaeus's and Augustine's readings – as between the premillennialist and postmillennialist readings – stems from a decision concerning the narrative flow of these chapters. Does 20.1–10 continue a narrative progression from chapters 17—19 or does it take us back in time? There is precedent for the latter, as the action of Revelation 12.1–6 clearly precedes the action of Revelation 10.1—11.19, taking the reader back to the Incarnation and Ascension of Jesus (Strimple 1999: 120–1). There are, however, some strong indications that the events of 20.1–15 continue a sequence begun in chapter 19 and completed in chapters 21—22. Prior to 20.1, Satan has been an active agent on the world stage (see 2.10, 13; 12.17; 16.13). Indeed, he had previously been expelled from heaven and confined to the earth (12.7–13); now he is expelled from the face of the earth and confined to the abyss, whose residents, like the locusts of 9.1–12, do not disturb those upon the earth unless and until they are released (9.2; 20.7; Blaising 1999: 217–18).[9] Satan had been

---

9   The binding of Satan recalls the story of the Watchers, rebel angels who were likewise bound with chains and shut up under the earth (see *1 Enoch* 6—16; *Jub.* 5.6, 10; Jude 6; 2 Pet. 2.4).

effectively deceiving the nations throughout chapters 12—19 by means of the agents he had summoned (12.9; 13.14; 18.23; 19.20); the hearers are told that he is imprisoned in the abyss so that he might *no longer* carry out this deceptive activity (20.3).

It is likely, then, that John's hearers would have understood 20.1–10 to provide a continuation of the narrative that had been developing since 12.1 and, in particular, to provide a continuation of the dragon's story as one of continuing, progressive downfall. John's repetition here of the titles bestowed on the dragon in 12.9 – 'the dragon, the ancient snake, who is the devil and Satan' – both recalls the earlier event and adds solemnity and gravity to this next phase of the enemy's defeat. The prime mover of the ills that the faithful followers of the Lamb have experienced under Roman domination – under the beasts and Babylon (forces with which God has already dealt decisively by this point) – will suffer further defeat, degradation and constraint. At the same time, his victims (that is, those whom Satan victimized through his beastly agents) will be ascendant in their thousand-year reign.

The verses pertinent to the thousand-year reign are roughly written (indeed, many modern translations hide the difficulties inherent in this scene):

> And I saw thrones and they sat upon them and judgement was given to/ for them, and [I saw] the souls of those who had been axed on account of the testimony of Jesus and on account of the word of God, and/even whoever did not worship the beast or its image and did not receive the mark upon their forehead and upon their right hand. And they lived and reigned with Christ for a thousand years.
> (Rev. 20.4)

Who is sitting upon the thrones? Is it the souls of the martyrs, whom John only names afterwards? Or is it the 24 elders, whom the hearers have encountered before on thrones in heaven (4.4; 11.16)? Is judgement given *to* those seated as a task for them to carry out (as in Wisd. 3.7–8; 1 Cor. 6.1–2), or is judgement (a verdict) given *for* them, in their favour – that is, do they now sit vindicated by God's judicial actions against their enemies (as in Dan. 7.22)? Who comes to life and reigns with Christ – the martyrs only, or a wider company of those who have resisted the worship of the beast and its image? In what realm does this reign take place (it is only in connection with 5.9–10 that we might place this reign 'on earth')?

The answers to these questions are not at all immediately apparent. The question of who will be so privileged (20.6), for example, depends on how one understands a very little word in Greek – *kai* – which could signify 'and' or 'even'. If it signified the former, John would be naming two groups: the narrower one, comprised of those who were executed for their testimony, and the broader one, comprised of all who resisted the worship of the beast and its mark, whether or not this eventuated in their deaths (Roloff 1984: 193; Prigent 1988: 310–11; Giessen 1997: 70). If it signified the latter, John would be further defining the martyrs as those who resisted the worship of the beast and its mark (Mounce 1997: 365–6; Böcher 1988a: 105). What *would* be immediately apparent to John's hearers is, again, that a tremendous privilege awaits those who resist the worship of the beast and its image and who refuse its mark, particularly those who endure execution on account of their witness.

Furthermore, it would be immediately apparent that the privilege will far outpace the perseverance in the present. Satan rages and the beast enjoys dominion for three and a half years (12.14; 13.5); the Lamb's faithful followers will enjoy vindication and dominion for a thousand! The numbers are clearly symbolic rather than indications of chronological time. Satan's 'three and a half years' began with Christ's exaltation and his own expulsion from heaven (12.5–13) and do not end until Christ's second coming (19.11–21). Rather, the proportion is the message (Koester 2014: 783).

The scene in 20.4–6 is linked to the scene of the Last Judgement in 20.11–15 in a clear sequence. Those who come to life and enjoy the thousand-year reign with Christ have participated in 'the first resurrection' (20.6). The 'rest of the dead did not live until the thousand years were completed' (20.5); when they *do* come to life, it is to stand before God's throne for God's verdict on each one's life in the body (20.12–13). The latter means, for many, to suffer 'the second death', namely to be plunged into the lake of fire (20.14), which retrospectively highlights once again the privilege of belonging to the group raised to life in 20.4–6, who can have complete confidence that 'the second death' has no authority over them (20.6).

The vision of the thousand-year reign assures John's hearers that the faithful – and, above all, those who are faithful unto death – will be vindicated, even as Christ was. They will 'come to life' (20.4) even as he 'came to life' and lives for ever (2.8; Koester 2014: 786), constituting the 'kingdom of priests' that God had decreed to be formed for himself since the exodus event (Exod. 19.5–6; Rev. 1.5–6; 5.9–10; 20.6). The vision of the thousand-year reign, then, is concerned primarily with God's justice towards his faithful and, above all, towards those who have sacrificed the most for the sake of their loyal obedience (Koester 2014: 749–50; Bauckham 1993b: 106–8). It provides further assurance to John's hearers that bearing testimony by word and deed, however costly in terms of the safe enjoyment of the present life, remains ever the more advantageous path since it leads to significantly greater and longer-lasting privileges in God's future.

At the conclusion of the thousand years, Satan, it is said, will be released. As a result, a massive force would be gathered from 'the four corners of the earth, Gog and Magog' and led against 'the beloved city', the 'camp of the holy ones' (20.7–9). The scene owes a great deal to Ezekiel's oracle predicting an assault on Israel by a confederacy of enemies under the leadership of 'Gog from the land of Magog' (Ezek. 38.2). A question that many have rightly asked, but that John does not clearly answer, is: why? Why should it be 'necessary' that Satan be released, even 'for a short time' (20.3)? Augustine's conjecture remains popular: Satan's activity after his release reveals the completeness of his own commitment to evil and also provides the faithful with one final opportunity to show their steadfastness (*Civ.* 20.8). Joseph Mangina offers an interesting alternative, focusing on the fact that, after a thousand years under new management, 'the great city' Babylon has been replaced over the course of the millennium by 'the beloved city', a 'human city, reconstituted, no longer as Babylon, but as the earthly counterpart of the new Jerusalem that will descend from heaven' (2010: 232). The final scene in this sequence serves to demonstrate the enduring quality of the 'beloved city' that God is building in Christ through the redemption of people from every nation, people, language and tribe. It is the heir of the assurances of the stability of Zion, 'which shall not be moved' (Ps. 46.5; Mangina 2010: 232).

Another question that is rightly asked is: whom does Satan deceive and gather? Who is *left* after 19.11–21? In keeping with his own more symbolic understanding of the millennium as the age of the Church, Augustine (*Civ.* 20.11–12) understood Gog and Magog to refer to all the nations extant at the end of the church age, who would join in persecuting the Church. Oecumenius (*Comm.* 20.8–10) believed Gog and Magog to be specific nations which either did not yet exist or were known by other names. This remained a popular direction for interpretation, particularly in regard to menaces looming large in the consciousness of the interpreters, as in Luther's selection of the Turks or Lindsey's selection of Russia (a chapter title in his *Late Great Planet Earth* is 'Russia is a Gog'). Futurists can also understand them as representative of groups of hostile people who would only be born during the future millennium (Lindsey 1975: 269). For all the questions the scene raises, John expresses an insight that has proven true: Satan would 'remain active even after the beast and its city are overthrown' (Koester 2014: 579) and, indeed, imperial Rome was not destined to be the *last* enemy of 'the camp of the holy ones' (20.9).

Judgement Day

The future John sees for the present age ends with a vision of universal judgement, when all – 'the great and the small' (20.12) – are held accountable before God. John augments the universality of the scene by cataloguing all the receptacles that yield their dead for the occasion, namely the sea, death and Hades (20.13).[10] Such an expectation for the point of transition between history and eternity was widely shared by authors standing in the tradition of the Jewish Scriptures. Those Scriptures themselves consistently nurtured the expectation that God would appear imminently on the scene to hold God's own people and their enemies to account in accordance with God's righteous standards revealed in the commandments. Frequently the prophets refer to this as 'the Day of the Lord' (Isa. 13.6, 9; Jer. 46.10; Ezek. 30.3; Joel 1.15; 2.1, 11; 3.14–16; Amos 5.18–20). While in most cases they have in mind a more immediate and local intervention in the affairs of Israel and Judah, the language often takes on cosmic and universal overtones (as in Isa. 13.6–13). In the worship life of Israel, this also takes on a more universal colour as God's coming to judge 'the world' and 'the peoples' is celebrated in anticipation (e.g. Pss. 96.10, 13; 98.9). In the later Second Temple period and the expectation of the early Church, this has become a fixed expectation of a universal judgement at the close of history before God or God's agent, often seated upon a throne (*1 Enoch* 69.26–29; Matt. 25.31–46; see also Acts 17.30–31; Rom. 2.5–11; 2 Cor. 5.9–10; 2 Tim. 4.1; 1 Pet. 4.5).

Who is present to be judged? What are the possible outcomes here? Such questions can only be raised because of John's distinctive vision of a 'first resurrection' involving 'the souls of those executed for their witness to Jesus' (20.4–6), a scene that does not appear in this form in any prior writing. Some readers take this to mean that *all* faithful followers of the Lamb take part in this event and are exempted from the judgement that follows the millennium. Other readers naturally place themselves in the scene of 20.11–15 (e.g. Beale 1999: 1032–3; Osborne 2002: 721–5; Koester 2014: 791). This would especially be true for readers who understood 20.4–6 to represent a special privilege accorded *martyrs*. John's hearers might indeed have heard 20.4–6 in such a way as to include them all, if they were to prove faithful in their situation as John defined fidelity, for John has also suggested that they would all need to contend against the forces that impelled them towards the

---

10 Compare the similar language in *1 Enoch* 51.1–2; *4 Ezra* 7.32; *2 Baruch* 50.2 and the discussion in Bauckham 1993a: 56–8.

worship of the beast and participation in the economy that served Babylon's incessant hunger. Even in this event, however, it is not clear that they would have exempted themselves from the picture of universal judgement in 20.11–15 just because they had 'come to life' beforehand – only that they would have knowledge in advance of how to secure a verdict of approval on that Day, a verdict that might potentially be given to them a thousand years in advance of that Day, if they heed John's summons. Fundamentally, the vision of judgement, like the vision of the thousand-year reign, would exercise a hortatory effect, providing further incentive to them to live so that they retain or *obtain* the 'works' that would follow them as a positive witness (2.2, 19, 26; 3.1–2, 8, 15; 14.13), live out the uncompromising witness to the One God and the Lamb that would place them beyond the power of 'the second death' (20.6) and do nothing to jeopardize their registration in the Scroll of Life (3.5; 13.8; 17.8).

Judgement is given to those standing before God's throne 'according to each person's deeds' (20.12, 13), with records consulted in the process: 'scrolls were opened, and another scroll was opened, which is the Scroll of Life, and the dead were judged on the basis of the things written in the books' (20.12). Several earlier texts express the conviction that heaven keeps a record of the deeds of human beings (*1 Enoch* 81.1–2; 90.20) and a register of the righteous (Dan. 12.1). As the scene is truly dealing with 'ultimate' things, what one believes ultimately to matter for one's deliverance tends to come to the fore in its interpretation. Augustine understood the 'scrolls' or 'books' symbolically as the two testaments that set forth the standard of judgement (*Civ.* 20.14) and 'the scroll of life' as 'a figure of the predestination of those who are to receive eternal life' (*Civ.* 20.15; tr. Weinrich 2005: 346). Protestant readers often express discomfort at the idea of *believers* being judged 'according to each one's works' and therefore are inclined to exempt them from this scene altogether or insist on their being 'saved by grace by having their names in the scroll of life' (Koester 2014: 780), which 'is the final basis for judgment' (Koester 2014: 781), in some cases denying *any* meaningful role to the other scrolls' contents (Wilkin 2013: 46–7).

John, however, prioritizes deeds over being entered in the scroll of life, because what one does or fails to do – even one who calls himself or herself a follower of the Lamb – can result in one's name being scratched out of the scroll of life, while 'overcoming' gives assurance that one's name will not be scratched out (3.5). Those who 'die in the Lord' can rest 'because their deeds follow them' (14.13), assuring their final vindication. Jesus, who indeed 'loved us and released us from our sins by his blood' (1.5) nevertheless remains at the same time 'the one who searches minds and hearts, and . . . will give to each person according to his or her deeds' (2.23). In his insistence 'that faith (what we believe) is inseparable from faithfulness (actions consistent with what we profess)' (Kraybill 2010: 162), John resonates with several other voices in the New Testament, including Jesus (Matt. 7.21; 25.31–46; Luke 6.46) and Paul (Rom. 2.6–11; 8.13–14; Gal. 5.19–21; 6.7–10; Eph. 5.5–6). Such a view is in keeping with John's goals, in which theological expressions serve pastoral aims, here the promotion of faithful witness and uncompromising obedience to God and the Messiah in the face of significant temporal pressures. As Harry Maier poignantly concludes, 'at the end, it is what you are doing in the meantime that counts' (2002: 132).

The last word of the scene is 'the lake of fire', wherein the beast, false prophet and dragon had previously been deposited. They are now joined by all who had been led astray through the ages to belong to their party. D. H. Lawrence (1931: 117) excoriated John for his 'lake of burning brimstone in which devils, demons, beasts, and bad men should frizzle and suffer for ever and ever and ever, Amen!' The notion of post-mortem punishment, especially continuing torment, is no less a stumbling block to Christian thinking today.[11] There are two significant factors behind John's vision of a lake of fire rather than the complete annihilation of those who had lived in defiance of the One God's commandments and refused allegiance to God's Messiah. The first is simply that he inherited this conviction. Jesus himself was remembered to have been quite the proponent of an 'eternal fire prepared for the devil and his angels', to which human beings who were judged worthy of such a fate would also be consigned (Matt. 13.41–43; 25.41–45 NRSV).

The second is that many in the ancient world denied any post-mortem existence. Epicurus, the third-century BC founder of an influential school of philosophical thought and ethics, taught that 'death . . . is nothing to us, since while we exist, death is not present, and whenever death is present, we do not exist . . . The dead no longer are' (*Letter to Menoeceus* 125). The popularity of this idea is attested by an inscription on many grave steles, 'I was not, I was, I am not, I care not' (*non fui, fui, non sum, non curo*), so common it came to be written merely as a kind of acronym (*N.F.F.N.S.N.C.*). In Epicurus's case, this conviction was meant to liberate one for a less troubled and anxious life that would nevertheless remain committed to virtuous living, since virtue made for a less troubled life as well. In practical consequence,

---

11   The immense popularity of Rob Bell's *Love Wins* (2011) attests to the desire to rid eschatology of a decisively final judgement and post-mortem punishment and suffering.

it could also lead to practices that subordinated the well-being of others to one's own gratification (see Wisd. 1.16—2.23). John stands on the other side of the debate, as it were, with those who *would* affirm post-mortem existence and the connection between one's practices here and one's destiny there in order to promote adherence to a particular code of living. The message of the lake of fire in such a context is simply a resounding affirmation: 'Death is not an escape' (Koester 2014: 793).

All things new

The present cosmos, hopelessly tainted by the evils it has witnessed, has 'fled' with the coming of the Day of the Lord (6.12–14; 20.11), and a new act of creation – a fresh start between God and humanity – takes its place. As early as Isaiah, the pious looked for a radical renewal of creation (Isa. 65.17; 66.22). By the later Second Temple period, the hope for a wholly new creation emerges more explicitly (e.g. *1 Enoch* 91.16). The vision of the new Jerusalem and the intimate experience of God that it provides represents the fulfilment of the cumulative hope of the Hebrew prophets. The voice from the throne gives expression to a pastiche of these promises at their long-awaited realization:

> Look! God's dwelling is with human beings
> and God will dwell with them
> and they will be his peoples,
> and God himself will be with them.
> And he will wipe every tear from their eyes
> and death will not exist any longer,
> nor will weeping or crying or distress exist any longer,
> because the former things went away.
> (Rev. 21.3–4)

God's declaration that Israel would be his people and he their God is central to the 'old covenant' revelation.[12] John significantly alters 'people' to 'peoples' in keeping with his own broad vision of the priestly kingdom God is drawing together in Christ from 'every tribe and language and people and nation' (Rev. 5.9; cf. 7.9). The promises that death, weeping, crying and distress would be set

---

12 See esp. Lev. 26.11–12; Ezek. 37.27; but also Jer. 7.23; 11.4; 24.7; 31.1, 33; 32.38; Ezek. 11.20; 14.11; 36.28; 37.23; Zech. 8.8; Bar. 2.35.

behind God's people for ever, together with the intimate assurance that God would wipe away the tears from every eye, carry forward Isaiah's promises of the same (see Isa. 25.8; 65.17–19). Indeed, references to Isaiah's and Ezekiel's visions of the restored and glorified Jerusalem pervade John's vision of the new Jerusalem.[13] Just as John relinquishes none of the hope for justice and vindication that his heritage has bequeathed him, so he relinquishes none of the hope for a new kind of existence beyond the reach of 'the destroyers of the earth' (11.18).

Even though John's hearers would be likely to set Babylon and New Jerusalem over against each other in their minds, John helps assure the comparison by introducing the vision of each city with a long string of identical words (the correspondences in the English here, shown in bold, fairly represent the correspondences in the original Greek):

And one of the seven angels having the seven bowls came and spoke with me, saying, 'Come, I will show you the judgement of the great prostitute seated over many waters.'
(Rev. 17.1)

And one of the seven angels having the seven bowls full of the seven last plagues **came and spoke with me, saying, 'Come, I will show you** the bride, the wife of the Lamb.'
(Rev. 21.9)

New Jerusalem is John's expression of the 'ideal' against which all humanly wrought societies, beginning with the Roman imperial order, are weighed and found wanting. The community of the redeemed remains a *community*, however, planted in the cities of Roman Asia and perfected in the new Jerusalem (Kraybill 2010: 177).[14] Access to the Edenic tree of life, the guarantor of immortality, is restored (Rev. 22.2), but now in a perfected city rather than a primitive garden (Peterson 1969: 139).

Not least among the incentives John gives his hearers to long for the new Jerusalem is the promise that all things presently experienced as

---

13 The Venerable Bede said of this vision: 'there is a considerable harmony between this book and the prophets, not only in their meanings but also in their vocabulary. For what verse can you find that is not from Isaiah or Zechariah or another of the prophets?' (*Exp.* 22.9; Weinrich 2011b: 193).

14 Augustine had seen in the new Jerusalem a reflection both of the Church now and of the community of the redeemed in the age to come. It has been coming down from heaven as its roster of citizens grows in every generation of the faithful but would one day appear in its unmixed glory (*Civ.* 20.17).

threatening – those things that render life insecure, that represent the worm at the core of existence – will no longer exist. 'Death will no longer be, nor mourning nor crying nor distress, because the former things passed away' (21.4); 'night will no longer exist' (21.25); 'every curse will no longer exist' (22.3); there will be 'no more sea' (21.1). Many of these recall the curses in Genesis 3 and primordial chaos (Hansen 2014: 79; Moo 2009: 165). There will also be no more night, such that the threats to a people's security that cause city gates to be closed at night will no longer exist (21.25). Those whose practices constitute an assault on the Christ-followers' convictions and sensibilities will no longer be present, banned from entering the city (21.8, 27; 22.15) even as 'no strange cults or other detestable practices' were allowed to draw nearer to the city of Rome than its sacred boundary, the *pomerium* set at a mile (1.5 km) from Rome's walls, so as not to disturb its sacred peace and harmony (Livy, *History of Rome* 1.44; Kraybill 1996: 212). Who would not long for a place that exists beyond threat, beyond harm, beyond fear?

The positive counterpart to the absence of all things that threaten is the immanent presence of God and the Lamb, the all-powerful and all-providing allies and patrons of the believing community. Indeed, their sheltering presence is perhaps the most prominent feature of the new Jerusalem:

> See! The tent of God is with humanity, and God will pitch his tent with them, and they will be God's peoples, and God will be with them, and will wipe away every tear from their eyes.
> (Rev. 21.3–4)

> And I did not see a temple in it, for the Lord God Almighty and the Lamb are its temple . . . The glory of God illumines it, and the Lamb is its light.
> (Rev. 21.22–23; cf. 22.5)

> The throne of God and of the Lamb will be in it, and his slaves will worship him, and they will see God's face.
> (Rev. 22.3–4)

God's presence fills the city with 'the glory of God', its jasper-like lustre (21.11) a sign of God's pervasive glory, which had also been compared with the lustre of jasper (4.3; Tõniste 2014: 282). This portrait of their future connection with God assures John's hearers that God is 'for them' here and now, empowering them to persevere in their faithful obedience in the face of the lesser forces that are 'against' them.

While John draws extensively on Ezekiel's vision concerning the new Temple in the restored Jerusalem (Ezek. 40—48),[15] at the same time he departs from Ezekiel in one stunning respect given the earlier text's focus. There is no Temple in the new Jerusalem because God's presence fills the whole. The shape of the new Jerusalem – a cube – recalls the dimensions of the holy of holies in the Solomonic Temple (1 Kings 6.20), the chamber in which God's full and holy presence manifested itself. That presence now pervades the whole, and all the city's residents are welcomed into the presence once figuratively limited to the innermost sanctum. This reflects upon the people who have a place in the city as well: 'The true people of God are completely holy, like the holy of holies of the temple, which was also a cube' (Tõniste 2014: 288).[16]

The splendour of the new Jerusalem as John describes it is designed to awaken 'awe' – a holy marvelling in contrast with John's marvelling after Babylon and the earth's marvelling after the beast (17.6–8). Augustus may have found Rome a city of brick and left it a city of marble (Suetonius, *Aug.* 28.3), but Rome's greatest glory is nothing in comparison with the city of God. John draws on prophetic and Second Temple period traditions about the future splendour of Zion (Isa. 54.11–12, which promised a Jerusalem restored with sapphire and precious stones; Tobit 13.17, which envisages the restored Jerusalem's building and paving materials to include 'sapphire and emerald and precious stones' as well as 'pure gold') as he describes the splendour of the new Jerusalem that descends from heaven beyond this creation (Rev. 21.18–21).[17]

From the earliest periods, the description of the new Jerusalem has been understood as 'theology expressed through architecture' (Tõniste 2014: 275). Describing an as-yet unrealized space invites hearers to imagine the new values and social relationships that are nurtured by and within that space (Tõniste 2014: 280). Early Christian interpreters found all manner of theological significations in the numbers and materials associated with the new Jerusalem's features. Bede is representative of the early Western tradition when he asserts that the three gates on each of the four sides of the city

---

15 See especially Ezek. 40.2–16; 41.4–5; 42.15–20; 43.2–5; 45.2; 48.18, 20, 30–35 and the careful study in Mathewson 2003.

16 Other significations of the shape of the new Jerusalem have, of course, been offered in the history of interpretation. Bede (*Exp.* 21.16) and Oecumenius (*Comm.* 21.15–22), for example, found here a figure for the stability of the blessedness of the saints.

17 See, further, Lee 2001: 6–52; Skemp 2005: 47–51. 'That the materials are not only valuable, but also pure . . . is emphasized three times in this segment (verses 18–21) recalling the idea of holiness' (Tõniste 2014: 290).

represent 'the faith in the holy Trinity . . . made known to the four corners of the earth' (*Exp.* 21.13; Weinrich 2011b: 184; so also the Greek father Oecumenius, *Comm.* 21.9–14). Aspringius ingeniously breaks down the measure of the wall's thickness, 144 cubits, to find its symbolic meaning(s). The figure represents the sum of 10 times 10 for the Decalogue, plus 4 tens and 4 units both for 'the fourfold truth of the gospel'. Alternatively, he suggests that it is the product of 24 (the number of patriarchs + apostles) times six (the days of the week of the present creation; *Tract. in Apoc.* 21.17; Weinrich 2005: 371). Bede explains the number more simply as 'the total of the number twelve squared . . . [which] signifies the immovable perfection of the holy city' (*Exp.* 21.17; Weinrich 2011b: 184).

The precious stones of which each of the city's 12 foundations were made attracted special attention as well. Andrew of Caesarea noticed that eight of the 12 stones correlated with eight of those on the Israelite high priest's breastplate, which originally represented each of the 12 tribes of Israel (Exod. 28.17). These eight, then, signified the old covenant, while the four that are new to the mix show 'the agreement of the new with the old and the superiority of the things brought to light in it' (*Comm. in Apoc.* 21.19; Weinrich 2005: 373). Bede interprets each of the foundation stones at great length as symbols of virtues that the people of God are to exhibit. He summarizes:

> Jasper, therefore, symbolizes the greenness of faith, and the sapphire suggests the height of celestial hope. Chalcedony indicates the fire of inner love, while the emerald is a figure of the confession of a strong faith in the midst of adversity. Sardonyx symbolizes the virtue of humility in the saints, and sardion indicates the glorious blood of the martyrs. Chrysolite symbolizes spiritual preaching with signs, while beryl suggests the perfected work of those who preach. Topaz demonstrates their fervent contemplation, while chrysoprase indicates both the work and the reward of the blessed martyrs. Hyacinth symbolizes the seeking after heavenly things by those who teach as well as their humble service for the sake of human weakness, and the amethyst designates the memory of the heavenly kingdom that is always in the mind of the humble.
> (*Exp.* 20.20; Weinrich 2011b: 190)

Andrew of Caesarea (*Comm. in Apoc.* 21.19–20) further connects each of the stones to one of the apostles (plus Paul, minus Judas) by some quality symbolically shared by each. As elsewhere in regard to Revelation's meaning, one is again left to wonder if the significance is to be found in the interpretation of each discrete detail or in the overall impression and impact of the images.

The cities in which John and his congregations lived and moved were full of dedicatory inscriptions over gates, on pillars, and across the architraves of temples and civic buildings, as any visitor to any of the sites today still cannot fail to notice. Generally these celebrate the benefactors who contributed to the erection of the edifices and the greater benefactors to whom these financiers wished to dedicate their own gifts. The dedicatory inscriptions in the new Jerusalem name the 12 apostles of the Lamb and the 12 tribes of Israel, named after their eponymous ancestors (21.12, 14). It may be noteworthy that the names so prominent in the inscriptions in Ephesus or Pergamum – the gods, the emperors, the local patrons who also staffed the priesthoods of their cults – are nowhere to be found (Koester 2014: 829). The community that God will bring into being, where all people will walk in the light of God and the light of the Lamb, retains its continuity with the historic people of God, Israel, which had borne sole witness to the One God for the entire period preceding the Incarnation and the birth of the Church. This is seen both in the presence of the names of the 12 patriarchs over the city's gates and in the many points of connection between the new Jerusalem and the hope articulated by the Hebrew prophets. It is also built upon the work of the Lamb's apostles, whose lives and witness stand at the foundations of the city's walls. John's vision of the community of the redeemed is far from narrow and parochial: 'The scope of salvation is enormous' (Kraybill 2010: 177), requiring a city whose dimensions are 1,500 miles (2,400 km) *cubed*.

John offers his vision of such a homeland as an incentive to his hearers to maintain a response of faithful obedience to God in the midst of their particular challenges, both laying out the conditions for entry into the new Jerusalem and the causes for exclusion therefrom (21.7–8, 27; 22.14–15). By means of such passages, the vision as a whole keeps before John's audiences the question of what kind of witness and practice they will adopt so that they might attain the desired ends and avoid the undesired consequences. The attributes and practices that lead to exclusion from the new Jerusalem are not merely those of a stock list of vices. Rather, 'every category John mentions is connected with the struggle of the church and the witness of the church against emperor worship' (Boesak 1987: 133; see also Pattemore 2004: 210; Tõniste 2014: 286). Each attribute – cowardice, faithlessness, a willingness to entangle oneself in the 'fornication' and idolatries of the empire, to allow oneself to fall under the 'spells' of the age and participate in the web of lies that public discourse spins (21.8; 22.15) – represents some form of compromising one's Christian loyalties and witness (as well as relevant facets of the behaviour of non-Christians).[18] 'The Holy City', a song written by Frederic Weatherly (lyrics) and Stephen Adams (music) in 1892 that remained popular throughout the twentieth century, says of the new Jerusalem: 'And all who would might enter, and no one was denied.' The song is not true at this point to John's vision, though it was in keeping with the emerging liberal Protestantism of the period. These verses, so important in John's context, are also carefully de-selected in the readings from Revelation 21 and 22 in the Revised Common Lectionary.

The attentive hearer will be surprised to find the kings of the earth bringing the glory of the nations into the new Jerusalem (21.24–26) and the leaves of the tree of life existing for 'the healing of the nations' (22.2 NRSV). This stands in considerable tension with the utter destruction of the nations and their kings in 19.17–21; 20.7–9. On the one hand, John inherits these images connected with the restored Jerusalem's glory from Isaiah (see esp. 60.3, 5, 11; Fekkes 1994: 282). On the other, he is clearly not using them without intentionality, for he modifies them in substantial ways (the kings enter voluntarily in Revelation but are *led* in a procession celebrating their subjugation in Isaiah). The tension emerges also between the casting of all those whose names were not found in the Scroll of Life into the lake of fire (20.15) and the presence of those – of *any* – 'outside' the new Jerusalem (22.15; Maier 2002: 150–2).

While some have taken the more positive verses (esp. 21.25) as an indication that John foresees universal salvation (Caird 1966: 279), the many texts that speak explicitly of the destruction and condemnation of those who gave their allegiance to the beast and to demons rather than to the One God (including the nearby 21.27!) should give interpreters pause before resolving the tension in a one-sided manner. The tension itself suggests that John is not interested in making absolute statements about the future beyond time. Rather, he is interested in depicting alternative consequences to alternative courses of action available in the present, which is precisely what he does in his other visions of 'the end' (19.11—22.5; cf. also 6.12–17; 7.9–17; 14.9–11, 14–20). The *present* moment of hearing John's Revelation faces one with 'the decision either to choose a life of costly testimony or to refuse it', to marvel after the beast or to follow the Lamb wherever he leads (Maier 2002: 152).[19] Will one live now so as to be welcomed into the new Jerusalem, or so as to be shut out? Will the nations persist in being duped into joining Satan's rebellion, or will they bring their glory into the new Jerusalem? Will the followers of the Lamb bear the bold witness

---

18   Kraybill 1996: 199. Kraybill sees informers who denounce Christians in the 'murderers' in the list.
19   See also Bauckham 1993b: 102–3; Koester 2014: 766, 768, 788.

that makes it possible for many among 'every tribe and people and language and nation' (13.7 NRSV) to shake off the spell that has been cast upon them by the agents of the great deceiver, the dragon?

John's vision of the new Jerusalem is another passage that, like the visions of the worship surrounding God's throne in chapters 4—5, has exercised a profound influence upon the hymnody of the Church throughout the centuries. Its imprint is clearly seen in such hymns as Philip Nicolai's 'Wake, Awake, for Night Is Flying' (*Wachet auf, ruft uns die Stimme*, 1599), John Newton's 'Glorious Things of Thee Are Spoken' (1779), Robert Lowry's 'Shall We Gather at the River' (1864), and Walter Russell Bowie's 'O Holy City, Seen of John' (1909), as well as African-American spirituals like 'Walk in Jerusalem Just Like John' (date unknown). These and other such hymns and songs have kept the hope of the future and eternal community of God's people before the followers of the Lamb in every century. None, however, seem to have captured so precisely the posture of withdrawal, longing and witness that John sought to nurture as Peter Abelard in his twelfth-century hymn, 'O What Their Joy and Their Glory Must Be' (*O quanta qualia*):

Now, in the meanwhile, with hearts raised on high,
we for that country must yearn and must sigh;
seeking Jerusalem, dear native land,
through our long exile on Babylon's strand.

12
Conclusions: Interpreting Revelation today

'Blessed is the person who keeps the words of the prophetic message of this book' (Rev. 22.7). Not every reader of Revelation has been convinced that the book does indeed contain a 'prophetic message', at least not from a respectable deity. The question of whether or *not* to 'keep the words' that we read – to allow them to shape our mindset, our values, our responses – is acutely raised in regard to Revelation as to few other books in the scriptural canon: 'Should we resist Revelation on account of its authoritarianism, violence, and misogyny, or should we embrace it as a voice that inspires resistance against injustice?' (Carey 2006: 169). Even if we choose the latter option (as Carey himself does), the history of interpretation down to the present day offers a broad variety of ways in which to listen to John's voice and to think about how it connects to our situation and the life of faithful witness in our situation. As Kovacs and Rowland have rightly asserted, 'No book in the Bible raises the question of the nature of the exegetical task more acutely than the Apocalypse' (2004: 11). And different decisions about the *kind* of book Revelation is, the *kind* of message it contains, will lead to a wider variety of modes of interpretation where this book is concerned than is typical for the writings of the Jewish and Christian canons.

Looking for 'fulfilment' in one-to-one correspondences

The most popular approach to interpreting Revelation remains that of looking for one-to-one correspondences between Revelation's characters and events and the past, present or future flow of historical persons, states and occurrences. Some who employ this approach remain very general in their application of Revelation's details rather than naming a particular person, institution or nation the 'beast' or 'Babylon', or presuming to have identified some particular practice or identification card or tracking device as 'the mark of the beast'. Instead, they essentially seek only to keep themselves and their audiences on high alert for the signs of the fulfilment of these 'prophecies' and, above all, of the approach of Christ's coming.

Such a reading is *potentially* appropriate insofar as it often replicates in a modern context the particular focus that John sought to nurture in his own context, namely prioritizing preparedness for encountering Christ at his return, since 'the time is near' (1.3; 22.10), so that one is found to have been living in faithful witness and obedience in this 'meanwhile'. At its best, however, this reading only considers Revelation as 'prophecy' – and that only in its sense of '*fore*telling' and not in its more commonly exhibited sense of '*forth*telling'. This is not to impugn the prophetic insight of John both in terms of forthtelling *and* foretelling. There is certainly a sense in which John accurately foresaw a critically important facet of the course of the two centuries that would follow his visionary experiences. His visions of a time of witness during which Christians would 'love not their lives unto death' as they stood up for and, thus, stood *beside* the Lamb whose testimony they bore and in whose steps they followed – wherever it might lead – well characterized the situation of the Christian Church through the rise of Constantine and the edicts of toleration. But 'foretelling' is certainly not all that John does in Revelation, and he gives every indication that this is not even the principal thing that his work offers.

This interpretative approach also does not take seriously the other cues John gives when he writes a 'letter' to specific (and ancient!) audiences and when he writes a kind of revelatory literature – an 'apocalypse', as the genre has come to be called – that typically seeks to lift the veil from the major forces and challenges within that ancient audience's landscape. Perhaps the greatest loss of this approach – if we set aside the literal body count that has resulted from the misapplication of Revelation – is the time and energy taken away from genuine discernment of the challenges to faithful witness and obedience in one's situation and from constructive change in the direction of deepening that witness and obedience, all for the sake of speculation that has proved empty time and times and half a time again.

Unfortunately, such interpretations rarely stay so general. Instead, they often attach John's images and labels, together with all the negative rhetorical power and theological weight that they carry, to people, institutions and practices that John never saw or imagined. Thus it remains popular among Protestant interpreters of Revelation to brand the Roman Catholic Church – and its leader, the pope, in particular – as 'the beast from the sea' and thereby to orient the interpreter's audience towards a heavy third of the global Christian Church as if it were a demonic agent. It remains popular to regard the United

States of America as 'the beast from the land' and to orient the interpreter's audience towards potentially wholesome developments in interdenominational cooperation as an attempt to create a one-world religion and enforce some demonic perversion of the faith. It remains popular to regard 'the mark of the beast' as branding Christians who gather on the first day of the week (Sunday) to worship the risen Lord rather than Saturday, allegedly the Sabbath still set apart by God for those who 'are no longer under the Torah but under grace' (Rom. 6.14; cf. Gal. 3.19–25), again reinforcing sectarian identity and sectarian boundaries within the Christian Church at the expense of the harmony and unity of the whole body of Christ.

Theological interpretation

Another approach to Revelation has been to sift through the text's affirmations and reflect upon its story for the book's contributions to theology. This is often pursued as an alternative to reading Revelation as predictive prophecy, particularly among those who have serious reservations about the overall soundness and the questionable fruit of that approach, though it is not inherently *incompatible* with any of the other approaches discussed here. Revelation has a great deal to contribute to our thinking about the character of God and God's interventions; the character of Jesus and the nature of his achievement; and the perennial problem of individual and systemic evil, its sources, and its eventual defeat by the just and judging God. One of the great theological contributions of Revelation is the manner in which it reveals that the God of Jesus Christ still remains the God of the exodus and the God of the prophets, whose character and commitment to justice proven so frequently in the past – holding both God's people and God's people's oppressors accountable to God's commandments – remains constant, and whose reliability to fulfil all that has been promised remains unshaken.[1]

One of the drawbacks of this approach, as the history of interpretation has shown us, is that theological interpretation can mean 'discovering' in Revelation theological and ethical convictions already known from elsewhere, attaching meaning to Revelation's images by means of the most tenuous and artificial connections. This has been particularly apparent in some interpretations of the orders of beings in heaven or the details of the new Jerusalem. This approach also runs the risk of not thinking sufficiently about the significance

---

1 Resources that foreground the theological contributions of Revelation include Bauckham 1993b; deSilva 2009: 158–74; Mangina 2010; Duvall 2016.

of *all* of John's reading cues for the interpretation of what he has written, although it tends to do justice to more of these cues than the first approach. It can do justice to Revelation as **prophetic word** – both as 'forthtelling' (insofar as it listens for what the text says about God's values and actions) and as 'foretelling' (insofar as it continues to engage constructively with New Testament eschatology, or the New Testament 'account of the last things'). It is also often informed by thinking about Revelation as an **apocalypse**, particularly in regard to what the larger cosmic story and the larger cosmic picture say about God, God's Messiah and God's interventions in the human scene from creation to consummation. Reading for essentially timeless theological truths, however, does not tend to nurture attentiveness to listening to the text as a **letter** written by a first-century Christian leader to a number of first-century Christian churches with a view to affecting their view of their situation and the possible responses to elements of that situation before them. Nor does it inherently press the interpreter and reading community to seek how to achieve in their new situation what John's word sought to accomplish among *his* reading communities, namely the 'apocalyptic adjustment' to their understanding of the challenges and opportunities of their very time- and place-specific setting in life.

Discernment on the basis of analysis and analogy

Every generation has had its interpreters who have identified that generation's 'antichrists' and claimed, in their new context, '*Here* at last is John's "beast" or 'John's "Babylon".' Despite his own strong disagreement with that approach, H. H. Rowley affirmed that 'beneath the mistaken hopes we can see a sound instinct' (Rowley 1963: 174), since the dragon continues to advance his agenda against God and continues to rage against the ever-new generations of 'those who keep God's commandments and hold fast to Jesus' testimony' (Rev. 12.17). The question is: how does Revelation assist us in unveiling that agenda at work in generations and situations far beyond John's own explicated audience and *its* generation and situation? Those who are most fully immersed in thinking about Revelation as **letter, prophetic word** and **apocalypse** tend to be united in their response. Revelation provides interpreters with 'the criteria to discern where the monster, the beast, and the false prophet are in our present situation, and where God is as well' (Richard 1995: 173). Revelation's 'value in today's world, therefore, lies not primarily in its predictive power, but in its diagnostic ability' (Paulien 2003: 159).

The interpretation that this volume has promoted involves us in (1) immersing ourselves as fully as possible into the social, economic, political, religious and ideological situations of John and his congregations; (2) discovering within those situations what John takes issue with and how he calls Christ-followers to respond; and (3) seeking to understand on what basis he makes those determinations. On the basis of this **exegetical** task, interpreters are then in a position to undertake the **hermeneutical** task, namely looking closely into the social, economic, political, religious and ideological situations that confront them and their reading communities and trying to discern where dynamics in those situations that are similar or analogous to those addressed by John would invite similar critiques and summonses to response. Such an approach to interpretation nurtures the critical and self-reflective practices that allow disciples in any modern context to gain the necessary, critical distance from the roles, scripts, values and knowledge that their society seeks continually to imprint upon them and, thereby, to find the space in which to formulate a more authentically Christ-shaped walk and witness. By seeking out analogous dangers to faithful response in the modern world, speaking prophetically against these dangers, and discovering the stance among those realities that reflects faithfulness to the scriptural tradition and to the God to which it witnesses, John's prophecy can still be 'kept' (and this in sharp contrast to the more popular method of trying to identify John's images with particular people or events in the modern or pre-modern world).

Allan Boesak's *Comfort and Protest* (Boesak 1987) represents just such an approach to Revelation as prophetic paradigm on the basis of which to diagnose and confront evil in a new situation – in his case, late-apartheid South Africa. He provides an excellent example of an historical reading of Revelation as first-century resistance literature that opens up avenues for contemporary discernment and resistance. William Stringfellow (1973), Wes Howard-Brook and Anthony Gwyther (1999) and Nelson Kraybill (2010) each do the same in regard to the situation in contemporary North America and Western Europe, each masterfully using an historically contextual reading of Revelation to learn how to ask new and penetrating questions about the degree to which modern political, economic and other arrangements contribute to fostering practices that stand opposed to those embraced – and strongly defended and ultimately secured – by the God of the prophets, Jesus and Revelation. The result is 'a relevance for our own generation that is every bit as real and every bit as powerful as that of the "popular" approach' (Russell 1994: 9), but built on the same, solid hermeneutical principles that guide our interpretation of every book of the scriptural canon. As Nelson Kraybill observes,

'the symbol of the beast in preaching and teaching can open our eyes to systemic and structural evil in our world' (2010: 136). John's critique of the
Roman imperial economy – its human cost, its warping of human desire and
relationships, its provision of some with gross abundance while leaving many
in want – calls us to be just as circumspect about the economies in which we
live and participate. John's call to disentangle oneself from violence and exploitative economics and from enjoying the benefits of unjust practices – his
call to 'come out' from Babylonish ways of ordering society – remains just as
urgent so that Christians in modern societies can both witness to God's justice *and* avoid falling afoul of God's justice.

In this regard, it may be further suggested that sound interpretation and application of Revelation includes not only historical study of the contents of this
one text and explorations of how it still provides an 'apocalyptic adjustment'
to the values and practices that surround the interpretative community. It also
includes 'going and doing likewise', as it were. Revelation is indeed not to be regarded as 'a secret message to be decoded', but it is also more than a text to be
responsibly, contextually interpreted and applied: it is 'a model to be emulated'
(Friesen 2001: 211). John invites interpreters not only to read what he has written but also to do as he has done. He invites them to immerse themselves in
the whole witness of the canonical Scriptures until they see their world in the
light of the values and practices both nurtured and excoriated by those Scriptures. He invites them to immerse themselves in prayer and in worship
until they see their everyday situations and the players and dynamics that shape
them in the light of God's throne, God's rule and God's eternity. Revelation
now stands as part of that canonical corpus but, within that corpus, it is also
a model for how to arrive at and how to communicate a scripturally informed
analysis, discernment and critique of modern social, religious, economic and
other power structures and 'domination systems'.[2]

The importance of this larger canonical context for discernment emerges
even more forcefully as one considers the very different paradigms of Christian response to 'the state' – that is, to governmental authority and particular authorities – advanced in Romans and 1 Peter, on the one hand, and Revelation on the other. Each offers important counterpoint to the other. When
the state arouses fear in the wicked and punishes disobedience *as God counts
disobedience*, and when the state affirms and promotes 'the good', it uses its

---

2   On 'domination systems' in general, see the insightful works by Wink (1983; 1986; 1992) and White
    (1998). Stringfellow (1973) and Howard-Brook and Gwyther (1999) are also well attuned to these
    phenomena.

authority rightly and Christians are called to affirm and cooperate with its agents (Rom. 13.3–4). But when the one who practices 'the good' now finds himself or herself in fear of the authorities' threatening actions rather than enjoying their approval – when 'a government can use the sword not to establish justice but to maintain injustice; not to secure liberation but to maintain slavery; not to break down but to maintain structures of oppression and inhumanity' (Boesak 1987: 99) – then the state ceases to be 'God's servant' and becomes something else, something hostile to God's own purposes for it. In these instances, Revelation calls the Christian community to take up its task of prophetic critique of political and economic systems that secure the prosperity and well-being of some at the expense of others. A perennial challenge for Christians who live under generally tolerant and well-functioning governments is 'to recognize the good in society around us without being so enamored of it that we fail to see when our own country acts like a beast' (Kraybill 2010: 144).[3]

The full scope of Revelation suggests that the task before Christian interpreters involves far more than simply critiquing their society. Rather, John's visions of Christian witness and action – and, above all, his vision of the new Jerusalem – push interpreters in every generation to form a vision for human community reflective of God's desires for people. John urges disciples to learn how to live as aliens in a land that is not our own, looking away to our native land, the city that none of us has yet seen but that is the consummation of the Judeo-Christian witness. At the same time, he calls the people of God ever to discover and engage the acts of justice and righteousness that spin the fine linen in which the bride is robed (Rev. 19.8), to live 'lives of spirited public witness to the God incarnate in Jesus of Nazareth, who reveals a way of being human on terms other than the insatiable desire for more, military domination, and national security' (Maier 2002: 28).

John reminds us of the power of vision to expand our capacity to see past our present and to learn to desire a better future, a more just future, a future more reflective of the prophets' vision, Jesus' vision, the apostles' vision, *God's* vision for human community. Martin Luther King Jr clearly understood this, as his perhaps most powerful speech – 'I have a dream' – demonstrates. His verbal description of that future in which people of different races experience

---

3 'Something beastly is at work, for example, in a world where people starve to death or die of preventable disease while nations spend billions on weapons and leisure. Jesus reassured believers who pray for divine intervention: "Will not God grant justice to his chosen ones who cry out to him day and night? Will he delay long in helping them? I tell you, he will quickly grant justice to them"' (Kraybill 2010: 137).

shalom together was a singularly effective vehicle by which to focus his audience's longing and motivate them to speak and to act in line with that vision for the future in absolute commitment to its realization. Revelation's own final visions continue to call interpreters to this task of allowing God to shape their imaginations as well – and, with these, their longings and their commitments to speak and to act – with a view to envisaging and striving towards God's promised future rather than continuing to serve the future towards which domination systems drive their subjects.

Bibliography

Allison, Dale C. 2009. *The Historical Christ and the Theological Jesus*. Grand Rapids, MI: Eerdmans.

Alnor, William M. 1989. *Soothsayers of the Second Advent*. Old Tappan, NJ: Revell.

Aune, David E. 1983a. 'The influence of Roman imperial court ceremonial on the Apocalypse of John.' *BR* 28: 5–26.

——. 1983b. *Prophecy in Early Christianity and the Ancient Mediterranean World*. Grand Rapids, MI: Eerdmans.

——. 1986. 'The Apocalypse of John and the problem of genre.' *Semeia* 36: 65–96.

——. 1989. 'The prophetic circle of John of Patmos and the exegesis of Revelation 22.16.' *JSNT* 37: 103–16.

——. 1990. 'The form and function of the proclamations to the seven churches (Revelation 2–3).' *NTS* 36: 182–204.

——. 1997. *Revelation 1–5*. WBC 52A; Dallas, TX: Word.

——. 1998a. *Revelation 6–16*. WBC 52B; Nashville, TN: Thomas Nelson.

——. 1998b. *Revelation 17–22*. WBC 52C; Nashville, TN: Thomas Nelson.

——. 2006. *Apocalypticism, Prophecy and Magic in Early Christianity*. Grand Rapids, MI: Baker Academic.

Backus, Irena. 2000. *Reformation Readings of the Apocalypse: Geneva, Zurich, and Wittenberg*. New York, NY and Oxford: Oxford University Press.

Balch, David L. 2006. '"A woman clothed with the sun" and the "great red dragon" seeking to "devour her child" (Rev 12:1, 4) in Roman domestic art.' Pp. 287–314 in John Fotopoulos, ed., *The New Testament and Early Christian Literature in Greco-Roman Context: Studies in honor of David E. Aune*. Supplements to Novum Testamentum 122. Leiden: Brill.

Barnett, Paul. 1989. 'Polemical parallelism: some further reflections on the Apocalypse.' *JSNT* 35: 111–20.

Barnhill, Gregory M. 2017. 'Seeing Christ through hearing the Apocalypse: an exploration of John's use of *ekphrasis* in Revelation 1 and 19.' *JSNT* 39: 235–357.

Barr, D. L. 1984. 'The Apocalypse as a symbolic transformation of the world: a literary analysis.' *Interpretation* 38: 39–50.

——. 2003a. 'Doing violence: moral issues in reading John's Apocalypse.' Pp. 97–108 in D. L. Barr, ed., *Reading the Book of Revelation: A resource for students.* Resources for Biblical Study 44. Atlanta, GA: Society of Biblical Literature.

——. 2003b. 'Introduction.' Pp. 1–9 in D. L. Barr, ed., *Reading the Book of Revelation: A resource for students.* Resources for Biblical Study 44. Atlanta, GA: Society of Biblical Literature.

——. 2003c. 'The story John told.' Pp. 11–23 in D. L. Barr, ed., *Reading the Book of Revelation: A resource for students.* Resources for Biblical Study 44. Atlanta, GA: Society of Biblical Literature.

——. 2012 [1998]. *Tales of the End: A narrative commentary on the book of Revelation.* 2nd edn. Salem, OR: Polebridge Press.

Barr, D. L., ed. 2003. *Reading the Book of Revelation: A resource for students.* Resources for Biblical Study 44. Atlanta, GA: Society of Biblical Literature.

——. 2006. *The Reality of Apocalypse: Rhetoric and politics in the book of Revelation.* Symposium Series 39. Atlanta, GA: Society of Biblical Literature.

Bauckham, Richard. 1993a. *The Climax of Prophecy: Studies in the book of Revelation.* Edinburgh: T&T Clark.

——. 1993b. *Theology of the Book of Revelation.* Cambridge: Cambridge University Press.

Beagley, Alan James. 1987. *The 'Sitz im Leben' of the Apocalypse with particular reference to the role of the Church's enemies.* Berlin: Walter de Gruyter.

Beale, G. K. 1998. *John's Use of the Old Testament in Revelation.* JSNTSup 166. Sheffield: Sheffield Academic Press.

——. 1999. *The Book of Revelation.* New International Greek Testament Commentary. Grand Rapids, MI: Eerdmans.

Beasley-Murray, G. R. 1978. *Revelation.* Rev. edn. New Century Bible. London: Marshall, Morgan & Scott.

Beckwith, I. T. 1919. *The Apocalypse of John.* New York, NY: Macmillan.

Beitzel, Barry, ed. 2019. *Lexham Geographic Commentary on Acts through Revelation.* Bellingham, WA: Lexham Press.

Bell, Daniel M., Jr. 2012. *The Economy of Desire: Christianity and capitalism in a postmodern world.* Grand Rapids, MI: Baker Academic.

Bell, Rob. 2011. *Love Wins: A book about heaven, hell, and the fate of every person who ever lived.* New York, NY: HarperOne.

Berrigan, Daniel. 1983. *The Nightmare of God.* Portland, OR: Sunburst.

Biguzzi, G. 1998. 'Ephesus, its Artemision, its temple to the Flavian emperors, and idolatry in Revelation.' *NovT* 40: 276–90.

Blaising, Craig A. 1999. 'Premillennialism.' Pp. 155–227 in Darrell L. Bock, gen. ed., *Three Views on the Millennium and Beyond*. Grand Rapids, MI: Zondervan.

Bloom, Harold. 1988. *The Revelation of St. John the Divine*. Modern Critical Interpretations. New York, NY: Chelsea House.

Blount, Brian. 2000. 'Reading Revelation today: witness as active resistance.' *Interpretation* 54: 398–415.

——. 2005. *Can I Get A Witness? Reading Revelation through African American culture*. Louisville, KY: Westminster John Knox Press.

——. 2009. *Revelation: A commentary*. New Testament Library. Louisville, KY: Westminster John Knox Press.

Böcher, Otto. 1988a. *Die Johannesapokalypse*. Erträge der Forschung 41. 4th edn. Darmstadt: Wissentschaftliche Buchgesellschaft.

——. 1988b. 'Die Johannes-Apokalypse in der neueren Forschung.' Pp. 3850–93 in Wolfgang Haase, ed., *Aufstieg und Niedergang der römischen Welt* 2.25.5. Berlin: de Gruyter.

Bock, Darrell L., ed. 1999. *Three Views on the Millennium and Beyond*. Grand Rapids, MI: Zondervan.

Boesak, Allan. 1987. *Comfort and Protest: The Apocalypse from a South African perspective*. Philadelphia, PA: Westminster Press.

Booth, Wayne. 1983 [1961]. *The Rhetoric of Fiction*. 2nd edn. Chicago, IL: University of Chicago Press.

Boring, M. Eugene. 1989. *Revelation*. Interpretation. Louisville, KY: John Knox Press.

Bousset, Wilhelm. 1906. *Die Offenbarung Johannis*. 6th edn. Göttingen: Vandenhoeck & Ruprecht.

Bowersock, G. W. 1982. 'The imperial cult: perceptions and persistence.' Pp. 171–83 in B. F. Meyer and E. P. Sanders, eds, *Jewish and Christian Self-Definition*, vol. 3. Philadelphia, PA: Fortress Press.

Boxall, Ian. 2006. *The Revelation of St. John*. Black's New Testament Commentary. London: Continuum and Peabody, MA: Hendrickson.

——. 2010. 'Reading the Apocalypse on the island of Patmos.' *Scripture Bulletin* 40: 22–33.

——. 2013. *Patmos in the Reception History of the Apocalypse*. Oxford Theology and Religion Monographs. New York, NY and Oxford: Oxford University Press.

Brighton, Louis A. 1999. *Revelation*. Concordia Commentary. St Louis, MO: Concordia.

Buchanan, G. W. 1993. *The Book of Revelation: Its introduction and prophecy*. Lewiston, NY: Edwin Mellen.

Bultmann, Rudolf. 1984. *Theologie des Neuen Testaments*. 9th edn. Tübingen: Mohr Siebeck.

Caird, G. B. 1966. *A Commentary on the Revelation of Saint John the Divine*. New York, NY: Harper & Row.

Callahan, Allen D. 1995. 'The language of Apocalypse.' *HTR* 88: 453–70.

Carey, Greg. 1999. *Elusive Apocalypse: Reading authority in the Revelation to John*. Studies in American Biblical Hermeneutics 15. Macon, GA: Mercer University Press.

———. 2005. *Ultimate Things: An introduction to Jewish and Christian apocalyptic literature*. St Louis, MO: Chalice Press.

———. 2006. 'Symptoms of resistance in the book of Revelation.' Pp. 169–80 in David Barr, ed., *The Reality of Apocalypse: Rhetoric and politics in the book of Revelation*. Symposium Series 39. Atlanta, GA: Society of Biblical Literature.

———. 2008. 'The book of Revelation as counter-imperial script.' Pp. 157–76 in Richard Horsley, ed., *In the Shadow of Empire: Reclaiming the Bible as a history of faithful resistance*. Louisville, KY: Westminster John Knox Press.

Carvalho, Corrine L. 2009. *Primer on Biblical Methods*. Winona, MN: Anselm Academic.

Casson, Lionel. 1989. *The Periplus Maris Erythraei: Text with introduction, translation, and commentary*. Princeton, NJ: Princeton University Press.

Charles, R. H. 1920. *A Critical and Exegetical Commentary on the Revelation of St. John*. 2 vols. Edinburgh: T&T Clark.

Chilton, Bruce. 2013. *Visions of the Apocalypse: Reception of John's Revelation in Western imagination*. Waco, TX: Baylor University Press.

Claridge, Amanda. 2010. *Rome: An Oxford archaeological guide*. 2nd edn. New York, NY and Oxford: Oxford University Press.

Collins, J. J., ed. 1979. *Apocalypse: The morphology of a genre*. Semeia 14. Missoula, MT: Scholars Press.

Comfort, Philip W. 2008. *New Testament Text and Translation Commentary*. Carol Stream, IL: Tyndale House.

Cooley, Alison E. 2009. *Res Gestae Divi Augusti: Text, translation, and commentary*. Cambridge: Cambridge University Press.

Court, J. M. 1979. *Myth and History in the Book of Revelation*. London: SPCK.

Cullmann, Oscar. 1956. *The State in the New Testament*. New York, NY: Charles Scribner's Sons.

Cuss, Dominique. 1974. *Imperial Cult and Honorary Terms in the New Testament*. Fribourg: University Press.

Danker, F. W. 1982. *Benefactor: An epigraphic study of a Graeco-Roman and New Testament semantic field*. St Louis, MO: Clayton House.

Deissman, Adolf. 1910. *Light from the Ancient East*. Tr. L. R. M. Strachan. London: Hodder & Stoughton.

Delorme, Jean, and Isabelle Donegani. 2010. *L'Apocalypse de Jean: Révélation pour le temps de la violence et du désir*. 2 vols. Paris: Cerf.

deSilva, D. A. 1991. 'The image of the beast and the Christians in Asia Minor.' *Trinity Journal* 12 (n.s.): 185–206.

——. 1992. 'The social setting of the Apocalypse of John: conflicts within, fears without.' *WTJ* 54: 273–302.

——. 1993. 'The construction and social function of a counter-cosmos in the Revelation of John.' *Forum* 9: 47–61.

——. 1995. *Despising Shame: Honor discourse and community maintenance in the epistle to the Hebrews*. Atlanta, GA: Society of Biblical Literature.

——. 1998. 'Honor discourse and the rhetorical strategy of the Apocalypse of John.' *JSNT* 71: 79–110.

——. 1999. 'A socio-rhetorical investigation of Revelation 14:6–13: a call to act justly toward the just and judging God.' *Bulletin for Biblical Research* 9: 65–117.

——. 2000. *Honor, Patronage, Kinship and Purity: Unlocking New Testament culture*. Downers Grove, IL: InterVarsity Press.

——. 2002a. 'Final topics: the rhetorical functions of intertexture in Revelation 14:14—16:21.' Pp. 215–41 in D. F. Watson, ed., *The Intertexture of Apocalyptic Discourse in the New Testament*. SBL Symposium Series 14. Atlanta, GA: Scholars Press.

——. 2002b. *Introducing the Apocrypha: Message, context, and significance*. Grand Rapids, MI: Baker Academic.

——. 2003. 'Toward a socio-rhetorical taxonomy of divine intervention: miracle discourse in the Revelation to John.' Pp. 303–16 in D. B. Gowler, L. G. Bloomquist and D. F. Watson, eds, *Fabrics of Discourse: Essays in honor of Vernon K. Robbins*. Harrisburg, PA: Trinity Press International.

——. 2007. 'X marks the spot? A critique of the use of chiasm in macro-structural analyses of Revelation.' *JSNT* 30: 343–71.

——. 2008a. 'The strategic arousal of emotions in the Apocalypse of John: a rhetorical-critical investigation of the oracles to the seven churches.' *NTS* 54: 90–114.

——. 2008b. 'What has Athens to do with Patmos? Rhetorical criticism of the Revelation of John (1980–2005).' *Currents in Biblical Research* 6: 256–89.

——. 2009. *Seeing Things John's Way: The rhetoric of the book of Revelation*. Louisville, KY: Westminster John Knox Press.

——. 2012. *The Jewish Teachers of Jesus, James, and Jude: What earliest Christianity learned from the Apocrypha and Pseudepigrapha*. New York, NY: Oxford University Press.

——. 2013a. 'Reading Revelation in Sri Lanka.' *Asia Journal of Theology* 27: 21–37.

——. 2013b. *Unholy Allegiances: Heeding Revelation's warning*. Peabody, MA: Hendrickson.

——. 2014. 'Revelation.' Pp. 215–20 in *Oxford Encyclopedia of Bible and Ethics*, vol. 2. Robert Brawley, gen. ed. New York, NY and Oxford: Oxford University Press.

——. 2018 [2004]. *An Introduction to the New Testament: Contexts, methods and ministry formation*. Rev. edn. Downers Grove, IL: InterVarsity Press.

——. 2020a. 'Rhetorical features of the book of Revelation.' Pp. 69–84 in *The Oxford Handbook of the Book of Revelation*. Craig Koester, ed. New York, NY and Oxford: Oxford University Press.

——. 2020b. *A Week in the Life of Ephesus*. Downers Grove, IL: InterVarsity Press.

Drury, John. 2002. *Painting the Word: Christian pictures and their meanings*. New Haven, CT: Yale University Press.

Duff, Paul B. 2001. *Who Rides the Beast? Prophetic rivalry and the rhetoric of crisis in the churches of the Apocalypse*. New York, NY and Oxford: Oxford University Press.

Duvall, J. Scott. 2016. *The Heart of Revelation: Understanding the ten essential themes of the Bible's final book*. Grand Rapids, MI: Baker.

Eagleton, Terry. 1996. *Literary Theory: An introduction*. 2nd edn. Minneapolis, MN: University of Minnesota Press.

Edwards, James B. 2018. 'The rider on the white horse, the thigh inscription, and Apollo: Revelation 19:16.' *JBL* 137: 519–36.

Emmerson, Richard K., and Bernard McGinn, eds. 1992. *The Apocalypse in the Middle Ages*. Ithaca, NY: Cornell University Press.

Erdkamp, Paul, ed. 2013. *The Cambridge Companion to Ancient Rome*. Cambridge: Cambridge University Press.

Etheridge, J. W. 1862–5. *The Targums of Onkelos and Jonathan ben Uzziel on the Pentateuch: With the fragments of the Jerusalem Targum*. London: Longman, Green, Longman, and Roberts.

Fairchild, Mark D. 2017. *Christian Origins in Ephesus and Asia Minor*. Peabody, MA: Hendrickson.

Fee, Gordon D. 2011. *Revelation*. New Covenant Commentary Series. Eugene, OR: Cascade.

Fekkes, Jan. 1994. *Isaiah and the Prophetic Traditions in the Book of Revelation: Visionary antecedents and their development*. JSNTSup 93. Sheffield: Sheffield Academic Press.

Ford, Josephine M. 1975. *Revelation*. AB 38; Garden City, NY: Doubleday.

Frey, Jörg. 2006. 'The relevance of the Roman imperial cult for the book of Revelation.' Pp. 231–55 in John Fotopoulos, ed., *The New Testament and Early Christian Literature in Greco-Roman Context: Studies in honor of David E. Aune*. Leiden and Boston, MA: Brill.

Friesen, Steven. 1993. *Twice Neokoros: Ephesus, Asia and the cult of the Flavian imperial family*. Leiden: Brill.

——. 2001. *Imperial Cults and the Apocalypse of John: Reading Revelation in the ruins*. Oxford: Oxford University Press.

——. 2003. 'The beast from the land: Revelation 13:11–18 and social setting.' Pp. 49–64 in D. L. Barr, ed., *Reading the Book of Revelation: A resource for students*. Resources for Biblical Study 44. Atlanta, GA: Society of Biblical Literature.

——. 2006. 'Sarcasm in Revelation 2–3: churches, Christians, true Jews, and satanic synagogues.' Pp. 127–44 in D. L. Barr, ed., *The Reality of Apocalypse: Rhetoric and politics in the book of Revelation*. Symposium Series 39. Atlanta, GA: Society of Biblical Literature.

Gentry, Kenneth L., Jr. 1998. *Before Jerusalem Fell: Dating the book of Revelation*. 3rd edn. Fountain Inn, SC: Victorious Hope.

——. 1999. 'Postmillennialism.' Pp. 13–57 in Darrell L. Bock, gen. ed., *Three Views on the Millennium and Beyond*. Grand Rapids, MI: Zondervan.

Giblin, C. H. 1984. 'Revelation 11.1–13: its form, function, and contextual integration.' *NTS* 30: 433–59.

Giesen, Heinz. 1997. *Die Offenbarung des Johannes*. Regensburger Neues Testament. Regensburg: Pustet.

Glancy, Jennifer A., and Stephen D. Moore. 2011. 'How typical a Roman prostitute is Revelation's great whore?' *JBL* 130: 551–69.

Gregg, Steve, ed. 1997. *Revelation: Four views. A parallel commentary*. Nashville, TN: Thomas Nelson.

Griffin, Miriam. 2000. 'The Flavians.' Pp. 1–83 in Alan K. Bowman, Peter Garnsey and Dominic Rathbone, eds, *Cambridge Ancient History, vol. 11: The High Empire, AD 70–192*. 2nd edn. Cambridge: Cambridge University Press.

Gumerlock, Francis X. 2000. *The Day and the Hour: A chronicle of Christianity's perennial fascination with predicting the end of the world*. Powder Springs, GA: American Vision.

——. 2006. 'Nero Antichrist: patristic evidence for the use of Nero's naming in calculating the number of the beast (Rev 13:18).' *WTJ* 68: 347–60.

——. 2009. *The Seven Seals of the Apocalypse: Medieval texts in translation.* Kalamazoo, MI: Western Michigan University Medieval Institute Publications.

——. 2016. *Early Latin Commentaries on the Apocalypse.* Kalamazoo, MI: Western Michigan University Medieval Institute Publications.

Hansen, Ryan Leif. 2014. *Silence and Praise: Rhetorical cosmology and political theology in the book of Revelation.* Minneapolis, MN: Fortress Press.

Hanson, K. C. 1996. 'How honorable! How shameful! A cultural analysis of Matthew's makarisms and reproaches.' *Semeia* 68: 81–111.

Harrington, Wilfrid. 1993. *Revelation.* Sacra Pagina 16. Collegeville, MN: Liturgical Press.

Hartlib, Samuel, and John Drury. 1651. *Clavis apocalyptica, or, the revelation revealed in which the great mysteries in the Revelation of St. John and the prophet Daniel are opened: it being made apparent that the prophetical numbers come to an end with the year of our Lord 1655.* London: Printed by W. D. for Tho. Matthewes.

Harvey, Barry A. 1999. *Another City: An ecclesiological primer for a post-Christian world.* Harrisburg, PA: Trinity Press International.

Hawk, L. Daniel. 2019. *The Violence of the Biblical God: Canonical narrative and Christian faith.* Grand Rapids, MI: Eerdmans.

Hemer, Colin J. 1986. *The Letters to the Seven Churches of Asia in Their Local Setting.* Sheffield: JSOT Press.

Hernandez, Juan, Jr. 2011. 'The relevance of Andrew of Caesarea for New Testament textual criticism.' *JBL* 130: 183–96.

Hirsch, E. D. 1967. *Validity in Interpretation.* New Haven, CT: Yale University Press.

Horsley, Richard, ed. 2008. *In the Shadow of Empire: Reclaiming the Bible as a history of faithful resistance.* Louisville, KY: Westminster John Knox Press.

Howard-Brook, Wes, and Anthony Gwyther. 1999. *Unveiling Empire: Reading Revelation then and now.* New York, NY: Orbis.

Humphrey, Edith M. 2003. 'A tale of two cities and (at least) three women.' Pp. 81–96 in D. L. Barr, ed., *Reading the Book of Revelation: A resource for students.* Resources for Biblical Study 44. Atlanta, GA: Society of Biblical Literature.

——. 2007. *And I Turned to See the Voice: The rhetoric of vision in the New Testament.* Grand Rapids, MI: Baker Academic.

Jauhiainen, Marko. 2005. *The Use of Zechariah in Revelation*. WUNT 2/199. Tübingen: Mohr Siebeck.

Johns, Loren L. 2003. *The Lamb Christology of the Apocalypse of John: An investigation into its origins and rhetorical force*. WUNT 2/167. Tübingen: Mohr Siebeck.

Jung, Carl G. 1960. *Answer to Job*. Translated by R. F. C. Hull. Cleveland and New York: World Publishing.

Karrer, Martin. 1986. *Die Johannesoffenbarung als Brief: Studien zu ihrem literarischen historischen und theologischen Ort*. FRLANT 140. Göttingen: Vandenhoeck & Ruprecht.

Kästner, Volker. 1998. 'The architecture of the Great Altar of Pergamum.' Pp. 137–61 in Helmut Koester, ed., *Pergamon: Citadel of the gods*. Harvard Theological Studies 46. Harrisburg, PA: Trinity Press International.

Keener, Craig. 2000. *Revelation*. New International Version Application Commentary. Grand Rapids, MI: Zondervan.

Kennedy, George Alexander, ed. 2003. *Progymnasmata: Greek textbooks of prose composition and rhetoric*. Leiden: Brill and Atlanta, GA: Society of Biblical Literature.

Kirby, John T. 1988. 'The rhetorical situations of Revelation 1–3.' *NTS* 34: 197–207.

Klassen, William. 1966. 'Vengeance in the Apocalypse of John.' *CBQ* 28: 300–11.

Koester, Craig. 2001. *Revelation and the End of All Things*. Grand Rapids, MI: Eerdmans.

———. 2014. *Revelation*. Anchor Yale Bible. New Haven, CT: Yale University Press.

Koester, Helmut, ed. 1995. *Ephesos: Metropolis of Asia*. Harvard Theological Studies 41. Valley Forge, PA: Trinity Press International.

———. 1998. *Pergamon: Citadel of the gods*. Harvard Theological Studies 46. Harrisburg, PA: Trinity Press International.

Kovacs, Judith, and Christopher Rowland. 2004. *Revelation: The Apocalypse of Jesus Christ*. Blackwell Bible Commentaries. London: Blackwell.

Kraft, H. 1974. *Die Offenbarung des Johannes*. HNT 16a. Tübingen: Mohr Siebeck.

Kraybill, Nelson. 1996. *Imperial Cult and Commerce in John's Apocalypse*. JSNTSup 132. Sheffield: Sheffield Academic Press.

———. 2010. *Apocalypse and Allegiance: Worship, politics, and devotion in the book of Revelation*. Grand Rapids, MI: Brazos Press.

LaHaye, Tim. 1999. *Revelation Unveiled*. Grand Rapids, MI: Zondervan Academic.

LaHaye, Tim, and Jerry B. Jenkins. 1995. *Left Behind: A novel of the earth's last days*. Carol Stream, IL: Tyndale House.

Lawrence, D. H. 1931. *Apocalypse*. New York, NY: A. A. Knopf.

Laws, Sophie. 1988. *In the Light of the Lamb: Imagery, parody, and theology in the Apocalypse of John*. Wilmington, DE: Michael Glazier.

Lee, Pilchan. 2001. *The New Jerusalem in the Book of Revelation. A study of Revelation 21–22 in the light of its background in Jewish tradition*. WUNT 2/129. Tübingen: Mohr Siebeck.

Leon, Harry J. 1995. *The Jews of Ancient Rome*. Updated edn. Peabody, MA: Hendrickson.

Levine, Amy-Jill, with Maria Mayo Robbins, eds. 2009. *A Feminist Companion to the Apocalypse of John*. London: T&T Clark.

Levison, John R. 1999. *Of Two Minds: Ecstasy and inspired interpretation in the New Testament world*. North Richland Hills, TX: BIBAL Press.

Lewis, I. M. 1971. *Ecstatic Religion: An anthropological study of spirit possession and shamanism*. Harmondsworth and Baltimore, MD: Penguin.

Lilje, Hans. 1957. *The Last Book of the Bible*. Philadelphia, PA: Muhlenberg Press.

Lindsey, Hal. 1975. *There's a New World Coming: A prophetic odyssey*. New York, NY: Bantam.

Lindsey, Hal, with Carole C. Carlson. 1970. *The Late Great Planet Earth: A penetrating look at incredible prophecies involving this generation*. Grand Rapids, MI: Zondervan.

Lohmeyer, E. 1970. *Die Offenbarung des Johannes*. HNT 16. Tübingen: Mohr Siebeck.

Lohse, Eduard. 1988a. *Die Offenbarung des Johannes*. Das Neue Testament Deutsch 11. Göttingen: Vandenhoeck & Ruprecht.

——. 1988b. 'Wie christliche ist die Offenbarung des Johannes?' *NTS* 34: 312–38.

Loisy, Alfred. 1923. *L'Apocalypse de Jean*. Paris: Nourry.

Longenecker, Bruce W. 2001. '"Linked like a chain": Rev 22.6–9 in light of an ancient transition technique.' *NTS* 47: 105–17.

McGinn, Bernard. 1979. *Visions of the End: Apocalyptic traditions in the Middle Ages*. New York, NY: Columbia University Press.

——. 1994. *Antichrist: Two thousand years of the human fascination with evil*. San Francisco, CA: HarperSanFrancisco.

Magie, David. 1950. *Roman Rule in Asia Minor to the End of the Third Century after Christ*. 2 vols. Princeton, NJ: Princeton University Press.

Maier, Charles S. 2006. *Among Empires: American ascendancy and its predecessors*. Cambridge, MA: Harvard University Press.

Maier, Harry O. 2002. *Apocalypse Recalled: The book of Revelation after Christendom*. Minneapolis, MN: Fortress Press.

Mangina, Joseph L. 2010. *Revelation*. Brazos Theological Commentary on the Bible. Grand Rapids, MI: Brazos Press.

Mathewson, David L. 1992. 'Revelation in recent genre criticism: some implications for interpretation.' *Trinity Journal* 13: 193–213.

——. 2003. *A New Heaven and a New Earth: The meaning and function of the Old Testament in Revelation 21.1–22.5*. JSNTSup 238. London: Sheffield Academic Press.

——. 2016. *Revelation: A handbook on the Greek text*. Waco, TX: Baylor University Press.

Mede, Joseph. 1627. *Clavis apocalyptica*. London: n.p.

Mellor, R. 1975. *ΘΕΑ ΡΩΜΗ: The worship of the goddess Roma in the Greek world*. Hypomnemata 42. Göttingen: Vandenhoeck & Ruprecht.

Moo, Jonathan. 2009. 'The sea that is no more: Revelation 21:1 and the function of sea imagery in the Apocalypse of John.' *NovT* 51: 148–67.

Morton, Russell. 2001. 'Glory to God and to the Lamb: John's use of Jewish and Hellenistic/Roman themes in formatting his theology in Revelation 4–5.' *JSNT* 24: 89–109.

——. 2007. *One upon the Throne and the Lamb: A tradition historical/theological analysis of Revelation 4–5*. Studies in Biblical Literature 110. New York, NY: Peter Lang.

——. 2014. *Recent Research on Revelation*. Recent Research in Biblical Studies 7. Sheffield: Sheffield Phoenix Press.

Mounce, Robert H. 1997 [1977]. *The Book of Revelation*. NICNT. Grand Rapids, MI: Eerdmans.

Moyise, Steven. 1995. *The Old Testament in the Book of Revelation*. JSNTSup 115. Sheffield: Sheffield Academic Press.

Mueller, Ekkehardt. 2002. 'The two witnesses of Revelation 11.' *Journal of the Adventist Theological Society* 13: 30–45.

Murphy, Frederick J. 1998. *Fallen Is Babylon: The Revelation to John*. New Testament in Context. Valley Forge, PA: Trinity Press International.

Murphy O'Connor, Jerome. 2008. *St. Paul's Ephesus: Texts and archaeology*. Collegeville, MN: Michael Glazier.

Newport, Kenneth G. C. 2000. *Apocalypse and Millennium: Studies in biblical exegesis*. Cambridge: Cambridge University Press.

Nietzsche, Friedrich. 1956. *The Birth of Tragedy and the Genealogy of Morals*. Garden City, NY: Doubleday.

O'Hear, Natasha, and Anthony O'Hear. 2015. *Picturing the Apocalypse: The book of Revelation in the arts over two millennia*. New York, NY and Oxford: Oxford University Press.

O'Leary, S. D. 1993. 'A dramatistic theory of apocalyptic rhetoric.' *Quarterly Journal of Speech* 79: 385–426.

Osborne, Grant R. 2002. *Revelation.* Baker Exegetical Commentary on the New Testament. Grand Rapids, MI: Baker Academic.

Pattemore, Stephen. 2004. *The People of God in the Apocalypse: Discourse, structure and exegesis.* SNTSMS 128. Cambridge: Cambridge University Press.

Paulien, Jon. 1988. 'Elusive allusions: the problematic use of the Old Testament in Revelation.' *BR* 33: 37–53.

——. 2003. 'The Lion/Lamb King: Reading the Apocalypse from popular culture.' Pp. 151–61 in D. L. Barr, ed., *Reading the Book of Revelation: A resource for students.* Resources for Biblical Study 44. Atlanta, GA: Society of Biblical Literature.

Perry, Peter S. 2009. *The Rhetoric of Digressions: Revelation 7:1–17 and 10:1–11:13 and ancient communications.* WUNT 2/268. Tübingen: Mohr Siebeck.

Petersen, Rodney L. 1993. *Preaching in the Last Days: The theme of the 'two witnesses' in the sixteenth and seventeenth centuries.* Oxford: Oxford University Press.

Peterson, Eugene H. 1969. 'Apocalypse: the medium is the message.' *Theology Today* 26: 133–41.

Pieters, Albertus. 1937. *The Lamb, the Woman and the Dragon: Studies in the Revelation of St. John.* Grand Rapids, MI: Zondervan.

Pippin, Tina. 1992. *Death and Desire: The rhetoric of gender in the Apocalypse of John.* Louisville, KY: Westminster John Knox Press.

Porter, S. E. 1989. 'The language of the Apocalypse in recent discussion.' *NTS* 35: 582–603.

Prévost, Jean-Pierre. 1993. *How to Read the Apocalypse.* New York, NY: Crossroad.

Price, S. R. F. 1984. *Rituals and Power: The Roman imperial cult in Asia Minor.* Cambridge: Cambridge University Press.

Prigent, Pierre. 1988. *L'Apocalypse de Saint Jean.* CNT 14. Geneva: Labor et Fides.

——. 2001. *Commentary on the Apocalypse of St. John.* Tr. Wendy Pradels. Tübingen: Mohr Siebeck.

Ramsey, W. M. 1904. *The Letters to the Seven Churches of Asia.* London: Hodder & Stoughton.

Rapske, Brian Mark. 2012. 'Exiles, islands, and the identity and perspective of John in Revelation.' Pp. 311–46 in S. E. Porter and A. W. Pitts, eds,

Christian Origins and Greco-Roman Culture: Social and literary contexts for the New Testament. Leiden: Brill.

Reddish, Mitchell G. 2001. *Revelation*. Smyth & Helwys Bible Commentary. Macon. GA: Smyth & Helwys.

Resseguie, James L. 1998. *Revelation Unsealed: A narrative-critical approach to John's Apocalypse*. Leiden: Brill.

——. 2009. *The Revelation of John: A narrative commentary*. Grand Rapids, MI: Baker Academic.

Rhoads, David, ed. 2005. *From Every People and Nation: The book of Revelation in intercultural perspective*. Minneapolis, MN: Fortress Press.

Richard, Pablo. 1995. *Apocalypse: A people's commentary on the book of Revelation*. Maryknoll, NY: Orbis.

Robinson, John A. T. 1976. *Redating the New Testament*. Philadelphia, PA: Westminster Press.

Roloff, Jürgen. 1984. *Die Offenbarung des Johannes*. Zürcher Bibelkommentare, Neues Testament 18. Zurich: Theologischer Verlag.

——. 1993. *The Revelation of John*. Tr. John E. Alsup. Continental Commentaries. Minneapolis, MN: Fortress Press.

Rossetti, Christina. 1892. *The Face of the Deep: A devotional commentary on the Apocalypse*. London: SPCK.

Rossing, Barbara R. 1999. *The Choice between Two Cities: Whore, bride, and empire in the Apocalypse*. Harvard Theological Studies 48. Harrisburg, PA: Trinity Press International.

Rowley, H. H. 1963. *The Relevance of Apocalyptic*. Rev. edn. Cambridge: Lutterworth Press.

Royalty, Robert. 1998. *The Streets of Heaven: The ideology of wealth in the Apocalypse of John*. Macon, GA: Mercer University Press.

——. 2004. 'Don't touch *this* book! Revelation 22:18–19 and the rhetoric of reading (in) the Apocalypse of John.' *Biblical Interpretation* 12: 282–99.

Ruiz, Jean Pierre. 1989. *Ezekiel in the Apocalypse: The transformation of prophetic language in Revelation 16,17–19,10*. Frankfurt am Main: Peter Lang.

Russell, D. S. 1994. *Prophecy and the Apocalyptic Dream: Protest and promise*. Peabody, MA: Hendrickson.

Ryrie, Charles C., ed. 1978. *The Ryrie Study Bible*. Chicago, IL: Moody.

Saffrey, H. D. 1975. 'Relire L'Apocalypse à Patmos.' *RB* 82: 385–417.

Satake, Akira. 2008. *Die Offenbarung des Johannes*. Meyer Kommentar 16a. Göttingen: Vandenhoeck & Ruprecht.

Scheidel, Walter, ed. 2012. *The Cambridge Companion to the Roman Economy*. Cambridge: Cambridge University Press.

Scherrer, Peter. 2000. *Ephesus: The new guide*. Istanbul: Ege Yayınları.

Scherrer, Steven J. 1984. 'Signs and wonders in the imperial cult: a new look at a Roman religious institution in the light of Rev 13:13–15.' *JBL* 103: 599–610.

Schüssler Fiorenza, Elisabeth. 1985. *The Book of Revelation: Justice and judgment*. Philadelphia, PA: Fortress Press.

——. 1991. *Revelation: Vision of a just world*. Proclamation Commentaries. Minneapolis, MN: Fortress Press.

——. 2007. *The Power of the Word: Scripture and the rhetoric of empire*. Minneapolis, MN: Fortress Press.

Scofield, Cyrus I., ed. 1909. *The Scofield Reference Bible*. Oxford: Oxford University Press.

——. 1917. *The Scofield Reference Bible. New and improved edn*. Oxford: Oxford University Press.

Skemp, Vincent. 2005. 'Avenues of intertextuality between Tobit and the New Testament.' Pp. 43–70 in Jeremy Corley and Vincent Skemp, eds, *Intertextual Studies in Ben Sira and Tobit: Essays in honor of Alexander A. Di Lella, O.F.M.* CBQMS 38. Washington, DC: Catholic Biblical Association.

Slater, T. B. 1998. 'On the social setting of the Revelation.' *NTS* 44: 232–56.

Smalley, Stephen S. 2005. *The Revelation to John: A commentary on the Greek text of the Apocalypse*. Downers Grove, IL: InterVarsity Press.

Smallwood, E. M. 1976. *The Jews under Roman Rule: From Pompey to Diocletian*. Leiden: Brill.

Smith, Ian. 2002. 'A rational choice model of the book of Revelation.' *JSNT* 85: 97–116.

Smith, R. R. R. 1987. 'The imperial reliefs from the Sebasteion at Aphrodisias.' *Journal of Roman Studies* 77: 88–138.

Spaeth, Barbette Stanley, ed. 2013. *The Cambridge Companion to Ancient Mediterranean Religions*. Cambridge: Cambridge University Press.

Sparks, H. F. D., ed. 1984. *The Apocryphal Old Testament*. Oxford: Clarendon Press.

Spilsbury, Paul. 2002. *The Throne, the Lamb and the Dragon: A reader's guide to the book of Revelation*. Downers Grove, IL: InterVarsity Press.

Stauffer, Ethelbert. 1955. *Christ and the Caesars*. Philadelphia, PA: Westminster Press.

Stenström, Hanna. 2009. '"They have not defiled themselves with women . . .": Christian identity according to the book of Revelation.' Pp. 33–54 in Amy-Jill Levine, with Maria Mayo Robbins, eds, *A Feminist Companion to the Apocalypse of John*. London: T&T Clark, 2009.

Stevens, Gerald L. 2014. *Revelation: The past and future of John's Apocalypse.* Eugene, OR: Pickwick.

Stevens, Gerald L., ed. 2010. *Essays on Revelation: Appropriating yesterday's Apocalypse in today's world.* Eugene, OR: Pickwick.

Stewart, Alexander E. 2017. '*Ekphrasis*, fear, and motivation in the Apocalypse of John.' *BBR* 27.2: 227–40.

Strimple, Robert B. 1999. 'Amillennialism.' Pp. 81–129 in Darrell L. Bock, gen. ed., *Three Views on the Millennium and Beyond.* Grand Rapids, MI: Zondervan.

Stringfellow, William. 1973. *An Ethic for Christians and Other Aliens in a Strange Land.* Waco, TX: Word.

Talbert, C. H. 1994. *The Apocalypse: A reading of the Revelation of John.* Louisville, KY: Westminster John Knox Press.

Tate, W. Randolph. 2008. *Biblical Interpretation: An integrated approach.* 3rd edn. Grand Rapids, MI: Baker Academic.

Taylor, Lily Ross. 1931. *The Divinity of the Roman Emperor.* Middletown, CT: American Philological Association.

Thompson, Leonard L. 1990. *The Book of Revelation: Apocalypse and empire.* Oxford: Oxford University Press.

——. 2003a. 'Ordinary lives: John and his first readers.' Pp. 25–47 in D. L. Barr, ed., *Reading the Book of Revelation: A resource for students.* Atlanta, GA: Society of Biblical Literature.

——. 2003b. 'Spirit possession.' Pp. 137–50 in D. L. Barr, ed., *Reading the Book of Revelation: A resource for students.* Resources for Biblical Study 44. Atlanta, GA: Society of Biblical Literature.

Trebilco, Paul. 2007. *The Early Christians in Ephesus from Paul to Ignatius.* Grand Rapids, MI: Eerdmans.

Tõniste, Külli. 2014. 'Measuring the holy city: architectural rhetoric in Revelation 21:9–21.' *Conversations with the Biblical World* 34: 269–93.

Tyconius. 2017. *Exposition of the Apocalypse.* Tr. Francis X. Gumerlock with introduction and notes by David C. Robinson. Fathers of the Church 134. Washington, DC: Catholic University of America Press.

van Henten, Jan Willem. 2006. 'Dragon myth and imperial ideology in Revelation 12–13.' Pp. 181–203 in David L. Barr, ed., *The Reality of Apocalypse: Rhetoric and politics in the book of Revelation.* Symposium Series 39. Atlanta: SBL.

Vos, L. A. 1965. *The Synoptic Traditions in the Apocalypse.* Kampen: Kok.

Wainwright, Arthur W. 1993. *Mysterious Apocalypse: Interpreting the book of Revelation.* Nashville, TN: Abingdon Press.

Walvoord, John F. 1966. *The Revelation of Jesus Christ: A commentary*. Chicago, IL: Moody Press.

Weinrich, William C., ed. 2005. *Revelation*. Ancient Christian Commentary on Scripture: New Testament 12. Downers Grove, IL: InterVarsity Press.

——. 2011a. *Greek Commentaries on Revelation*. Ancient Christian Texts. Downers Grove, IL: InterVarsity Press.

——. 2011b. *Latin Commentaries on Revelation*. Ancient Christian Texts. Downers Grove, IL: InterVarsity Press.

Wettstein, Joannes Jacobus. 1752. *Novum Testamentum Graecum*. 2 vols. Amsterdam: Officina Dommeriana.

Whitaker, Robyn J. 2015. *Ekphrasis, Vision, and Persuasion in the Book of Revelation*. WUNT 2/410. Tübingen: Mohr Siebeck.

White, C. Dale. 1998. *Making a Just Peace: Human rights and domination systems*. Nashville, TN: Abingdon Press.

White, Ellen G. 1950 [1911]. *The Great Controversy between Christ and Satan*. Mountain View, CA: Pacific Press.

Wilder, Amos N. 1971. 'The rhetoric of ancient and modern apocalyptic.' *Interpretation* 25: 436–53.

Wilkin, Robert N. 2013. 'Christians will be judged according to their works at the *Rewards* Judgment, but *not* at the *Final* Judgment.' Pp. 25–50 in Alan P. Stanley, ed., *The Role of Works at the Final Judgment*. Grand Rapids, MI: Zondervan.

Wilson, Mark. 2007a. *Revelation*. Zondervan Illustrated Bible Backgrounds Commentary. Grand Rapids, MI: Zondervan.

——. 2007b. *The Victor Sayings in the Book of Revelation*. Eugene, OR: Wipf & Stock.

——. 2010. *Biblical Turkey: A guide to the Jewish and Christian sites of Asia Minor*. Istanbul: Ege Yayınları.

Wimsatt, W. K., and M. C. Beardsley. 1954. *The Verbal Icon: Studies in the meaning of poetry*. Louisville, KY: University Press of Kentucky.

Wink, Walter. 1983. *Naming the Powers: The language of power in the New Testament*. Minneapolis, MN: Fortress Press.

——. 1986. *Unmasking the Powers: The invisible forces that determine human existence*. Minneapolis, MN: Fortress Press.

——. 1992. *Engaging the Powers: Discernment and resistance in a world of domination*. Minneapolis, MN: Fortress Press.

Witherington, Ben, III. 2003. *Revelation*. New Cambridge Bible Commentary. Cambridge: Cambridge University Press.

Wold, Benjamin, G. 2009. 'Revelation's plague septets: new exodus and exile.' Pp. 279–97 in F. García Martínez, ed., *Echoes from the Caves: Qumran and the New Testament*. STDJ 85. Leiden and Boston, MA: Brill.

Worth, Roland H., Jr. 1999a. *The Seven Cities of the Apocalypse and Greco-Asian Culture*. Mahwah, NJ: Paulist Press.

——. 1999b. *The Seven Cities of the Apocalypse and Roman Culture*. Mahwah, NJ: Paulist Press.

Yarbro Collins, Adela. 1976. *The Combat Myth in the Book of Revelation*. Harvard Dissertations in Religion 9. Missoula, MT: Scholars Press.

——. 1980. 'Revelation 18: taunt-song or dirge?' Pp. 185–204 in J. Lambrecht, ed., *L'Apocalypse johannique et l'apocalyptique dans le Nouveau Testament*. Bibliotheca ephemeridum theologicarum lovaniensium 53. Louvain: Leuven University Press.

——. 1984. *Crisis and Catharsis: The power of the Apocalypse*. Philadelphia, PA: Westminster Press.

——. 1986. 'Reading the book of Revelation in the twentieth century.' *Interpretation* 40: 229–42.

——. 1993. 'Feminine symbolism in the book of Revelation.' *Biblical Interpretation* 1: 20–33. Reprinted as pp. 121–30 in Amy-Jill Levine, with Maria Mayo Robbins, eds, *A Feminist Companion to the Apocalypse of John*. London: T&T Clark, 2009.

Yeates, Paul Henry. 2017. 'Blaspheming heaven: Revelation 13:4–8 and the competition for heaven in Roman imperial ideology and the visions of John.' *NovT* 59: 31–51.

Zanker, Paul. 1990. *The Power of Images in the Age of Augustus*. Ann Arbor, MI: University of Michigan Press.

Index of Scripture references and ancient authors

Index of Scripture references and ancient authors

Index of Scripture references and ancient authors

Index of modern authors

Index of subjects

Index of subjects

Index of subjects